M000025710

An Introduction to Multicultural Education

From Theory to Practice

Chinaka Samuel DomNwachukwu

ROWMAN & LITTLEFIELD PUBLISHERS, INC.
Lanham • New York • Toronto • Plymouth, UK

Rowman & Littlefield Publishers, Inc.
A wholly owned subsidiary of The Rowman & Littlefield Publishing Group, Inc.
4501 Forbes Boulevard, Suite 200, Lanham, Maryland 20706
http://www.rowmanlittlefield.com

Estover Road, Plymouth PL6 7PY, United Kingdom

Copyright © 2010 by Chinaka Samuel DomNwachukwu

All rights reserved. No part of this book may be reproduced in any form or by
any electronic or mechanical means, including information storage and retrieval
systems, without written permission from the publisher, except by a reviewer who
may quote passages in a review.

British Library Cataloguing in Publication Information Available

Library of Congress Cataloging-in-Publication Data

DomNwachukwu, Chinaka Samuel, 1964–
  An introduction to multicultural education : from theory to practice / Chinaka
Samuel DomNwachukwu.
     p. cm.
  Includes bibliographical references and index.
  ISBN 978-1-60709-683-2 (cloth : alk. paper) — ISBN 978-1-60709-684-9 (pbk. :
alk. paper) — ISBN 978-1-60709-685-6 (electronic)
  1. Multicultural education—United States. I. Title.
  LC1099.3.D66 2009
  370.1170973—dc22

                                                    2009042842

♾ ™ The paper used in this publication meets the minimum requirements of
American National Standard for Information Sciences—Permanence of
Paper for Printed Library Materials, ANSI/NISO Z39.48-1992.

Printed in the United States of America

Contents

List of Figures and Tables

FIGURES

TABLES

Preface

This book is my attempt to meet the needs of graduate students who are taking classes in cultural diversity towards meeting requirements for the California Cross-Cultural Language and Academic Development Certification required of all California teachers. Students often struggle with the textbooks required for the class, either because the writers are too confrontational or even offensive to differing worldviews or because candidates can't see the foundational principles within those texts that would prepare them to accept and engage this required course work from a positive mindset. This volume attempts to provide strong historical and pedagogical principles for multicultural education as foundational resources, as well as present the basic principles of multicultural education in a language that students are able to relate to.

The book begins with a call for educators to look within themselves and to explore our collective humanity and our collective journey as cultural beings. Personal narratives are used to illustrate the significance of our cultural identities, so as to give educators an opportunity to appreciate the value and significance of their students' cultural experiences. It is written with the American cultural milieu in mind, so a deliberate attempt was made to analyze and engage the American cultural mosaic, as well as the issues around crises of cross-cultural encounters.

In order to lay a firm foundation for the relevance and significance of multicultural education in the American educational context, this book addresses the historical forces that have shaped the American society and that make multicultural education an educational imperative. It discusses the history of prejudice and racism, multilingual and bilingual rights and opportunities, religious rights and liberties, and women's rights. From

American history we establish an indisputable ground for multicultural education as an essential part of the school curriculum rather than just as part of a politically correct agenda.

This book goes beyond theories and principles to provide step-by-step approaches for implementing multicultural education in the K–12 classrooms. Model lessons, support materials, and activities make this book user friendly and further strengthen the practical tips. It is my hope that readers find this book useful and engaging.

Writing this book has been a fulfilling experience. Some people may view teaching as a job and others as a vocation. I tend to share the latter perspective, for I see in teaching a divine calling to make a difference in society. Schools are one of the most powerful institutions for social reconstruction, and the role teachers play have great significance in any society. Multicultural education may be a newcomer to the educational discourse, but its significance in the twenty-first-century classroom is immeasurable.

The world of this century is not like the world of the centuries before it. We live in a globalized world, where we are confronted with an inescapable convergence of human populations, cultures, worldviews, and political and economic structures. To think that we can live and operate in purely homogenous cultural environments is unrealistic, and the promise of the decades ahead is that of an inescapable mixing of human populations in measures and degrees greater than ever.

In light of the present and future realities of our social and cultural convergence, the need to prepare students to competently live and function in a multicultural world becomes an essential aspect of the educational curriculum at a global level. It will take teachers who are culturally competent to educate and equip diverse populations in our present school systems and to help construct a social arrangement that will make the social realities of the future relevant and in sync with our increasing diverse cultural and worldview trends.

ACKNOWLEDGMENTS

Azusa Pacific University, an evangelical private Christian university, has provided me with a comfortable context for honest discussion of diversity issues for the years I have been here. Like many U.S. universities, this institution is still on a journey toward cultural synergy, but its leadership (president, provost, and the cabinets) has been intentional in making diversity discussions possible in classrooms, cafeterias, and anywhere students and faculty can gather for honest conversation.

Dean of the School of Education, Helen Easterling Williams, and my faculty colleagues at the School of Education have been inspirational in their commitment to excellence and the desire to prepare the best equipped teachers for the twenty-first century. The support of my able administrative assistant and office manager for our Teacher Education Department, Mona Girgis, and the faculty members in my department were very supportive during the writing of this book. Dr. Gail Reeder, my professional colleague, gave her precious time to read through my manuscript and made helpful suggestions.

My students in the Cultural Diversity course, who were not willing to settle with a one-sided view of social justice but constantly demanded better ways to see and utilize the principles and strategies of multicultural education, deserve my thanks. They inspired me to continue to think, work, and attempt new ways to explain things that have already been explained. When finally they saw and heard these issues present in my own words as reflected in this book, they gave their resounding endorsement. It's my prayer that they reach personal fulfilment as they undertake the task of reconstructing and enhancing the current social arrangements and making it better than what was handed down to us.

My children, Osinachi, Chinonso, Naedum, and Nissi, made sacrifices toward the making of this book. Those late nights in the office and times in my study away from them at home were sacrifices for children their age. I owe them my gratitude and hope to find meaningful ways to make it up for them. Finally I must dedicate this book to my wife, Nkechi, who has been my ally and best critic for the past nineteen years. As a science teacher in a low-income school system, her skills and experiences have had significant impact on the way I articulate issues and ideas to students who are preparing to be teachers, and they have indeed influenced the contents of this book in significant ways.

Chapter One

Humans as Cultural Beings

Foundations for Multicultural Education

Chapter Objectives:

The purpose of this chapter is to expose readers to the concept of culture and cultural identity using personal narratives, rather than abstract concepts and lectures on culture and worldview. Combining the insights from this chapter and their personal experiences, readers will be able to:

1. articulate an understanding of multicultural education as a learner-centered pedagogy
2. reflect on the concept of culture from their personal experiences
3. articulate a cultural autobiography
4. develop a personal appreciation of cultural diversity, seeing it as an asset, not a liability, within the field of education

The teaching and learning of diversity and diversity issues are anchored on people—teachers and students. One of the most positive experiences of this author as a teacher of social equity and justice as well as multiculturalism, has been the process of helping students come to terms with their cultural identity. Many native-born Caucasian Americans (commonly called "whites," a term that does not accurately describe the pigmentation of any human group) assume that beyond being white and being American there are no other cultural constructs that distinguish them from other people within American society. When these individuals are persuaded (as is often the case) to dig deeper into their cultural roots, they discover, to their amazement, that Caucasian could be Anglo, Dutch, Greek, Russian, Jewish, Arab, Iranian, or any of several other ethnicities. "White" is not a valid cultural identity. The reality of multicultural education, however, is that it takes one who knows who he or she is within a cultural setting to enhance other people's cultural awareness and promote diversity. Thus, the question is: Who am I within my culture?" Identity negotiation is a critical aspect of the intercultural experience, and teachers who work in multicultural settings go through this negotiation just as their students do.

In this chapter, we will examine some ways individuals within American educational systems have attempted to describe their cultural identity. Before articulating individual understandings of cultural identity, we need to discuss what it means to be human within the context of multicultural education.

WHAT DOES IT MEAN TO BE HUMAN?

The quest for the definition of what it means to be human has been the pre-occupation of philosophers and scientists since the time of Socrates. We are generally regarded by scientists and anthropologists as *Homo sapiens*, or human individuals. Some theorists have attempted to define us on the basis of our self-consciousness, or what we call the ego. Norman Ford made a definitive statement that humans are social beings by nature. According to Ford, awareness of the self, or personal ego, is only possible as a result of one's conscious activities. These activities can be corporeal or noncorporeal. Among the different forms in which this sense of self is manifested are cultural and social activities.[1]

Harold H. Titus, in his *Living Issues in Philosophy*, gave a definition that encapsulates what it means to be human much better than any other sources consulted on this topic. He defines the human being as a part of nature, who partakes in nature's ways, yet appears to transcend nature and exercises control over it.[2] He writes about the human being, "he is no less than what he is—a self-conscious being with unique characteristics. The nature and character of a thing is determined not so much by its beginning as by its end. Man's aspirations give him his place and his importance. . . . He also has great adaptive powers and the capacity to exert some control over his own development."[3] Titus presents three perspectives from which we can look at the human person, namely, (1) the classical, rationalistic view of man; (2) the religious view of man; (3) and the scientific interpretation of man.

The classical Greek view is built around the ideas of great philosophers such as Plato, Aristotle and Protagoras. Whereas Plato thinks that reason is the highest part of the human soul, whose function is to guide conduct, Aristotle sees reason as our prized faculty, which sets us apart from subhuman nature. This classical interpretation sees humans primarily from the viewpoint of nature and our unique rational ability.This view can be stretched to its humanistic conclusion in which Protagoras suggests that the human being is the measure of all things.[4]

The religious view, which according to Titus is represented by Judeo-Christian, Islamic, and Hindu traditions, looks at humans from a pair of spiritual lenses. The Judeo-Christian perspective looks at human beings primarily from the point of view of their divine origin. Humans transcend the natural condition and reach their highest potential when in harmony with God. Islam sees our duty as loyalty to God and his divine laws, and that is the essence of our being. Hinduism sees humans as subject not object and explains our consciousness as a reflection of the consciousness of the supreme spirit.[5] Titus's point is that these religions all have their individual perception of the human person.

There is also no unified scientific interpretation of human beings. There is, instead, a biological perspective, a physiological perspective, and an anthropological perspective. Science distinguishes between humans and other creatures on the basis of our "advanced anatomical and physiological complexity and . . . more elaborate behavioral patterns."[6]

The conclusion that Titus draws on what it means to be human, however, has great significance for us as we attempt to address human multiculturalism and its impact on the American educational system. He states, "Any purportedly comprehensive interpretation of man that neglects or ignores his ideas and ideals, his self-consciousness, his power of abstract thought, his powers of ethical discrimination and aesthetic appreciation, and his need for worship and companionship is incomplete and inadequate."[7]

This view lends itself to a holistic interpretation of the human person and compels the present work to go a step further to investigate the ethical, aesthetic, and religious dimension of the human person in the educational process.

In light of the insights from Titus, let's attempt a definition of the human person as *a biological being who is inherently spiritual as well as culturally determined.* To be human, therefore, would involve an attempt to fully articulate our biological, spiritual, and cultural attributes as one functional unit, called personality, which is able to be creative, reflective, and sociable.

A question that must be addressed in light of this definition of the human person, therefore, is: What does it mean to be a human being within the educational process, either as a learner or as a teacher?

THE LEARNER AS A SOCIAL BEING

Every child in a classroom comes from a social setting called family.[8] In twenty-first-century America, the definition of family has changed drastically. The nineteenth and early twentieth centuries' definition of family was father, mother, and children. In the latter half of the twentieth century, the family began to be gradually redefined, as divorce became a normal part of life in society. Many schoolchildren began to come from homes made up of a mother, a stepfather, and both biological and step-siblings. Some have come from homes with father, stepmother, and step-siblings. Yet others were being raised by a single mother or single father. Some children started to be raised by grandparents, either because biological parents were incarcerated or because they were deemed incompetent to raise them due to one social problem or another. Toward the turn of the twenty-first century, we were already grappling with the question of gay and lesbian parenting. Today it is not very much an issue; gays and lesbians are both adopting and raising children.

Thus, the definition of family as we knew it has changed forever. This shift in social pattern has generated lots of arguments from both the conservative and liberal fronts. The former calls for a return to the original definition of family, while the latter calls for a complete overhaul of social norms and expectations, to widen them to be more inclusive of these new forms and expressions of family. The liberal approach has called for a restructuring of educational curricula to ensure a fair representation of the diversity that defines our twenty-first-century society.

Although the religious conservative view has lots of validity to it, as some of the factors that have led to the new forms of family reflect a departure from the religious and moral norms that formed the foundation of this society, a learner-centered pedagogy calls for a critical look at the implications of these shifts for the schoolchild. Does a child being raised in a gay or lesbian family see any oddity in the structure of his or her family? The argument may be stretched one way or the other. Should the classroom be the context for approving or disapproving one family structure or another?

Again, the argument may be stretched even further. A more important question would be whether every child, irrespective of his or her family structure has a right to be in the classroom and to be taught well. To this question, it will be odd to hear a negative response.

The question should therefore be: How does the learner-centered classroom provide every child a safe and healthy learning environment, void of the intrusions of the divergent social views that influence the widening structure of the family? This is the task that today's educators must confront. Learning takes place in a social context, and fortunately or unfortunately, American society happens to be the most divergent social arrangement of our time. Is it possible, then, to work toward synergy amid our diversity? The questions raised in this chapter may never find one answer that fits all situations. These may be questions that would have to be answered within the collective arrangement of the school communities and their value systems. This may be one area in which the original community-oriented school governance that formed the educational structures of America becomes our best court of appeal. Communities must be empowered to explore what constitutes the best interest of their constituents, without violating the rights of the minorities. Is there a way the interest of both the majority and the minority can be protected? These are questions that must be continuously asked as every stakeholder in a school site collaborates to find lasting solutions to these social problems. The idea of the learner as a social being will come up again for discussion.

THE LEARNER AS A CULTURAL BEING

Recently the topic of Ebonics as an alternative language for African American students took the forefront in the news media. The significance of this debate does not rest exclusively on the problems posed by the uniqueness of the African American version of the English language, but reflects an acknowledgment that African American culture is distinct and different from the mainstream Anglo-Saxon Protestant culture.

American society is a mosaic of cultures. Right from the birth of this nation, diversity was its very essence. Native Americans who had roamed the land centuries before the Europeans arrived were themselves a diverse group of people. They were made up of many different ethnicities with different languages, cultures, and social arrangements. The Europeans who came into what is now the United States were homogeneous only for a short while. No sooner had the earliest British colonists settled down than other Western Europeans joined them. Africans were brought in as slaves to become part of the manpower that gave this nation its social arrangement, government, and economic structure. Over the years, different events brought Eastern and Southern Europeans in as well. With the discovery of gold, people from all over the world, from as far away as China, made their way to the United States. With the construction of the transcontinental railroad, the Chinese came in even larger numbers. As for the Spanish-speaking Americans, considering the fact that California and Texas were once part of Mexico, it is difficult to regard them as immigrant groups. One certain reality thus confronts us, namely, that the United States of America is and always has been a land of divergent groups of people.

One of the most disconcerting elements of contemporary educational structures remains the inability of some educators to come to terms with the diversity of our land and its educational environment. A learner-centered pedagogy does not call for mere tolerance, because the language of tolerance is insulting and disrespectful to the many Americans whose ancestors have paid high prices in servitude, extreme hardships, and death to make this country what it is today. All Americans have a right to be seen as Americans and respected for their contributions to this great nation and those of their ancestors. The right language, therefore, is that of inclusion and equal opportunity. A learner-centered pedagogy must come to terms with the right of every child in the American classroom to be there and to be taught well so as to maximize his or her full potential. Instruction must be provided in the language and format that is most comprehensible to the child, to enable that child achieve the desired academic goal.

American history is filled with struggles and conflicts between different ethnicities: whites versus Indians; Western versus Eastern, Central, and Southern Europeans; whites versus Hispanics; Hispanics versus African Americans; and so on. These are struggles and conflicts that must come to an end in the twenty-first century for us to build a united nation. These are struggles and conflicts that must become conspicuously absent in American classrooms.

In American society, teachers are the front line in the program of acculturating newcomers to American society. For some students, their teachers are the first and only adults outside their immediate homes who are able to influence their adaptation to the new culture called America. Given the fact that teachers know, to some extent, that this is their responsibility, they tend to adopt one of two approaches to doing the job.

Teachers as Assimilators

Some teachers see themselves as agents of assimilation. They uphold the melting-pot ideology, in which the student is expected to get rid of everything ethnic and become "American," as the claim goes. Students whose beliefs and behaviors do not match those of successful mainstream students are seen as lacking in "ability, prior knowledge, motivation, or communication skills."[9] This mind-set often leads to attitudes of disrespect toward these students, which consequently leads these students to develop feelings of rejection, low self-esteem, and poor academic achievement.

Teachers as Accommodators

When teachers see themselves as accommodators, they tend to make accommodations in their teaching to facilitate learning for the nonmainstream students. They tend to exhibit respect toward these students, and this translates to the students seeing themselves as capable, only needing to catch up with the way things are said and done in this new culture. This is a classroom that has the interest and development of the child as its primary commitment, not the perpetuation of a dominant culture, which is seen as in competition with other microcultures. The teacher's role is not that of the culture police, but that of an educator, a friend, and an ally to the learner, who is on a journey toward self-development and self-realization.

To effectively educate students from diverse backgrounds, the teacher must first of all come to terms with his or her humanity and cultural identity, and then go the next step of affirming the humanity of the students in his or her classrooms, as well as affirming their individual cultural identities. In order to attain this goal, one of the exercises I take my teacher candidates through is a cultural autobiography project titled, "Who Am I in My Culture?" In this project, students take time to research their own cultural heritage as well as other cultural influences that have made them who they are. They write their autobiography and come to class with it, along with important artifacts that represent their cultures. These are shared with the whole class, and this ends up being one of the most intriguing parts of our diversity class. In the section below I want to share a few samples of what these teacher candidates have written and we will also discuss them.

WHO AM I IN MY CULTURE?

All of the candidates responding to this question are student teachers who are engaging the question of their cultural identity within the first two weeks of their first diversity class in a teacher education program. As you will come to discover through the write-ups, some candidates already have a very broad understanding of culture and are very much in tune with their cultural identity. The most revealing aspect of these narratives is the fact that somehow within those first two weeks of class; these individuals come to terms with the fact that they possess unique cultural identities that make them who they are within the larger U.S. society. With the permission of the students, these narratives are presented here to illustrate the strength of individual cultural experiences and how much they help in defining who we are.

Narrative Number One: Meet Marcos Garcia

Hello, I am the product of parents who met in the vineyards of Ukiah, California. I am a brown boy in a white world, ashamed of my skin and of my Spanish-speaking father.

I am the one who answered a Spanish question in English.

I am the one who wished I could be anyone but me.

I am the one who, in high school, was Mexican to the white kids and American to the brown kids. To which side do I lay claim?

I am the one whose parents said, "Follow your dreams, you don't want to work like we do." I am the one who worked construction with my father and found college to be a better place. His hard work withered the feelings of embarrassment.

I am the one who took a Mexican/American literature course and found out that Mexican people actually wrote books and that I was not alone with my feelings. I am the one who minored in Chicano Studies, read book after book, and finally found something to shatter the pretenses. I am the one who is proud of being Chicano and refuses to use the term hisPANIC.

I am the one who does not need to eat with a fork, tortillas will do, *Gracias*. I am the one everyone looks at when they need a Spanish translator. Yes, I do speak Spanish by the way. I am the one who went to film school to make films that showcased the realities of my culture. I am the one who, at the time, was the only Chicano directing rap music videos.

I am the one who continues to write in an effort to get our stories up on the silver screen. I am the one who got into teaching to show students that they can be what they want to be. That they are not limited to the stereotypes and menial jobs the media portrays. I am the one who needs to lead by example and instill in my students the power of having dreams and the satisfaction of realizing them.

I am a son, a brother, an uncle, a *nino*, a *chicano*, a writer, a teacher. I am Marcos Angelberto Garcia. Pleased to meet you.

Man is never closer to himself than when he is close to his community. This is the best way to illustrate how I began to transition from a shameful sense of history to a proud past. A variety of people and experiences have helped shape my thoughts and feelings over the years. However, the browning of my skin begins with my parents.

I remember the instance that laid the first coat. I was sixteen; riding in the bed of a trusty red Toyota pick-up truck with a plastic shell nestled over my head. My family and I were returning from a Sunday afternoon at the Redondo Beach Pier. My brother and sister rode along side me, exhausted. Suddenly, I heard my father beat the horn and pound the brakes. An Anglo man nearly sideswiped our truck. My father yelled for him to watch where he was going in his Spanish accent. The man retaliated with, "You fucking wetback!" WET-BACK! Wetback! All other sounds faded to a whisper. Wetback?

It sounded so heavy, so unbearable; it forced me to breathe a rapid breath, like I was suffocating. I remember wondering, who are we?' I knew then I did not belong to an American community.

Other incidents also occurred to family and neighbors that caused me to question who I was. But my parents were always there to instill me with con-fidence, "If they want to call us wetbacks, so what? We know who we are!" They made sure to let me know people will call us names but never to be sorry for who I am. This is the price they paid to live a better life, one out of the fields and integrated into an American society. I was beginning to listen with the darkening of my skin.

I then entered my senior year in high school. I had to take English 1B with Frank Zepeda. He was different from any other teacher on campus. He was Mexican. He spoke to us in *Spanglish*, called us "*chuntaros*" and we liked it. It was strange to see someone who looked like a relative teaching a class, es-pecially mine. He helped us believe in ourselves as young Chicanos. He spoke about things that happened in our homes. He was one of us. He once wrote on one of my essays, "I like your writing style." The simplest of comments can

last a lifetime. He made me realize that anyone in our community could succeed if they had the desire.

I went on to enroll at Mt. San Antonio College a few years later. At the urging of a friend, I registered for Mexican/American Literature. It was literally
shocking to find out how many books were written by Latinos. I felt betrayed
by the American public school system for not allowing me the opportunity to
be aware these books ever existed. Professor Julian Medina challenged us to
debate issues and topics facing the Chicano community. We read books, poems, watched films and discussed the feelings of the authors. Some shared my
sentiments. I was relieved to know I was not alone.

I was not the only one without knowledge of my past. I began to look at the
people in my community with a new familiarity. There was hope for me yet to
still grow a shade darker.

I later transferred to California State University, Long Beach, to major in
Film Production. After the eye-opening experience in the literature class, I also
majored in Chicano Studies. I needed to learn about the people who opened
the doors for me to succeed, about where my mother and father came from and
why they hold their beliefs. I began to learn the other side of history and what
was done to the people of Mexico.

I learned about injustice and racism and why people think my father is a
wetback and why he will never be one. Again, I felt betrayed by the school
system. Why do we not know at least a portion of our history? Why do we not
know about the origins of our community? The more I read, the closer I grew
to my community; the closer I grew to knowing who I am, being browned by
the rays of experience.

I do not feel this transition could have happened any other way. It could not
have happened sooner, it could not have happened at the urging of others. It
had to take place within the realm of my own destiny. I now know the history
of the faces in my community. I know the struggles, the pride and the will to
survive. I know because I am one of them.

This opening piece is one of the most revealing pieces written by these student teachers. I chose to preserve the original names because I believe that
this is a story worth telling in its truest form. Marcos did not only write about
his cultural identity, he went further to elaborate on his journey toward that
cultural identity. The realism that this piece presents to us is the struggle of
cultural identity that children born into immigrant homes go through as they
grow up in American society. Such struggles are rarely considered a major
issue by the schools and educators, yet this case demonstrates the extent
to which they shape the individuals' lives and perspectives. The crises of

cultural self-awareness are major issues that must begin to be addressed if multicultural education is to take a deep root in our educational settings.

Cultural awareness and self-identity is not a struggle for immigrant American children only, it is a major issue that other groups of American children deal with. A white teacher candidate wrote concerning her own cultural identity. Some of these names have been altered to protect the characters, so let's call her Sherri.

Narrative Number Two: Meet Sherri

My grandparents were immigrants from both Poland and Italy.
They came to Ellis Island at the turn of the 20th century.
Matthew and Sophia Mocniak settled in a Pennsylvania coal-mining town.
Pneumonia claimed Matthew soon after, from his labors underground.
Pascal and Nelie Pacino stayed in New York to raise a family.
They built a thriving business in Bronx's "Little Italy."
My parents met each other in their melting-pot neighborhood.
Mike and Josephina both excelled by working as hard as they could.
Their honeymoon was a stay out West, where my father built his career.
He became a most sought-after, brilliant Aerospace Engineer.
Orange, California, was the suburb chosen to make their home.
My two brothers and I had plenty of freedom, and lots of space to roam.
As I reflect back on the experiences that are ingrained in me,
I see a comfortable childhood, full of opportunities.
I was born in 1960, and given a soap-opera star's name.
Sherri Diane Mocniak via Diane Cannon's fame.
Religious faith, love, and togetherness created family unity.
Caring for and working within, strengthened our community.
We were taught to respect our elders, and those of every color, shape, and size.
We were exposed to the downtrodden, their plight to recognize.
I married John at 19, too young many did say.
I knew he was the "one for me," and we are together to this day.
My husband is a mixture of ethnicities gently stirred.
As for our two daughters, the lines have all been blurred.
We too moved to the country, to raise our family, with hopes that we could capture some of the ways it used to be.

Here we see a classic case of a descendant of a set of European immigrants who fully captured the American dream, and whose descendants have also done very well. This woman would be the typical American girl. Yet she confronts one glaring truth about her culture and heritage, "the lines have all been blurred." The fact of cultural identity within the American white population is more challenging today than among many other groups. In a typical class of fifteen to twenty students, more than 60 percent would be white, and when we undertake this exercise of cultural self-discovery, more than 70 percent of these white students would confess to the lines being blurred as far as racial and cultural identity is concerned. For most of these students, cultural identity is no longer anchored on a European descent, since the European blood has mixed with African, Native American, Jewish, and sometimes Asian blood; instead they have come to carve out for themselves a new cultural identity that is uniquely theirs and uniquely American. While some readers may be tempted to see this as a negative development, it may be that herein lies the strength of being truly *American*. The melting pot ideology, which has been espoused in the past history of this country may be somewhat of a reality, and it may have given America its unique cultural identity.

Americans of all ethnicities may attempt to trace their cultural heritage to somewhere outside the American shores, but there has been such a mingling within the American shores that our identities can no longer be exclusively defined in terms of our non-American ancestry.

The next case is from an African American woman. She has come to terms with the reality of her cultural identity in a very unique way.

Narrative Number Three: Meet Breygyndta

When you examine your place in your culture, a good first place to begin is your name. While your name can reveal your ethnicity or culture, how you choose to pronounce it reveals even more about how you *feel* about your cultural background. And then there are those names that just leave you guessing. That's my name. My birth name is Breygyndta Lilian Mary Warna Bertlow. My name is a significant part of my culture because African Americans value creativity. Being different is praiseworthy in dress style, music trends, and even name choice. It would be unheard of in African American culture to look to a name book, except to see what had already been taken. Like many African American women, my mother just made up my name. There is no other name like it, though the sounds are not in themselves unique. Unfortunately, the creativity of African American culture that has been displayed through creative names is experiencing a backlash. Some of the creative names have been seen as absurd and have been ridiculed in the public. Whereas having a unique name was at one time a symbol of pride, it has, in mainstream American culture, become more of a burden and a stigma. These creative names are now considered "ghetto," evoking images of welfare mothers and illiterate children. Anyone with hopes of professional success has to now seriously consider how their names affect people's perceptions of their abilities and intellect. Names like Shavonia and Tyloquiesha are not only unique, but they also carry a stigma.

For the most part, I have been able to evade such considerations. For almost all of my life, I have gone by "Rey" because people have a hard time saying *Breygyndta*.

The second thing that my name tells about my culture is the significance of the matriarchs. I am named after two of my grandmothers, Warna and Mari, giving honor and homage to the generations that came before my mother.

In African American culture, the matriarchs are very important. The strength that African American women have had to possess in order to survive and protect their families in a white-male-dominated society has become a legend. "Being strong" is a noble characteristic and a compliment that every African American woman would want to have (true for all groups, I'm sure, but especially true in African American culture).

It is this name that I believe truly sums up who I am in my culture. My husband's last name, Dirakavit, is Thai, though he is not (another interesting, but unrelated, story). And the middle name that we both chose to take is Badilika, which is Swahili for "to be changed." My name is multicultural—it reflects my personal and familial heritage, and my distant ancestors, but also an acceptance of other groups. Living in Southern California, I have been blessed with the opportunity to be immersed in many different cultures: from East LA (mostly Latino) to Claremont (mostly white) to Baldwin Village (mostly African American). Each of these groups has shaped my cultural identity. So, I like to think that my new name reflects, to a greater extent, the multicultural nature of my life and experiences. While I am African American culturally, my culture is more than just African American.

In this short write-up, Breygyndta gives us a classic case of one who has come to a full grasp of the dynamics of her cultural identity. Here is an African American woman who goes beyond conventional racial identity to seek a definition of her cultural identity deep within the experiential, historical, as well as environmental factors that have shaped her life and that of her cultural group. This is a dimension that most Americans are reluctant to explore. Those who venture into this sphere, however, are mostly those who have suffered one kind of social deprivation or another based on their ethnic or cultural identity, especially those who are unable to "pass for white."[10] The question that arises, therefore, is whether we must wait for crises and oppressions to arouse the desire to establish our cultural identity. The beauty of the American cultural landscape is that it is a mosaic. We have those forces and principles that hold us together as one nation under God, and we also have those unique characteristics and heritages that provide the variety that makes America beautiful. Cultural diversity is indeed beautiful. The beauty of Old Town Pasadena, in the San Gabriel Valley of California, is the variety of restaurants that attract thousands of people from across the southland on a daily basis—Thai, Indian, Chinese, Cantonese, Italian, Mexican, French, Armenian, just name it. Each one thrives, patronized by Americans of a variety of ethnicities and races, suggesting that there is more to being American than skin color and ethnic heritage. The next candidate, a student teacher of Asian descent seems to be arriving at a state of equilibrium in terms of her cultural identity.

Narrative Number Four: Meet Kim

Chopsticks, Respecting of Elders, Piano, In 'N' Out Hamburgers, Shopping Malls, Independence. Such is the mixture of words that describe my eclectic background. When I think about my culture, I think Korean, American, Korean American. These two heritages have somehow fused together to make up who I am, to become my own unique heritage, and form a generation of people almost like me.

When I was younger, my schoolmates would ask me, "Where are you from?" To which I could not give an answer. If I said I was "American," they would further prod, "But then how come your eyes are so different?" Those students who were not so nice as to pose questions merely jeered "Go back to the country you came from!"

I did not know how to respond back to them that I was from the country of America. I had been born and raised in Los Angeles. I was at a loss to explain myself to my ignorant peers. Attending an all-white, middle-class private school did not help much. During my elementary and junior high years, I only remember about six other Asian students, all of whom were Korean like me.

My brother left after sixth grade to attend the public middle school; I always thought part of his reason for leaving was because of the racism he faced. The other Asian students also phased out eventually. I, however, felt comfortable at my school. But it was not until high school, when I attended a public high school, that I started acknowledging and interacting with other minority students in a school setting. The high school I attended had an ethnically diverse population of students. Going on to college, I took courses in Asian American and Ethnic studies, and finally started appreciating my background and culture for its full worth and value. I had found my identity.

I have visited Korea a couple of times recently. I always feel like a foreigner there. Even though my facial features and hair color make me fit into the homogenous mixture, and though I can speak the language quite fluently, I have never felt at home. On the other hand, in America, I am one of many minorities. Yet, for the most part, I feel like this country is my home, the place where I belong. I feel accepted and valued, and when I face ignorance, I like to teach rather than react negatively.

Asian Americans are victims of the "model-minority" myth. And even though I do play piano, and though I study diligently and sometimes drive recklessly, I am not particularly adept at math and science, nor do I know martial arts or consider myself exotic looking. If you were to ask me who I was within my culture, I would say I am "myself." I have been influenced by American cultural traditions and ideals, such as American food and independence, but I have also been influenced by my Asian cultural values, such as respecting my elders, having a hard work ethic, and the importance of family. These two cultures have fluidly joined together to form my own culture, an Asian American (or Korean American) culture, and it is within this culture that I find who I am.

In the United States, we have come into an age where our ethnicities and races must fuse with the other cultural factors that are uniquely American to define our individual cultural identities. That process may be easier for some because they have a lighter skin tone; all of us must, nevertheless, be prepared to confront this process of engaging our evolving new cultural identities as we all strive to build "one indivisible nation under God." The activities below will help you to interact personally with the issues raised in this chapter.

～

QUESTIONS AND APPLICATION

Activity: Who Am I in My Culture?

Articulate a personal statement of your cultural identity based on the insights gained from chapter 1. Describe your cultural identity beginning with your heritage and the cultural and worldview influences that have shaped you into becoming who you are today. Describe how your cultural identity will impact the way you function as a K–12 teacher.

Review Questions

1. Compare and contrast the different cultural experiences presented in this chapter. What common similarities and differences do you observe across the responses?
2. What are the distinguishing elements that make each of these individuals Americans? How do their ethnic roots enhance or detract from their American identity?
3. What other ways can K–12 teachers aid their students in their struggle for cultural self-awareness? Develop an action plan you can use in helping your students as they navigate through their personal struggles for cultural identity.

Strategies for Application

The following activities can be used in applying the principles and lessons of this chapter to a K–12 classroom situation.

1. Grades K–6: Students can work with their parents to write their family history, identifying their history of immigration to the United States and cultural mixes and intermarriages that may have taken place along their ancestral lines. These papers can be presented in class with parents (for K–3 students) or alone by students (for grades 4–6). This will allow for sharing of cultural heritage and family history with the whole class, creating a positive attitude toward cultural differences.
2. Grades 7–12: Students can research their cultural and family history and write research papers, do murals, or create other kinds of special projects to showcase their history and cultural heritage. This could be a way to excite students or their families to begin a family-tree project. A family history/cultural event day could be organized with multicultural food and exhibition of their projects.

Chapter Two

Engaging the American Cultural Mosaic

Chapter Objectives:

This chapter introduces and presents a critical analysis of American culture. At the end of this chapter, readers will be able to:

1. conceptualize the American culture as a mosaic
2. describe the historical factors that have shaped the American culture
3. explain the interactive nature of cultural structures and their effects on the dynamic shifts that take place within cultures and worldviews

WHAT IS CULTURE?

To properly understand the concept of culture, we must begin by articulating a clear definition of the word *culture*. Culture is a concept that has been defined in different ways by many different interests and disciplines; however, the desire here is not to compare definitions but to isolate those that make the concept of culture very clear and appropriate for our context. One of the definitions of culture that stands out within the field of multicultural education is by Sonia Nieto, who defined it as the values, traditions, social relationships, and worldviews created, shared, and transformed by a group of people.[1] Generally speaking, however, the field of cultural anthropology tends to provide a better and more precise definition of culture. Two anthropologists, Kroeber and Kluckhohn (1952) present a definition that provides a very clear insight to this concept of culture, which states:

> Culture consists of patterns, explicit and implicit, of and for behavior acquired
> and transmitted by symbols, constituting the distinctive achievement of human

groups, including their embodiments in artifacts; the essential core of culture consists of traditional (i.e., historically derived and selected) ideas and especially their attached values; culture systems may, on the one hand, be considered as products of action, on the other hand as conditioning elements of further action."[2]

It is important to note a concept of culture as implicit and explicit patterns of and for behavior, distinctive achievements, artifacts, ideas, and their attached values. These concepts of culture may not lend themselves readily to a regular and more contemporary definition of culture, but they present profound insights into what culture really means. It is appropriate to analyze this definition in order to appreciate its practicality and utility.

AMERICAN CULTURE AS A MOSAIC

Given the plurality of the American ethnic makeup, one would rightly question the validity of a reference to "American culture." The whole concept of American culture must be seen as pluralistic in its essence. American culture is more of a mosaic. Within the larger umbrella of the American cultural mosaic there is a macroculture, which serves as the glue or the frame that holds the rest of the microcultures in place. This macroculture is essentially the American flavor of Anglo-Saxon Protestant culture, which was the dominant culture of colonial America and has continued to be the dominant culture of modern-day America. Its dominance should not suggest the exclusion or marginalization of the rest of the microcultures, which in earlier days were Irish, German, Scottish, Polish, Italian, African, Chinese, Japanese, and Native American (not an exhaustive list). The contemporary face of American microcultures reveals a numberless array of cultures representing peoples of all countries on Earth. The idea of American culture as a mosaic stems from the fact that English remains the dominant language of commerce and trade as well as government, while other languages are affirmed as credible and valuable for commerce and diplomatic relations as well.

The American ideas and ideals that govern the way things are done here, such as freedom, equality, equal access to opportunities, capitalism, and free enterprise have remained the same over the more than two hundred years that this nation has been in existence. Second-generation children of immigrants mostly adopt this mainstream Anglo-Saxon Protestant culture, but they tend to keep their ancestral cultures as well. This tendency toward biculturalism is very much a dynamic of the American immigrant population and not a rejection of the mainstream culture. A cross-section of the American cultural matrix may, therefore, reveal a plurality of cultures, yet each microculture is only one small face within a larger mosaic glued together by the principles and practices that were established under a predominantly Anglo-Saxon Protestant culture. In this respect we can confidently speak about American culture without necessarily contradicting ourselves.

American Culture as Patterns of Behaviors/Practices

First, let's look at culture as consisting of patterns "of behavior, as well as providing patterns for behavior." Within every cultural group there are certain patterns of behavior that are unique to them. For many generations, when an American was walking down a street of Paris or Frankfurt, for example, an average European more often than not could tell that the individual was an American, even before the American opened his or her mouth. This may no longer be as prevalent as it used to be, due to a growing global trend of Americanization. Nevertheless, Americans carry themselves in a way that distinguishes them. They are often assertive and walk with broad shoulders. Americans know their rights and demand them, though sometimes their assertiveness is offensive to some non-Americans.[3] Some other cultures would be more yielding, even when their rights are being infringed upon, but an average American would not tolerate any appearance of humiliation or an infringement of his or her rights. Another behavior pattern that characterizes Americans is curiosity and a daredevil attitude. According to a Zimbabwean tourist guide at Victoria Falls, someone dies falling into the waterfall each year, and 90 percent of the time it is an American.

Indeed, each cultural group has behavior patterns that distinguish it from the others. A Nigerian friend told his story about walking into a shop in Mali, West Africa, and the shopkeeper sat leisurely in his seat, not bothering that he had a customer. After walking around for a few minutes and noticing that the shopkeeper was not going to come and assist him, my friend walked up to him and asked, "Mr. Man, are you selling these items or are they just for display? Haven't you noticed you have a customer?" The shopkeeper got up from his seat and said, "You must be a Nigerian. Nobody from around here will speak to me like that." He knew because patterns of behavior can be significantly different from one part of Africa to another.

American Culture as Symbols

A second focus within this definition of culture is the idea of culture being transmitted through symbols. Every cultural group has symbols that distinguish it from the rest of the world. Each country has its own flag, which is the most commonly shared symbol across the world. Other symbols, however, distinguish some cultures in unique ways. The Statue of Liberty has become a symbol of American freedom. Anywhere the image of that statue is seen across the world, it clearly identifies the United States, and no other nation. A less lofty example, the hamburger, has also become a cultural symbol, signifying the American fast pace of life.

America is one of the few countries of the world where it is acceptable for people to be walking along the street with a cup of Starbucks coffee or a soda can and possibly a hamburger to go with it, or driving with one hand and eating with the other. In some cultures, etiquette despises such behaviors. On the flip side, many French people and people of former French colonies still observe a two-hour afternoon lunch, which goes with a siesta. The average American would look at that as a reckless waste of productivity and manpower. Life seems slower paced in many European countries compared to America as symbolized by the hamburger.

American Culture as Human Achievement

Every country of the world has museums that are filled with statues, monuments, images, and publications about national heroes and cultural icons. What makes an individual a hero or icon varies from society to society. Accomplishments that bring lots of recognition among some peoples may not attract any serious attention from others. For many countries in Africa and Central and South America, soccer players have the highest honor a sports person can possibly achieve. People in the United States, however, honor football, baseball, and basketball players, games that are hardly noticed in most of the countries that value soccer. Human achievements thus tell us about different cultures and ways of life. The history and culture of the United States have been heavily influenced and shaped by the Revolutionary War. Monuments have been erected for George Washington, and the significance of the achievements of Washington and his comrades can be seen in the American spirit of fearlessness, tenacity, and courage. America does not shy away from wars, because there is a legacy of victory as well as the need for self-preservation. In fact, it is said that the earliest American flag had the symbol of a rattlesnake on it, sending the message, "Don't step on me or you will be bitten." That message shaped America's response to Pearl Harbor and the most recent attack of September 11, 2001.

A monument was also erected to honor Abraham Lincoln, America's leader in one of the most difficult times in its history. Lincoln's bravery, ingenuity, and leadership skills were primary factors in the Union's victory in the Civil War, as well as in America's ability to forge ahead as one nation despite that war.

More recently, a monument was commissioned to honor Martin Luther King, Jr. At the commissioning ceremony, George W. Bush, the U.S. president at the time, stated in his speech that it was not coincidental that Martin Luther King's memorial was being erected in the same area where both Washington's and Lincoln's memorials stand. He stated that whereas Washington fought for the promise of America's freedom, Lincoln extended that freedom to all Americans, but Martin Luther King, Jr., made that promise a reality. In effect, therefore, each one of these monuments must be seen as a celebration of achievements within the American cultural ideal of freedom.

Apart from these monuments, we also have all kinds of halls of fame. The Football Hall of Fame, the Broadcasting Hall of Fame, and various music halls of fame are just a few. We have the Hollywood Walk of Fame as well, which celebrates the achievements of individuals who have made significant contributions to the entertainment industry. It is part of the American culture to celebrate human achievements.

The American Culture as Sets of Ideas and Belief Systems

Some of the most significant ideas that have shaped the American cultural landscape include the ideas of freedom, equality, and happiness.[4] The earliest Europeans who came to America came in search of freedom, and that idea of freedom was behind the resistance to the English throne that led to the American Revolution. The American concept of freedom is reflected in the way an average American lives his or her life. One of the cultural shocks that immigrants from Asia, Africa, and South America face on coming to America is the extent of freedom that America's children enjoy. The authority with which parents from developing countries rule their families is drastically reduced once they step onto American soil. Individual freedom is a highly prized asset, and American culture respects it more than anything else. On the matter of equality, whereas Americans can be rightfully accused of scoring very poorly in the historical past in terms of human rights and social equality, it has emerged in the last few decades at the forefront of the global battle for equity and fair play. Such progress is possible because the U.S. Constitution assumes that "all men are created equal, and endowed with such inalienable rights as life, liberty, and the pursuit of happiness" (First Amendment). This idea is the bedrock on which the structures of equality that have become part of everyday life in America have been built and on which the battles for human rights have been fought. It is an ideology that has indeed shaped America throughout its history and continues to do so.

Lastly, the idea of happiness is one that most writers rarely pay close attention to. This ideology, however, is fundamental to the American way of life. Is it not significant that the United States may be the only country on Earth that includes the idea of happiness in its constitution? Americans have grown to love a life of pursuing happiness. We love big cars, big homes, big television screens, and whatever else we believe can make us happy. The sad part of the influence of this idea of happiness is the effect it has had on family structure in recent years. Men and women are no longer willing to work on difficult relationships. People quickly exit a marriage once they sense that their happiness is threatened.

Kroeber and Kluckhohn's definition of culture, therefore, presents us with an exhaustive survey that takes the concept beyond the conventional one of traditions, beliefs, and practices. Based on their definition, we can conclude that a more precise way to look at culture would be to conceptualize it as *a given set of ideas, belief systems, worldviews, practices, and artifacts that define a people as well as distinguish them from others.*

A CROSS-SECTION OF THE AMERICAN CULTURAL ARRANGEMENT

Within any society, culture must be conceptualized as an arrangement, a structure, and an organized system. Culture is learned, shared, adaptable, and dynamic.[5] Culture is made up of internal and superficial elements, concrete and symbolic elements. The superficial and symbolic aspects of the culture often deceive visitors and newcomers, who may fail to probe its internal and concrete aspects. Strict discipline and engagement is required for newcomers to a cultural arrangement in order to fully understand the intricacies of the setting.

In this work, however, we prefer to look at the elements or contents of culture as arranged in an intricate web of relationships. To fully understand culture, we need to look at it as one unit of an intricate set of arrangements. Then we will dissect it and look at each component on the basis of its significance and merit, and subsequently at each one in relationship to the others. Charles Kraft discusses cultural patterning and the centralization of worldview in this kind of arrangement.[6] He identifies four significant components of culture as religious structures, social structure, technological structure, and linguistic structure, with worldview as the core, which he labels the organizer of conceptualization.

Whereas sociologists categorize religious and economic structures as well as political and family structures as parts of social institutions and structures, Kraft separated these structures and made social structure a category among others (religious, linguistic, and technological). It makes sense to speak of culture as a more embracing concept, with social structure as the aspect that deals with family structures, regulation of human behaviors, values and norms, social relationships, associations, and other similar arrangements. In the present work, therefore, we have chosen to build on Kraft's ideas and attempt to conceptualize culture as a sphere with a core and six different components (see figure 2.1). The core is worldview, Kraft's organizer of conceptualizations.

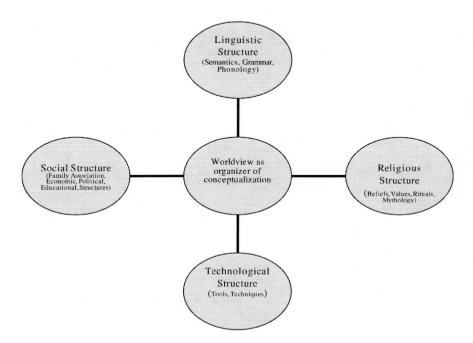

Figure 2.1.   Charles Kraft's Cultural Patterns

The components of culture are expanded to six in order to separate the political and economic subcultures from the social, since these are very complex structures in and of themselves. Sociologists identify specific areas within which basic human needs are met in society, and those include the family sector; educational institutions; and the economic, religious, and political sectors.[7]

Therefore, we have the following substructures: religious, political, economic, linguistic, technological, and social arrangements. These structures can enable us to engage the American culture and worldview. The web of cultural patterning that represents this is illustrated in figure 2.2.

The Structure of American Macroculture

In this section we will focus on the structure of the mainstream American culture, to which all Americans, regardless of race and ethnicity subscribe. The substructure we have presented above represents this macroculture. In order to appreciate the unique significance of each substructure within this macroculture, we will engage each one as an individual part of the unit.

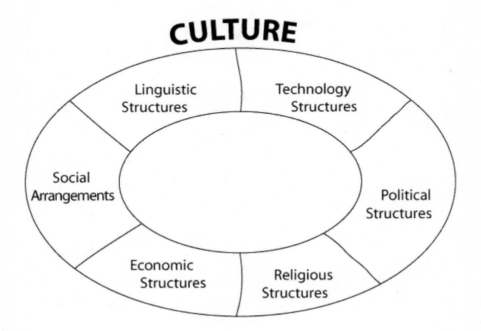

Figure 2.2.   American Cultural Patterning

A group of sociologists wrote the following words just a few years ago, "A description of American social structure would indicate the presence of monogamy along with Judeo-Christian values and norms and the institutionalization of economic competition and of democratic political organizations."[8] This statement is less than adequate in describing the American social structure, since along with the monogamous family structure, you have Mormon polygamist practices along with rampant divorces and remarriages, which can now been seen as serial polygamy. The Judeo-Christian values are presently being challenged by a secular humanistic worldview that is pervading the American moral and spiritual landscape. These substructures—religious substructures, political substructures, economic substructures, linguistic substructures, technological substructures, and social arrangements—must be examined in depth.

The U.S. Religious Substructure

Émile Durkheim defines religion as "a unified system of beliefs and practices relative to sacred things, that is so to say, things set apart and forbidden— beliefs and practices which unites into one single moral community called a Church."[9] America in the twenty-first century is religiously pluralistic. The history of this nation points back to a beginning steeped in Anglo-Saxon Protestant heritage. This heritage, while still very strong and enduring, has gradually yielded to a more inclusive religious atmosphere in keeping with the Bill of Rights, which entitles every American to a choice of religion without any governmental interference.

The Anglo-Saxon Protestant ethic, however, strongly influenced both the legal and political arrangements of America, and it has remained a very strong influence. Today, along with it, are myriad Eastern religions such as Buddhism, Hinduism, Confucianism, and Islam. America in the twentieth century actually saw the birth of a new religious expression known as the New Age movement, along with other ideologies that some have chosen to classify as religious despite strong objections from the adherents. Such ideologies include the cults of American patriotism, atheism, Secular Humanism, and many other philosophical ideologies, some of which have become almost militant. America has, therefore, become a land where you have the right to worship anything you choose. America even floats an organized Church of Satan. Religious tolerance, therefore, distinguishes the United States from many other nations, where citizens are compelled to adhere to specific religious traditions. Some fundamentalist Christians are always talking about a return to our Christian roots; such a return may be practically impossible, given the unique cultural characteristics of twenty-first-century America. The United States will continue to be a land of freedom of religious expression, but the dominance of one religion over others may be impracticable.

Political Substructure

The American political system is rooted in representative government. Office holders are empowered by the citizens (electorates) through an electoral process to serve, thus giving them legal mandate to hold public office and maintain public liberties.[10] The idea of freedom has been established as the basic principle that led to the founding of this nation as well as a principle that led to the fighting and winning of the American Revolution. That principle set the stage for America's political arrangement. The U.S. Declaration of Independence states, "We hold these truths to be self-evident, that all men are created equal, that they are endowed by their creator with certain unalienable Rights, which among these are Life, Liberty and pursuit of Happiness."[11] Americans pride themselves in being seen as the architects of the modern democratic system of government. In the American Revolution they rejected the tyrannical sway of the British Crown and set up their own government, raising a farmer and former military general (George Washington) to a rank equal to that of kings, yet making sure he did not see himself as one.

The three arms of government (the executive, legislative, and judicial) provide checks and balances, and ensure that the people continue to have a voice in the way their nation is run. Abraham Lincoln later encapsulated the concept of democracy as "government of the people, by the people and for the people."[12] This concept is very much American. In the twenty-first century we have seen democracy at work in the United States as George Bush, in the wake of the terrorist activity of September 11, 2001, had to lobby the U.S. Congress to give him authorization before he could go to war against the Taliban in Afghanistan. Despite the fact that he was the chief executive, he needed to avoid a unilateral decision when it came to putting America's young people in harm's way. The common citizens got involved in this decision process as many congressmen and congresswomen sent out questionnaires to their constituents to find out what they thought about going to war against Iraq before they could vote yes or no. This is democracy at its best, and no country seems to exemplify these principles today the way America does.

The Economic Substructure

The concept of American freedom and independence is best embodied in the spirit of the frontier movement: one individual venturing out with his family and setting up a homestead in the middle of nowhere. The frontiersman could take this risk because he knew that when he tilled the land and planted his tobacco, corn, or cotton, he could harvest the farm proceeds and keep the whole profit. The American capitalist system is seen as liberating. It is a major factor that has placed America at the forefront of the international market economy. Some historians believe that all human actions, and consequently culture and social development, derive from a people's economic conditions. This idea holds that "all social standing and political power is based on one's level of prosperity."[13] Individual ownership of property encourages adventure and economic initiatives.

The American marketplace features all levels of entrepreneurs. Through tax cuts and other incentives, the government encourages the average American to enter the marketplace as sellers, not just buyers. This encouragement is absent in many other countries, where the line between the "haves" and "have-nots" has been drawn. Rags-to-riches stories characterize the American social arena. By the end of 2003, The United States could boast of an average of 3,500,000 millionaires.[14] Sadly, this number was reduced following the economic crisis of 2008–2009. In 2003, it was said that the two wealthiest men in America were richer than the sixty of the world's poorest countries combined. The nature of the American marketplace makes that possible.

The Technological Substructure

In the 1990s, Alvin Toffler said that "the control of knowledge is the crux of tomorrow's worldwide struggle for power."[15] Through technological advancements the United States has earned a central position in the marketplace of the control of knowledge. It is the world's leading superpower, and this is largely due to its place at the forefront of technological advancements, leading the world in commercial aviation, the computer industry, as well as space exploration. The United States furnish the world's leading specialists in all of these fields and more. The recent war in Iraq launched a new level of technological advancement that no other country of the world has been able to match: cluster bombs, night-vision goggles, global positioning satellites, and much more. America furnishes warships whose dimensions are unimaginable in many civilized nations. Any random poll of American students will reveal that an average student in American classrooms comes from a home with at least two computers with Internet connection, while a study in 2004 showed that only about 2 percent of the entire world population has regular access to the Internet.[16] Life in the United States is becoming more and more technology dependent, while many parts of the world are still playing catch up in the technology game. The boost in technology has pushed commerce in the United States to a higher level, as technology has practically destroyed geographical limitations: video conferences, mobile phones with Internet connectivity, iPods, podcasting, wi-fi, Twitter, Facebook, and many more innovations are the order of the day.

Linguistic Structures

One of the nations whose language has undergone the most dynamic transformation in this century may be the United States. The *dominant language* of English has long departed from its roots in terms of grammar, syntax, and even lexical structures. Significant variations now exist between British and American meanings of certain words and sentences. Spelling has changed, and new vocabularies that were not previously English have been incorporated. Americans speak a version of the English language that is exclusively American.

It is always a funny irony to hear Americans accuse the English of speaking with an accent. The possibility of that irony validates the fact that American English has taken its own unique identity. Even within American societies we notice slight regional variations that further illustrate the significance of language as a cultural construct. The English language has become a major tool for spreading American culture to many parts of the world. English-language studies are popular in many nations who want to do business with America.

Social Arrangement

Over the years the term *social institutions* has been used by sociologists to suggest many different things. One sociologist gives it a concise definition, part of the which states that social institutions are "purposive, regulatory, and consequently primary cultural configurations, formed unconsciously and/or deliberately, to satisfy individual wants and social needs bound up with the efficient operation of any plurality of persons."[17] Within what was known as social institutions, such things as family structure, political arrangements, and educational programs are all included. For the purpose of this work, the term *social arrangement* is used instead of *social institution*, in order to avoid the term *institution* being taken as an abstraction rather than a perceived reality.[18] Social arrangements would, therefore, include family structures, housing, educational programs, institutions, and structures dealing with human welfare and coexistence.

Traditional American society was clearly identifiable as constituting communities of families. Homogeneity was a factor that pulled people together. Being a nation of immigrants, each immigrant population tended to settle in the same area to provide support and protection to their kind. A family was a man, his wife, and children. Schools were locally controlled, as they were initially the creation of the individual communities, not the government. Certain elements of these social structures remain a big part of American social identity today. Schools remain a community-based effort, despite the current attempts by the state and federal governments to regulate and supervise educational practices. The most powerful decision-making body in the school system remains the local school board, publicly elected by the people to run the schools. Given the steady urbanization process and the end of legally protected institutional discrimination in America, the makeup of communities is changing as people are now free to live wherever they choose. Some smaller communities continue to resist this change by refusing housing to the "out group" despite federal and state laws that prohibit such practices. The structure of the family has also changed. The American family is now a mosaic. Some are made up of a mom, dad, and children, others by a man and woman with no children, yet others by just a mom and children or dad and children. It could be grandparents and grandchildren, two moms and children, two dads and children, just to name a few possibilities.

With the increasing rise in urbanization, American society has continued to become more and more individualistic. The individualism of the twenty-first century may be said to be significantly different from that of the twentieth century. In previous centuries Americans cared about what neighbors would say and how the community would react to certain behaviors and lifestyles, but today's America seems to care less. As long as the lifestyle or behavior does not hurt anyone else, the individual feels it is his or her constitutional right to carry on with it, even if the whole community frowns at it. Such a radical shift has made gay and lesbian marriages, which were practically unheard of, front-page news in twenty-first-century America. So the American family structure has changed forever.

THE INTERACTIONS BETWEEN
AMERICAN CULTURAL SYSTEMS

There is a dynamic interaction that takes place between American cultural systems. These systems are so interrelated that any change in one affects what goes on in the other structures. Figure 2.3 illustrates this interaction.

Let's start with the technological structures that we mentioned earlier. The rapid advancement in American technology is only possible because

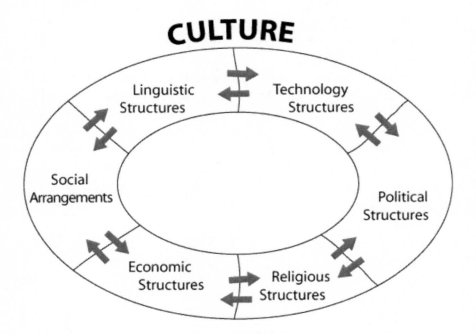

Figure 2.3.   Interactions of Cultural Structures in the American Cultural Systems

of the kind of capitalist economic system available in American society. American citizens and corporations know that they have a free market economy. Whatever they invent is theirs, and the government cannot take it away from them. The American government actually facilitates entrepreneurial spirit and invention, as the government is about the largest market for American corporations, with a defense budget at one point that was larger than the combined national budgets of the ten next most-developed countries (the Iraqi war years).[19] Much of this money is spent on defense technology, which is usually outsourced to American corporations like Boeing and Halliburton.

America is proud to produce men like Bill Gates, who has taken the world of technology to another level. Gates is willing to put all his energy and resources into technological advancements because he stands to benefit substantially from it. It has made him one of the wealthiest men on Earth, wealthier than many poor countries of the world combined.[20] American technological advancements have also affected its linguistic structures. Words that were unknown twenty to thirty years ago are now everyday language, for example, Internet, e-mail, Web page, Facebook, Twitter, MySpace, and many more.

The advancement in technology has its own ripple effect on the political landscape of the United States. The 2004 Democratic primary elections felt the power of technology as Vermont governor Howard Dean used the Internet to recruit a new breed of financiers for the Democratic Party that had otherwise been ignored. With the power of the Internet, he was thrown ahead of the other candidates for many weeks. Barack Obama built upon this breakthrough in 2008, raising more money and support than any other politician before him and receiving more votes than any other past president to become the first U.S. president of African descent. Electronic voting is another new addition to the American political landscape. It is believed that with this system being developed in many states, reliability of election results will be higher and more people will also be able to vote. However, there is also a higher possibility for election fraud, as computers can be programmed to swap votes. A radio broadcast recently featured a blind woman in California who was praising the electronic voting system as empowering to the blind because they would no longer need a third party to verify the content of their ballots before concluding their voting. So technology can empower or inhibit individual participation in the electoral process, and consequently affect who is voted into office.

As the political structure is being affected, it is, on the other hand, affecting the social arrangement. In 2004, the mayor of San Francisco opened city hall for gay marriages to be performed in violation of a state law that bans same-sex marriage. The mayor was confident in doing this because, having surveyed his constituents, he believed he had enough support to go ahead. Politicians who feel that their constituents agree with a social agenda will work hard to push that agenda, even if it goes contrary to traditionally held views that once defined the sociocultural landscape.

As politicians are empowering same-sex marriages through legislations and unilateral actions, traditional religious organizations are compelled to revise their positions on it. Denominations like the United Methodist Church, the Presbyterian Fellowship of America, and the Episcopal Church have all been fractured by elements that would take a progressive position over and against the traditional stance of these churches. The social landscape is being redrawn as gay marriages take place and churches open their doors to them. It is not only the social and political movements that are reshaping America's religious landscapes. Russell Chandler identifies such forces as immigration, ecology, education, the media, and the arts, as additional factors reshaping America's religious landscapes.[21]

THE AMERICAN WORLDVIEW AS THE CONDITIONING ELEMENTS OF CULTURE

Worldview is at the core of any cultural arrangement. Charles Kraft has defined worldview as "the central systematization of conceptions underlying the way a people view reality." He describes it as the factor to which the members of the culture (largely unconsciously) owe their conception of reality, and from which stems their value system."[22] Worldview, therefore, is the hub that drives the wheels of culture. Figure 2.4 portrays the place of worldview in the cultural arrangement.

First, in the diagram (figure 2.4), let's focus on the faint arrows going from the worldview into the different cultural structures. This illustrates how worldview quietly fashions these structures. The arrows are faint, suggesting the almost imperceptible nature of the process by which worldview structures and forms the cultural systems.

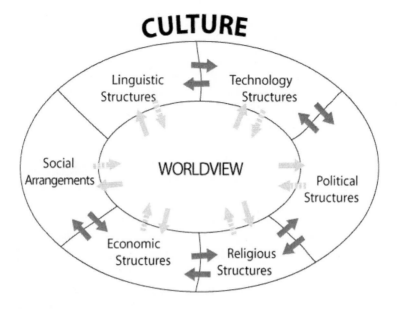

Figure 2.4. Worldview in Cultural Arrangements

To fully understand the nature of American worldview, we must isolate each of the cultural structures we have already identified above and discuss how worldview helped to shape them in the American cultural milieu.

American Worldview as the Conditioning Element of the American Social Structure

Above we identified culture as sets of ideas and belief systems. It is clear that ideas and belief systems are nontangible elements. Ideas, particularly, originate from worldview, and the place of worldview as the conditioning element of cultural structures is central. Values are one of the most visible elements of culture, yet these originate from the worldview level. Values cannot stand on their own without the concrete social structures that we call culture. Amitai Etzioni put it succinctly, that "values not mediated through concrete social structures tend to become tenuous, frail, and, in the long run, insupportable."[23] The idea of freedom led the first set of immigrants from Europe to leave their countries of birth in search of a new life in the New World. This idea of freedom originated from their interpretation of the Bible, which asserts the sovereignty of individual lives and the right of humans to serve God by choice.

This idea of freedom influenced the way these immigrants lived their lives in the New World. Coupled with that idea of freedom was the idea of individual right to property ownership. Aware that they were not under any governmental restriction to reside in any one locale or practice a specific kind of trade, these immigrants wandered into the American hinterlands. A man and his wife and children could go to the middle of nowhere, clear the bushes, erect a homestead, and establish a home. They were willing to fight off the natives alongside wild animals and other foes to establish themselves in a place of their own choosing. This sense of freedom and individuality has now translated to a more observable social structure of single homes. Children are desirous to leave the home once they are of age, in search of their own future.

Unlike many other cultures, American parents are not very much inclined to pushing their children toward one profession or the other. They tend to want to leave the children to make their choices as long as it would help them stay happy. This is one way the worldview of a people helps shape their social organization. Another example is the fact that individual freedom and rights is at the heart of the restructuring that is taking place in the marriage institution in America today. Many Americans do not like the homosexual lifestyle, but they recognize the rights of these individuals to live their lives the way they choose. The worldview that says they are free to make their choices and live their lives by their own standards is fundamental to the progressive thinking of today's America.

American Worldview: The Conditioning Element of the American Economy

At the heart of the American capitalist economic system is a Judeo-Christian, Protestant ethic on money and material property ownership. This worldview, which traces back to the Anglo-Saxon Protestant origin of the mainstream culture, is the defining worldview that gives American capitalism its form. Max Weber was probably the first person to categorically link capitalism to Protestantism. According to him, capitalism, "as an economic system is a creation of the Reformation."[24] Weber examined the writings of Benjamin Franklin as influential in shaping American capitalism,[25] and thus he described American capitalism in very unique, yet culturally specific, language. Weber saw American capitalism as the most naive and open form yet to exist. His interpretation of Franklin yielded unique perceptions of capitalism. The reality of capitalism is presented in the following writings,

> In capitalist economies, the making of money takes on the character of a purpose rather than a necessity. It becomes a value rather than something that happens by chance or something that wells out of the avarice of a particular individual. There develops a collective "spirit" which advocates the idea that each person is called upon to make the utmost of his life and, furthermore, that the form this should take is devotion to industry in this world.[26]

The spirit of American freedom and individuality once again resonates in this statement. The individual is of a paramount significance, not the system. The worth of the individual, however, did not become as significant in relation to the system until, at least, the Reformation when Luther advanced the place of the individual and his or her access to salvation by faith alone.[27] As a result of the Reformation, the significance of the individual rose above that of the system. Cuzzort and King, writing about Weber's discussion of American capitalism, stated, "Capitalism must be understood as a mass phenomenon. It is a culturally prescribed way of living; it is a complex of ideals; it is a change in the older moral order."[28]

Once again, the note of individualism resounds, a note that is very much a part of the American history and way of life. Some people would like to conceptualize the individual rights to property and individual freedom as "made in America." These are indeed fundamental human rights, which America, more than any other nation on Earth, helped push to the forefront of both political and economic ideologies. American capitalism, therefore, stems from America's view of life and reality—America's worldview.

The Judeo-Christian elements can be found in numberless Bible references that emphasize hard work and individual right to property. The parable of the vineyard workers in Matthew, chapter 20, addresses the case of a landowner who hired laborers to work in his vineyard. He hired the first set in the morning, negotiated a wage with them, and put them to work. At noon he hired another set and put them into the same field. Just an hour before the workday ended he hired yet another set of workers and put them in the same field. At the end he pays them the same wage. The earliest workers started to grumble and accuse him of unfairness. He asked them whether he paid them a penny less than their agreed wage, and they answered no. He then questioned why they would begrudge his generosity. He chose to use his money the way he pleased, and they had no reason to complain.

Another Bible parable talks about a master who gave his servants varying amounts of money, as he was about to travel. To one he gave five talents, to another three, and yet another one. The first two traded with their talents and made profits of the same amount, thus doubling their talents. The last one chose not to invest the money and quickly gave it back to the owner upon his return, claiming he was afraid of losing it. The owner scolded him and took the one he had and gave it to the one who had ten, thus making him richer (Matthew 25:14–30). Here is another classic illustration of the benefit of hard work and industry, as well as its accompanying benefit of keeping the whole profit, an underlying ideology of the American capitalist economy. The Judeo-Christian economic principles therefore are fundamental to the way Americans buy and sell.

American Worldview as the Conditioning Element for Our Technological Climate

Twenty-first-century America is the world's leader in the field of technology. Competition and the drive to be free, is at the root of American technological advancement. America is always afraid of the emergence of another world superpower that can overthrow its democracy and rob its citizens of their freedom. The need to safeguard freedom and democracy pushes America to invest invaluable resources and energy into technological advancements. When America went into Iraq a few years ago, it was practically sending a message to the rest of the world, and especially to other superpowers: "Look, we are still ahead, so don't get any ideas into your head." Such a war as the one in Iraq served as a testing ground for America's technological advancements.

A more significant insight is that much of these technological advances start at individual nongovernmental corporate levels. Businesses and corporations develop these technologies and then try to sell them to the government. In many other countries of the world, individual corporations cannot even attempt developing these technologies without the government authorizing them to. But a country based on a free market economy and individual rights like the United States provides a context for such excursions into the world of the technologically unknown.

American Worldview as the Conditioning Element
for Religious Plurality

The United States in the twenty-first century can be said to be religiously pluralistic. This is a statement many conservative Christians would rather not hear, but it is the reality of the American religious landscape. When in the First Amendment the founding fathers stated that, "Congress shall make no laws establishing religion or prohibiting the free exercise thereof," they entrenched in our national life and social structure, a pluralistic ideology as the defining element for the American religious landscape. It is possible that given the overwhelming Christian presence of that era, the full implications of this declaration were probably not evident, but as America matures and takes shape as a country of immigrants, the reality of the American pluralistic religious landscape has come into clear focus. An interpretation that has often been read into this part of the First Amendment is that when this open door to religious expression was established, most people in America thought of religion as differing expressions of Christianity and Judaism and secretive fraternities and sects that took some religious forms, such as Freemasonry.

Robert Nisbet in his interpretation of Émile Durkheim's views on religion attributes to him an assertion that religion exerts limitless influence on culture and personality.[29] The fundamental principle, however, is that the American founding fathers had a great regard for the sovereignty of the individual right to choose how to worship God. This understanding does not restrict this right to just Christians, but to every individual expression of worship or even a deliberate refusal to worship. At the heart of this declaration is a fundamental evangelistic interpretation of the Christian faith. The call to worship God, according to the New Testament, is a call to the individual. The gospels give the individual a choice to respond one way or the other to the call to faith. The gospels oppose the use of force in bringing anyone to faith in Jesus Christ. This understanding of worship is responsible for the Pilgrim's refusal to be restrained by the Church of England, hence the search for a land of freedom where they could exercise their faith without the intervention of government. Freedom of worship, therefore, is fundamental to the American way of life. It is at the heart of the founding principles of this land, and remains a principle that sets America apart from most nations on earth. This is a unique cultural element, brought about by a very strong Evangelical Christian worldview.

THE INTERACTIVE NATURE OF CULTURAL
STRUCTURES AND THEIR EFFECT ON WORLDVIEW

American cultural structures, like those of any people, are not independent entities. They are codependent, and we have established that fact. A more significant factor, however, is that these structures also interact to produce significant shifts and changes at the core of the society's worldview patterns. Worldview therefore is not a constant. It is subject to modifications, given a level of interaction with various cultural structures and societal forms. A significant change in one or more cultural structures can produce a major rearrangement of the worldview patterns and significantly alter the worldview.

In the case of the American cultural arrangement, the sudden invasion of religious pluralism has led to a rearrangement of the way American societies are expressing their religious freedom. There was a time in America when the worldview was significantly religious, and that religious worldview was essentially Christian. Over the years, gains made during the civil rights movement empowered some individuals to openly begin to express a nontheistic worldview. This movement has been further enhanced by advancements in the fields of science, as secular science gradually moves away from a religious explanation of the origin of life. An overtly religious explanation of divine intervention in life situations has practically given way to a more existential explanation in the American popular worldview. This is a major shift in the conceptualization of reality.

Another area where changes in the cultural structures have rearranged our worldview is in the area of social arrangements. The classic American concept of family until recently has been husband and wife, with or without children. In recent years, along with increased divorce rates and the fact that liberal minds have pushed same-gender unions as a civil right, the family has been redefined. As society allows civil rights to take precedence over the preservation of the status quo, the worldview on the definition of family has practically changed. It has become politically incorrect to see same-sex partnership as indecent—a previously respected way of viewing same-sex unions.

A constant dynamic of this nature of worldview rearrangement is that it is usually a painful process. The worldview is the most resistant arena of change in any cultural arrangement. Any issue that attempts to alter the way a people view reality—marriage, family, religion, humanity—is usually strongly resisted. In figure 2.5, the arrows from the individual cultural structures to the worldview are deliberately presented as faint and broken because

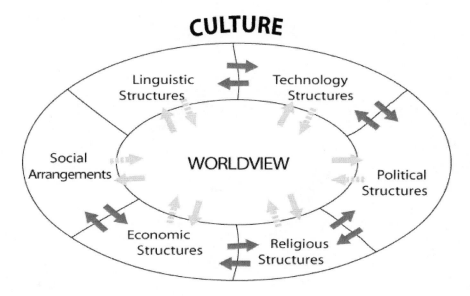

Figure 2.5. Worldview Alterations

the dynamics of change are never a straight shot, due to the nature of the opposition that any change encounters before it finally succeeds.

It is important, therefore, to be aware of the fact that when we aim at altering any individual structure within a cultural arrangement, we are not only changing that structure, but attempting to change the whole society's worldview. The broken arrows demonstrate how often the changes that take place in one simple cultural system can affect the whole worldview arrangement. Recently in America, there has been a battle between the gay rights movements and groups and individuals who hold to a traditional view of family and marriage.

For most people, when gays and lesbians ask for rights to be married and to be recognized and accepted by society as legitimate unions, it is simply a matter of civil rights. For others it is more than that. It is a matter of worldview alteration. A recognition of gay marriage as legitimate will affect the way society sees marriage and family for the endless future. Family trees will no longer be what we have traditionally known them to be. Our health care system will be more and more challenged in tracing family health history. These changes will affect our tax systems, religious expressions and doctrines, marketing strategies, and even our political structures.

Another example of this worldview restructuring might be taking place outside the United States, as we speak. Recently America undertook to overthrow Saddam Hussein's dictatorship and introduce democracy in Iraq. It sounded lofty and good, but the reality is that the introduction of democracy affects all the other structures of Iraqi society: economy (free market), language (English will become more commonly used), religion (Christian and non-Christian faiths will find inroads), technology (capitalism opens the door to more contemporary technology), social arrangement (the place of women and minorities will be redefined and improved). As these structures are being revised, the ways Iraqis view reality will be changed forever.

QUESTIONS AND APPLICATION

Case Study: The Cultural Rearrangement of Iraq

In April 2003 the United States, under President George W. Bush, began a war to oust Iraqi dictator and human rights violator Saddam Hussein. Lots of speculations have taken place in the attempt to come to terms with the real motive for this war, but the official position is that Saddam Hussein's administration posed a threat to the security of the United States, as it was suspected of ties with terrorists as well as engaged in the production and possible use of weapons of mass destruction. Another compelling government position was that his records of human rights violations demanded an end to Saddam's rule of tyranny and the ushering in of a new era of freedom and human rights protection in the spirit of America's concept of democracy.

By implication, therefore, the U.S. government was not entering Iraq with the sole purpose of removing Saddam, but with an added agenda of establishing a democratic political order in a country and region that have never experienced democracy.

Challenge Questions

1. In view of the fact that political arrangement is an essential part of a society's cultural structure, how would a foreign imposition of democracy into Iraq likely affect the culture and structure of the future Iraqi society?
2. Should the U.S. succeed in imposing a democratic government, what other cultural structures and institutions of Iraq would be altered positively?

3. Should the U.S. succeed in imposing a democratic government, what other cultural structures and institutions of Iraq would be altered negatively?
4. In what ways would a democratic government affect the worldview of Iraqis, which has been essentially egalitarian and theocratic?
5. Should the U.S. desire to establish democracy succeed, what factors are likely to provoke an Iraqi resentment and opposition to the U.S. government?

Activity

Describe the unique cultural factors within the American way of life that distinguishes it from other democracies of the world. Compare and contrast U.S. capitalism with the capitalism of Great Britain.

Strategies for Application

Many different activities can be used to apply lessons from this chapter to K–12 educational settings, namely,

1. Research Projects—Grades 4–12 students can research their city, county, or state, using U.S. census data to determine the ethnic distribution of people across their chosen locality. They can further investigate the history and immigration pattern of each group, finding out when the people began their immigration to the United States and why; how they have adjusted to U.S. culture over the years; and what social, political, economic, and cultural challenges they have had to deal with over the years.
2. Field Trips—Teachers of K–12 students can organize field trips through historical sites in their city, county, or state. During such field trips, the history and cultural experiences of the various peoples of the city, county, or state will be the focus of investigation and discussion. Also, field trips to science and technology museums can be used as a way to help K–12 students engage the impact of technology and technological advancement on the culture of a people.

Chapter Three

The Crises of
Cross-Cultural Encounters

Chapter Objectives:

The purpose of this chapter is to discuss the crises of cross-cultural encounters, bias, prejudice, and other factors that often result from variance in cultural values, and different levels of cultural values adjustment. Readers will be able to:

1. define cultural values and explain cultural values adjustment
2. explain the implications of cultural values adjustment and maladjustment for multicultural education
3. take a cultural values adjustment survey to determine the extent of their cultural adjustment

The need for multicultural education arises from the stress of cross-cultural encounters. Humans do not exist in isolated culturally homogeneous units any more. We live in a global age, where barriers of race, ethnicity, distance, and civilization are continuously crumbling. How we relate to one another in this global age, however, is often determined by the beliefs and ideas that we hold about the groups or individuals who are different from us. Prejudice and bias have remained major factors that have led to crises in cross-cultural encounters. In this chapter we will attempt to explain how we develop cultural prejudices and biases, as well as attempt to propose practical ways to engage them.

Figure 3.1.   Issues in Discrimination

CULTURAL VALUES ADJUSTMENT:
A THEORETICAL BASIS FOR ENGAGING
INTERETHNIC AND INTERCULTURAL ENCOUNTERS

Kent Koppelman and R. Lee Goodhart explain two different ways people attempt to account for prejudice: (1) the process of forming opinions without looking at relevant facts, and (2) being irrational.[1] In responding to the idea that prejudice is the process of forming an opinion without looking at relevant facts, they argue that often people with prejudice do examine relevant facts and simply interpret them to confirm their prejudices. For the view that prejudice is a set of irrational conclusions, they argue that rational people sometimes hold prejudices. They give examples of (1) Aristotle, who claimed that women were inferior to men; (2) Abraham Lincoln, who held that African American people were intellectually inferior to white people;[2] and (3) Martin Luther, the leader of the Protestant Reformation, who told German Christians, "Do not doubt that next to the devil you have no enemy more cruel, more venomous and virulent, than a true Jew." Each one of these men was an icon in their various fields. They were critical thinking people, yet highly prejudiced.

The question that arises from the realization that perfectly rational and well meaning people can be highly prejudiced is why it is so. Koppelman and Goodhart attempted to suggest factors that lead to prejudice. Among those are elitism and zero-sum attitudes:

1. Elitism: This is the belief that most people succeed in society because they possess what it takes to succeed, while those who fail to succeed are naturally flawed and their failure to succeed is nobody's fault. This leads to a sense of entitlement and a condescending attitude toward others.
2. The zero-sum attitude: The idea here is that sharing power is not in the best interest of the person in possession of power, since the assumption is that the personal gain of one individual means a loss to the other.[3]

Koppelman and Goodhart also mention the 1982 book by Jack and William Levin in which they identify four causes of prejudice, namely:

1. Personal frustration: Personal failures and frustrations often lead the frustrated individuals to scapegoating tendencies.
2. Uncertainty about the "out group": Humans are usually afraid of the unknown. Avoidance exacerbates prejudices. Distance creates fear.
3. Threat to one's self-esteem: U.S. society trains people to develop self-esteem by comparing themselves with others. People are encouraged to develop a superiority complex as a way of validating the self.
4. Competition: Competition for scarce resources like jobs, good homes, even prestige and recognition, create grounds for putting down others so as to elevate the self.[4]

With due respect to these views and explanations, it needs to be argued that a fundamental factor responsible for the perpetuation of prejudice and intolerance is conflicts in cultural values. In order to make this argument, we must understand the meaning of values, cultural values, and the crises of cultural values adjustment.

Values

Values can be defined as sets of highly regarded codes of conduct and behavior parameters adopted by an individual or society. These guide one's behaviors, interactions, and judgments. Stephen Covey defined values as "the worth or priority we place on people, things, ideas, or principles."[5] Values are self-chosen beliefs and ideals; internal and subjective, based on how we see the world. Values are shaped by upbringing, society, and personal reflections.

Cultural Values

Janet Kalven (1982) asserts that human values are formed through the rewards and punishments that our parents, teachers, and peers mete out to us.[6] Every child is born and raised within a cultural context. That context defines for the child what is good and bad, moral or immoral. This is what we call ethics. It also defines for the child acceptable and unacceptable public and private behaviors, which often fall within the realm of etiquette. Beyond these two, however, the sociocultural context also defines, for the child, boundaries of social interaction. It tells the child who belongs and who does not belong within the social arrangement, which defines him or her. The criteria for determining who is within and who is outside of this social arrangement would often be ethnic, racial, socioeconomic, religious, or other factors. This child grows up seeing the world exclusively from this perspective and believing that these arrangements are natural limits within which he or she must operate.

Raths, Harmin, and Simon put this in a more technical frame when they identified seven traditional approaches to teaching values:

- Setting an example: when parents and teachers model behaviors for their children or students.
- Rules and regulations: established to promote or discourage certain behaviors.
- Persuasion: use of reasonable arguments to convince an individual to adopt certain values.
- Appeal to conscience: parents and teachers use this approach to discourage or dissuade a youngster from accepting or adopting an inappropriate or unacceptable value.
- Limited choices: Parents and teachers manipulate behaviors by limiting choices children can make; for example, some American white parents have been known to tell their girls, "You are never to come home with an African American man to this house." You limit the choices for them up front.
- Inspiration: Values are reinforced or recommended through inspirational materials like lectures, books, films, music, and so on.
- Dogma: We teach cultural or religious dogma, which prescribes certain values and discourages others; for example, "This is how our family has always done it" or "That is what the Bible says."[7]

Cultural Values Adjustment

The idea of cultural values adjustment assumes that no cultural system is perfect in and of itself. Also, no cultural system exists in complete isolation. The fact of our imperfection and the necessity of social interaction with others demand that we adjust our worldviews and value systems to be more accommodating of people outside of our own cultural arrangements. The challenge of cultural values adjustment comes as a child is exposed to other cultural values and social factors outside of what he or she has been taught. These new cultural values and standards confront some children early in life if they are privileged to go to school in a multicultural environment. Merely by interaction with children from other sociocultural environments their cultural values are challenged, and if the school environment is such that it encourages diversity and social integration, they will begin to adjust their cultural values very early in life. For kids who are raised in culturally sheltered environments, such as what obtains in suburban America or some inner cities, where the population is homogenous, children do not get this opportunity very early in life. The opportunity comes again if they have the chance of attending college in a culturally diverse environment. Most kids who are raised in the inner cities and happen to go to college are able to experience this shift during college years because the chances are high that they will attend a college with a diverse student population.

For some white kids from suburban America, however, a good number of them end up attending schools where the majority of the student population is from their own ethnic and socioeconomic levels. These individuals miss out, once again, from any chance of having their cultural values challenged, so they keep holding on to the views they brought from their suburban communities. A few of these kids, however, who happen to attend college in ethnically and/or economically diverse contexts are confronted with new and different sets of cultural values, and they are challenged to adjust their previously held views in order to accommodate an expanded and more inclusive cultural value system. This challenge often comes from classes that are structured to engage these issues. Sometimes, however, they can come from students' personal interactions and encounters with people from different backgrounds.

If the pressure comes as a result of academic discourse, analysis and synthesis of social situations and issues of social injustice, students are able to make personal decisions that can result in a cultural values adjustment that enables them to be open, receptive, and accommodating of other cultures and worldviews. Depending on the nature of the academic discourse, some students actually shut down and refuse to open themselves up to any new cultural values that would differ from what they have brought from home.

Cultural values adjustment is most effective when it happens in the course of interpersonal encounters. These may result from sharing a dormitory room with students from other sociocultural backgrounds or belonging to the same sports team, study group, or sorority. As students get to know each other at a personal level, they are able to continuously adjust their cultural values to accommodate their new friends and ensure that they get along. The academic discourse in the classroom setting often serves to facilitate this, but it does not accomplish values adjustment single-handedly. The end product of cultural adjustment is individuals who have allowed their cultural values to expand to accommodate and include other cultures. In so doing they redefine for themselves a new cultural identity. They are no longer the individuals that left home to go to college; instead they are new personalities with new (enhanced) values that are expanding beyond their childhood cultural boundaries.

This is the kind of experience that makes it possible for some kids who are raised in culturally shielded environments to still find themselves in interethnic or interracial marriages. They have grown to acquire a new appreciation of some cultures that are outside of their own cultural boundaries.

More significantly, individuals who have undergone this adjustment process are able to function more effectively in a culturally diverse environment. Professionally they are able to work more collaboratively with individuals who are from different cultural backgrounds. If they are teachers, they are more capable of creating a diversity-sensitive learning environment in which all students feel affirmed and accepted. Rosa Hernandez-Sheets describes these teachers as culturally inclusive teachers.[8] They are culturally competent teachers who are able to facilitate learning for all children. Lindsey et al. refer to this level of competency as cultural proficiency.[9] It is important to discuss factors that inhibit this level of competency or proficiency in individuals as we explore avenues to promote cultural competency, hence the following discussion on cultural maladjustment.

Cultural Values Maladjustment

Cultural values maladjustment is found in individuals who have either been deprived of the proper exposure to other cultural values or have refused to allow their own previously held cultural values to be challenged and adjusted. In the first instance, when individuals are raised in a culturally shielded environment, they do not possess the necessary skills and dispositions to see any credible value in cultural views and expressions outside of their own. This is not necessarily their fault; rather, they are victims of a myopic and conservative upbringing. Some individuals live their entire lives at this level, avoiding everything that looks different from the values and cultural orientations that they have known all their lives. Those foreign elements threaten and create discomfort, so the human tendency is to avoid them.

On one side, this could be one of the factors responsible for the failure of some white public school teachers to embrace and promote diversity. At a personal level, they have not adjusted their cultural value systems to accommodate new cultures, so they are unable to promote diversity. On the other hand, it is also why some minority students, especially African American students from the inner cities, are unable to function effectively in some American academic environments. They see academics as a foreign culture, a white culture. Given the fact that their own cultural value systems have not been adjusted to see and embrace the good in the white culture, they tend to reject everything white in its entirety. Students who try to embrace academic pursuit are seen as selling out to the white culture, and consequently are ostracized.

Those people who have deliberately refused to allow their cultural values to be revised or adjusted represent the other category of people who are victims of cultural maladjustment. These are individuals who have been exposed to the other cultures, may have gone through diverse K–12 schools and taken college courses that promoted diversity, yet they resolved within themselves that their own cultural values are superior to all others and should be the only standard by which they live their lives and operate, even in professional environments. Such individuals would see academic courses in which their culture is critiqued as disrespectful and opposed to their culture, and they would take a defensive stance in such courses rather than allow themselves to critique their culture in light of insights from the course. Such people can finish a whole course in cultural diversity and conclude it was a complete waste of their time. They have a tendency to see the world exclusively in terms of "we" versus "them." Their cultural boundaries are immovable and almost cast in stone. In their private lives, they are those who refuse to walk across the street to get to know their neighbor who looks different. Society often brands such people as racists, but many of them do not fit that categorization. They do not want to cross their cultural boundaries to get to know you because it discomforts their cultural psyche, but they have no problems with your existence and opportunities.

These people are simply ethnocentric. The world as they know it is their cultural arrangement, and anything outside of it is foreign. In the United States, you will find people fitting this category among whites, African Americans, Hispanics, Asians, and other ethnicities. There might be a disparity in the distribution across ethnic groups, but nevertheless, they exist across the board.

Implications of Cultural Values Maladjustment for Multicultural Education

In the United States, although laws have been enacted to enforce integration in American schools, they have proved inadequate in establishing a cohesive society. Some state education boards in the United States have instituted mandatory diversity training for all teachers in an attempt to promote integration and cohesion, yet the success rate in cultural competency has not been significant. A fundamental factor responsible for this deficiency is the disproportion between the ethnic composition of the students that are taught and the teachers who teach them, especially in the inner cities. White males and females represent more than 80 percent of the teacher population in America's K–12 classrooms.[10] A very high percentage of this teacher population is raised in shielded suburban environments, thereby implying a need for cultural values adjustment. Whereas some of these teachers are willing to go and obtain the necessary training that would enable them to undergo this cultural values adjustment so as to function better in a progressively diverse school environment, some are closed to the idea, and refuse to allow their cultural comfort zones to be invaded.

When the state of California instituted the Cross-cultural Language and Academic Development (CLAD)[11] certification for all teachers, they mandated all practicing teachers to go back to school and get the certification or take an exam to waive the classes. Whereas some teachers immediately took advantage of the continuing education opportunity it offered, others who were nearing their retirement took early retirement or waited until the last year they could hold off and then retired. Some others decided to do nothing about it in the hopes that it would all go away with time. Such people have found themselves trapped, as the federal No Child Left Behind (NCLB) mandate has added teeth to this requirement, and their jobs have become threatened.

The big question is how one can expect teachers who are culturally maladjusted to teach multicultural student populations. This is basically what the educational system is doing today, and the proposition here is that we must first of all find ways to address this problem among teachers before we can expect them to teach multicultural populations. The section below provides a tool for measuring levels of personal cultural values adjustment. Follow the instruction and evaluate your level of personal values adjustment.

CULTURAL VALUES ADJUSTMENT SURVEY

Please choose only one option (a to e) that best represents you for each question.

1. Personal (unassigned) reading about other cultures and worldviews

    a. does not really appeal to me
    b. is something I would love to do
    c. is something I do on an ongoing basis
    d. has contributed significantly to my knowledge base about the world and other cultures
    e. significantly influences my lifestyle, professional practice, and social interactions with people from other backgrounds

2. Sharing living space with somebody from a different ethnic background or race

    a. has never really appealed to me
    b. is something I would love to do
    c. is something I have done in an arranged setting like dormitory rooms
    d. is something I have voluntarily undertaken once
    e. is something I have done by choice on repeated occasions

3. Educating others on cultural diversity and its benefits

    a. is something I have never thought of doing
    b. is something I would love to do if I have the skills
    c. is something I have always desired to do, given the skills I already possess
    d. is something I have been able to do in a formal (work-related) setting
    e. is something I do both formally and at a personal level

4. Sensitivity to how I interact with people from other cultures and ethnicity

    a. is something I have not really given much thought to

    b. is something I would love to be more conscious about

    c. is something I am becoming more conscious about

    d. is something that I have made part of the principles undergirding my social interactions

    e. has enabled me to make friends across ethnic groups and sociocultural boundaries

5. Rethinking my cultural value systems

    a. is something I have not really given much thought to

    b. is something I would love to be more conscious about

    c. is something I am becoming more conscious about

    d. is something that I have made part of the principles undergirding my social interactions

    e. has enabled me to make friends across ethnicities and sociocultural boundaries

6. Consciously rearranging the way I look at other cultures and peoples

    a. is something I have not really given much thought to

    b. is something I would love to be more conscious about

    c. is something I am becoming more conscious about

    d. is something that I have made part of the principles undergirding my social interactions

    e. has enabled me to make friends across ethnicities and sociocultural boundaries

7. Involvement in social action

    a. is something I have not really given much thought to

    b. is something I would love to be more conscious about

    c. is something I am becoming more conscious about

    d. is something that I have made part of the principles undergirding my social interactions

    e. has enabled me to make friends across ethnicities and sociocultural boundaries

8. Establishing and maintaining friendships with people of different cultural or ethnic origin from myself

a. is something I have never thought of doing
b. is something I would love to do if I have the opportunity
c. is something I have always desired to do, given the opportunities I already have
d. is something I have been able to do in formal (work-related) settings
e. is something I do both formally and at personal level

9. Taking action to mediate in situations where people are discriminated against on racial or ethnic basis

a. is something I have not really given much thought to
b. is something I would love to be more conscious about
c. is something I am becoming more conscious about
d. is something that I have made part of the principles undergirding my social interactions
e. has enabled me to make friends across ethnicities and sociocultural boundaries

10. Choosing to abstain from racially or ethnic offensive jokes and discussions

a. is something I have not really given much thought to
b. is something I would love to be more conscious about
c. is something I am becoming conscious about
d. is something that I have made part of the principles undergirding my social interactions
e. has enabled me to make friends across ethnicities and sociocultural boundaries

Valuation of Responses

The table below indicates the value of each response you picked in each question. Using this valuation key, tally the sum of your responses from questions 1 to 10.

A = 1
B = 2
C = 3
D = 4
E = 5

Each of the responses indicates a level of cultural values adjustment. The total value allocation gives you a general indication of where you are on cultural values adjustment. These levels are expected to change as you grow in cultural competency skills and abilities.

A = 1:   Level one—Adjustment deficiency
B = 2:   Level two—Openness
C = 3:   Level three—Knowledge
D = 4:   Level four—Respect and appreciation
E = 5:   Level five—Identification/Personal involvement and social action

Total Value Allocation

45–50 points: Highest level of cultural values adjustment. Well adjusted and personally involved in fights for social justice and equality.

35–44 points: High level of cultural values adjustment. Characterized by diversity appreciation, relatively good sense of social justice, and possible social action.

25–34 points: Moderately adjusted. Open-minded and willing to learn about other cultures and worldviews. Making progress.

15–24 points: Slightly adjusted. Closed-minded in certain areas, but open in some others. Very slow progress. Needs more assistance.

10–14 points: Not well adjusted. Closed-minded, resistant to change. Requires major paradigm shift.

THE EFFECTS OF WORLDVIEW IN THE DEVELOPMENT OF CROSS-CULTURAL IDEAS

Cultural values, ideas, and beliefs are not only developed in childhood, they are continuously shaped and reshaped as we interact with social situations and issues around us. Worldview provides the basis for this ongoing development of ideas and belief systems. The development of ideas follows a pattern.

Humans have a tendency to recognize familiar patterns very quickly. These familiar patterns eventually develop into belief systems. Ideas and belief systems thus developed form the basis for our stories. These stories are the tools for justifying our perceptions. When our perceptions are wrong,

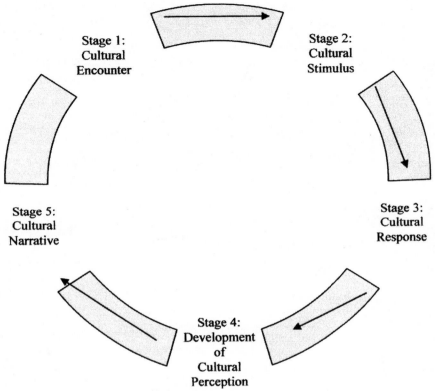

Stage 1:
Cultural
Encounter

Stage 2:
Cultural
Stimulus

Stage 5:
Cultural
Narrative

Stage 3:
Cultural
Response

Stage 4:
Development
of
Cultural
Perception

Figure 3.2.   Development of Cross-Cultural Ideas

it is difficult to see things differently because we have already developed a belief system that seems to be a logical by-product of our perception. Figure 3.2 below illustrates the pattern.

Culturally speaking, therefore, a good example of this process is the events of the terrorist acts on the United States that culminated in the destruction of the twin towers of the World Trade Center in New York on September 11, 2001. A critical cross-cultural encounter took place as Americans watched these "foreigners" fly passenger jets into the twin towers. It was a very painful encounter that stimulated anger, fear, a sense of vulnerability, and bitterness toward Arabs and Muslims.

The responses in many places were quick and sometimes deadly. It practically became a crime, and a capital crime in some parts, to travel or move around "while looking Arab or Muslim." Hate crimes immediately began to be carried out against these groups. On the more modest side, the average

American became uncomfortable at the sight of a Muslim or Arab. The government tightened safety measures in order to fend off future attacks. People were delayed and sometimes detained without any charges—by way of the Patriot Act. A more widespread cultural response was evident as American flags rose on homes, cars were decked with varieties of American flag decals, placards displayed all kinds of patriotic slogans, and young men volunteered for military service in order to go and get the enemy. A cultural perception of distrust and unease with Arab Muslims soon became a part of the American public mind-set, to the extent that the credibility of long-term allies like Saudi Arabia was questioned. Whereas many people consciously tried to isolate the terrorists from the rest of Arabs, the reality was that many more Americans became intolerant of Arab Muslims. Even Malaysians, Indians, and Pakistanis suffered from the backlash of hatred and resentment that was meant for Arabs, as they were often mistaken for Arabs. Individuals who carried out these acts of hatred and intolerance did it because they felt justified to do so on the basis of a cultural narrative that said, "Arab Muslims hate Americans, whether Saudis or Palestinians, they hate us. We cannot regard them as friends or Allies. We must not allow ourselves to be deceived into trusting them." If this line of thinking is left unchallenged, it could become an established cross-cultural belief system in America. This possibility requires us to evaluate the way we see cultures and different kinds of people over time.

CULTURAL AND PERSONAL BIASES
IN THE EDUCATIONAL SETTINGS

A primary inhibition to students' academic performance and social development in schools comes from biases that are evident in the classrooms and the general school environment. Biases have a variety of root causes. The causative factors include prejudice, stereotyping, ethnocentrism, and a number of other factors. Let's explore these root causes of bias in the schools and investigate the outward manifestations of bias in the educational setting.

Factors Responsible for Educational Biases

Prejudice may be the root cause of educational bias. Before we discuss prejudice, therefore, let's first define *bias*. Bias has been described as "any attitude, belief, or feelings that results in, and helps justify, unfair treatment of an individual because of his or her identity."[12] A dictionary definition of *prejudice*, on the other hand, says it is hatred or disrespect based on an inflexible generalization about a given people or an individual.[13]

Prejudice takes different forms. It could be exhibited in excessive pride in one's ethnic heritage, country, or culture, to the point that others outside that group tend to respond negatively to that group. In certain cases prejudice is based on fear of the unknown, fear of contamination, and the negative human tendency to separate rather than unite. The fundamental problem in combating prejudice and racism is that they are not based on logical or rational conclusions; rather, they are beliefs that have become stories, entirely a matter of perceived conclusions that were not subjected to any rational logical critique.

Prejudice in the educational setting manifests in the form of racism, sexism, and other negative attitudes. Students often get punished excessively because of their cultural or social identity rather than for their immediate behaviors. This happens when certain behaviors that would be overlooked in a child from the dominant culture would be disapproved of in a minority child. Lots of studies have focused recently on how much minority students get punished for certain behaviors compared to students from the dominant culture. Studies are done on how boys are treated in the classroom compared to girls. One study reported that boys receive between five and ten times more disciplinary actions than girls do at the elementary and middle school level. The same study points out that nearly two-thirds of the students in special education programs in the United States are boys.[14] Each one of these and related studies tend to reveal a new and troubling development in the educational system. The number of minority children in special education classes continues to rise while the white students continue to dominate the gifted and talented programs. These tendencies have been often criticized as prejudicial and unfair.

Prejudice, therefore, manifests itself every time a child is not looked at, treated, or interacted with on the basis of his or her personal merit and demerits, but instead on the basis of group or ethnic expectations and categorizations. Such treatment undermines the rights of that individual child to fair treatment and quality education, and it undermines the fundamental principles of this country's laws and constitution. It is illegal, it is immoral, it is wrong. Research has repeatedly shown that a teacher's effectiveness in promoting student achievement is intrinsically connected to that teacher's "deep-seated" beliefs and assumptions about the students, their character, potential, and intelligence.[15]

As a teacher educator, this writer has the special privilege of going from one classroom to another, supervising and encouraging new teachers on the path to professional growth. One of the assignments I require my student teachers to do during student teaching is to write a journal. They are required to write down special experiences and encounters that make their days challenging or rewarding. They are to take special notice of what goes on in the classroom and report back to me how they feel about them. One student wrote about the master teacher's attitude to the different categories of students. First he describes the two classes of students:

> The two classes I deal with, one "normal" and the other "gate," demonstrate a basic dilemma in terms of ethno-class stratification. This is more marked because for the most part average IQ and native mental abilities between the two groups appear to be unremarkably similar and probably just above average. The difference between the two groups appears to me as motivational, self-ego, with continuous social reinforcement, greater involvement, interest and enrichment by parents, fundamental differences in social values and ethos between predominantly Chinese American and Mexican American patterns of enculturation and socialization, and especially perhaps the different ways the two groups are treated by the master teacher.

One may want to question the basis on which this student teacher can make assumptions about these students' backgrounds and IQ, as well as his basis for delineating the basic differences between the two groups to essentially environmental and social rather than genetic. It is important to note that this is not a regular student teacher. This teacher candidate already held a doctorate in cultural anthropology and was a seasoned researcher who had come into the field of education as a second career. He had the credentials, the skills, and the knowledge base to make the assumptions and judgments he made. He wrote on the master teacher's expectations, attitudes, and treatment of these groups of students:

> Though they run on parallel schedules, in terms of their curriculum, it is clear that much more is expected from, and hence received from, the Gate group compared to the other, while the other tends to be scolded, admonished and shouted at far more frequently for transgressions that are minor and similar in kind and frequency for both groups. I do not think the teacher realizes she is

doing this, . . . she tends to try out new lessons on the "normal" class before modifying them to fit the Gate class. Both groups appear to have similar kinds of questions and problems with math work, and the rates and amount of information retention between the groups appear to be similar, though I would say because the Gate group tends to get greater and perhaps more consistent reinforcement in the home and in other extra-curricular contexts, they tend to revisit and retain a greater amount than the other group.

Does this master teacher know what she is doing? How can she claim to not know? She must know, but she may not know that it is unfair. She may not admit the bias that is so evident and entrenched. Antibias does not mean denying the need for differentiated curricula, but it calls for equal and quality education for all. Teachers must look for the potential in every child and seek ways to harness that potential.

Teacher expectations have significant impact on how students achieve. A study done by Ladson-Billings revealed that African American students are more sensitive to the perceptions of their teachers than white students, and consequently act to meet the teacher expectations.[16] The implication of this is that if the teacher's expectations are low, the students will act accordingly, and if the expectations are high, they will act accordingly. Teachers must be willing to dispel the tendency to place low expectations on students because of ethnicity or disability.

FORMS OF BIAS IN THE EDUCATIONAL SETTING

Teacher/Administrator's Attitudes and Language

Teachers and the administrative staff all take a stand on issues of race, equity, and social justice. Such stance is seldom spoken, yet very much pronounced. The way a teacher relates to students who are different from him or her ethnically, racially, or otherwise says something to other students in the classroom about how that teacher perceives ethnic or racial differences. Teachers and administrators often come down very hard on minority students for offences and infringements they let pass when students from the mainstream culture commit them. When that happens, the minority students see themselves as scapegoats, and they become resentful to the system. Students from the mainstream culture may take advantage of the bias to lure minority students into trouble, as they know they will most likely not be the ones who get punished.

Some teachers and administrators adopt the colorblind approach. They choose to dismiss issues of ethnic and racial differences and try to treat every student the same. As much as this is well intended, overlooking the crises faced by the minority students often means their unique needs go unmet. Kids from poor homes or single-parent homes are likely to struggle academically because of their domestic situations. When we adopt a colorblind approach, we miss the underlying social factors that have nothing to with ethnicity and that hamper academic progress.

Counselors' Attitudes and Language

Junior high and high school counselors may be the most influential people in students' journey to academic success. These counselors advise on course selections and also control the tracks students fall into. Sadly, some counselors categorize students based on their skin color or ethnic origin long before they even open their files to look at their academic abilities and other issues. A college counselor told a young African American girl, who recently graduated from a school in the University of California system, that the university was not for her type. He advised her to go to California State University at Dominguez Hills, because that's the school that is meant for her type. This straight-A student was a fighter who knew what she wanted in life, so she kept pushing until her admission to the institution she wanted was granted. The same woman was later admitted in the same university's medical school.[17] Many counselors inhibit the chances of minority students rather than enhance them by tracking them to particular schools or study programs.

Classroom Environments

Teachers need to pay special attention to how they arrange their classrooms. What cultural artifacts are displayed in your classroom? Do they represent the dominant culture, or are they inclusive? Many teachers fail to take into consideration the way their classroom environments speak about the conduciveness of the classroom learning for every child. K–6 teachers often go to pains to decorate the classroom with print-rich materials, photos, and cultural artifacts. More often than not, the cultural artifacts represent the teacher's cultural heritage and background much more than it speaks to the student population represented in the classroom. A culturally inclusive classroom environment projects artifacts, objects, and photos that every child in the classroom can connect with. The diversity of the classroom population must be reflected in the classroom environment.

Students' Attitudes to One Another (Hegemony vs. Minorities)

School culture often perpetuates divisiveness among students. Ethnic rivalry in schools often speaks to the general school climate. If the school climate is such that there is empowerment, cooperation, and collaboration, ethnic rivalry will be minimized. When white and African American or Hispanic students begin to fight each other purely across racial lines, it suggests that something is wrong in that school's culture. Students' attitudes toward one another can be improved if the administration is willing to invest in the development of an inclusive community. Simple steps toward this inclusion can be a collective celebration of ethnic holidays and events. Hispanic and African American students have no reason to fight against each other if they realize that they are both minorities and have similar issues that they are dealing with. When the school climate suggests to one group, no matter how subtly it is done, that they are better than the other, a seed of discord is sown.

OTHER ISSUES IN CROSS-CULTURAL ENCOUNTERS IN AMERICA

In this section we will briefly address a number of concepts and issues that multicultural educators must familiarize themselves with in the process of teaching in diverse learning environments. Our understanding of these issues and concepts, as well as our attitudes to facilitating or discouraging them, have great significance on how well we do in fostering cross-cultural harmony.

Enculturation

Enculturation is the process of inculcating into an individual a given set of ideas, belief systems, worldviews, practices, and artifacts of a given culture or a social group. This can be simply defined as the process of culture acquisition. The way we raise children in our families is an enculturation process. The English as a second language (ESOL) classes as well as the many Institutes for American Language and Culture across college campuses are all enculturation processes and programs. The goal is to enable recent immigrants to fit into the new society and function effectively.

Assimilation

This is the process by which individuals adopt the "behaviors, values, beliefs, and lifestyle of the dominant culture."[18] With assimilation, the individuals lose their own culture completely and adopt the culture of the dominant group. In the history of American cultural interactions, the "assimilationist" ideology characterized the time between the turn of the twentieth century and World War I. This was the time when the Anglo-Saxon Protestant culture emerged as the dominant U.S. culture. The ideal was for the immigrant population to give up all their ethnic characteristics and adopt the dominant culture. Two goals characterized the educational institutions of the time, namely: to rid ethnic groups of their unique traits and to force them to acquire Anglo-Saxon values and behaviors.

One of the leading educational minds of that age, Ellwood Patterson Cubberly, stated the major goal of common school thus:

> Our task is to break up these groups or settlements, to assimilate and amalgamate these people as part of our American race, and to implant in their children, as far as can be done, the Anglo-Saxon conception of righteousness, law and order, and popular government, and to awaken in them a reverence for our democratic institutions and for those things in our national life which we as a people hold to be of abiding worth."[19]

The assimilation perspective is the same as the "melting pot" ideology, wherein new immigrants from Europe were expected to submerge their cultural heritage and practices under the dominant Anglo-Saxon Protestant culture that had been established here in the United States. The fact that such thoughts and ideologies expressed above characterized individuals who have influenced the American educational system makes it more than imperative that we engage in a conscientious effort to redefine the goals of our educational structures in the twenty-first century, thus making multicultural education an indispensable aspect of our school curriculum.

Acculturation

This is the process by which individuals adopt the culture of the mainstream without necessarily giving up their own cultures. This was characteristic of the many early Eastern, Southern, and Central European peoples who came to the United States. Whereas they learned the English language and Anglo-Saxon ethics and etiquette, they maintained their cultures, as they lived in their own communities and built their own churches and schools. The possibility of retaining ethnic cultures while claiming to be American tends to pose a threat to some Americans who think that the ideal American image is the melting pot image. These people fail to realize that the melting pot metaphor refers to the melting pot of the nineteenth and twentieth centuries, which accepted Europeans of every stock but rejected Africans, Native Americans, Chinese, and Hispanics until the civil rights movement compelled the country to accept the fact that those groups are also Americans. The United States has been more of a salad bowl, where the lettuce, tomatoes, cabbage, carrots, and celery all retained their individual identities, but were willing to be part of one meal, which is blended into an edible unit by a liquid called salad dressing. When eaten as one unit the individual tastes combine to make the meal worth eating. That is indeed the reality of American ethnic diversity.

Accommodation

This is a two-way process by which members of the mainstream culture adapt to certain changes that come about as a result of the presence of a minority culture, while the minority culture also adjusts some of its ways in light of the dominant culture. The language of accommodation is often used loosely to suggest that the dominant culture is giving the immigrant culture an opportunity to thrive. It is often said to suggest that this is a favor being done the minority culture, for which they should be grateful. In the context of schooling, however, every child has equal right to be in school and to learn, and no child should ever be treated as though he or she is being done a favor by being allowed into the school and given an opportunity to succeed. Equal and quality education is a debt we owe all America's children, regardless of race, ethnicity, socioeconomic status, and gender.

Accommodation must be seen as a symbiotic relationship in which the various cultural expressions that constitute the United States accept the validity of each cultural group, their right to be, and the need for them to advance themselves, and then commit to contribute toward making it happen. We must see ourselves as codependent groups who need one another to become the best we are capable of becoming.

Cultural Pluralism

This has been defined as a situation in which "members of diverse cultural groups have equal opportunities for success, . . . in which cultural similarities and differences are valued, and in which students are provided cultural alternatives."[20] The America into which the earlier Western European immigrants and the later Eastern, Central, and Southern European immigrants lived together was not an assimilated America but a pluralistic America. The mere presence of these later European "peoples" threatened the earlier West European immigrants.

In 1917 and 1924 immigration acts were passed for the purpose of limiting the immigration of these non-Western Europeans to the United States. The effect of pure pluralism is ultimately seen in coexistences, intercultural (racial) marriages, integrated neighborhoods, integrated workplaces, and other avenues. These constitute the true vision of the American maxim, *E pluribus unum*—Out of many, one.[21]

Biculturalism

This is the situation in which an individual is able to function effectively in two cultures. It is the innate ability of the human species to function effectively in more than one platform. Some women are teachers, mothers, and wives as well. Some people like mashed potatoes with gravy on a turkey dinner and also love sushi. This is an example of what it means to be bicultural. Biculturalism is found among African Americans, Japanese Americans, and Mexican Americans. These are groups that have had to reconcile two different cultural heritages while still maintaining their individual identities. Biculturalism often comes with a price. Such a price was paid by Japanese Americans who were actively engaged fighting America's enemies during the World War II while their families at home in America were being displaced and sent to internment camps.

Many minority children in U.S. public and private schools are bicultural. They are as American as can be; the culture into which they were born and are being raised is essentially American, yet many of them are still affected by the cultures of their immigrant parents and grandparents. These children often see themselves first and foremost as Americans, before any ethnic label. It is society that often tells them that they are not American enough because their physical features resemble that of their Asian, Hispanic, or African parents. During my days as a public school teacher, my classroom was once visited by a friend from outside the country. As he was interacting with some of my students who were of Asian descent, I heard him ask the girls, "Where do you come from?" My students looked at him and asked, "What do you mean?" I watched him struggle to explain himself. He wanted to know whether they were of Japanese or Vietnamese or Chinese descent. The students, who did not like the question or its tone, said to him, "We are Americans."

Our schools are full of bicultural students who are patriotic Americans, yet we have curricula, policies, and procedures, as well as teachers whose conduct and words continuously tell these students that they are foreigners in their land of birth. The contemporary multicultural education goal is to remove these negative signals. We need to allow students to be the Americans they desire and are proud to be. Schools must help students realize that eating sushi or dim sum for breakfast instead of scrambled eggs and bacon does not make them any less American.

Racism

Racism can be defined as the assumption that certain traits possessed by a group of people distinguish them and make them either superior or inferior to others. Racism or racialism has been defined as a way of cognitively organizing perceptions of people around the world by certain immutable characteristics.[22] The problem with this definition is that these so-called immutable characteristics remain vague and hard to define. Kevin Cokley identified some of these immutable characteristics to include behavior, intellect, and temperament.[23] These characteristics have been argued and debated in academic and political circles. The debates have influenced policies on the use of IQ tests on minority students, given the fact that the whole assertion that intellectual and behavioral differences can be seen as immutable racial characteristics has not been scientifically proven. Skin pigmentation, more than any other characteristic, has been used as a defining physical factor that distinguishes African Americans from whites. Yet what is called African American or white has different shades and tones of skin color. Physical features have been used, in addition to skin color, to distinguish Asians from whites. But the fact remains that the basic characteristics that distinguish one race from another vary when races are compared to each other, thereby invalidating their immutability. What has been characterized as immutable in one context may actually be replaced by another feature or characteristic in other contexts. In light of this possibility, perhaps the only thing that has remained immutable in racial categorizations is the assumption of the members of one race that they are superior to others.[24]

Discrimination

This refers to unfair treatment of one person or group of persons because of prejudice about race, ethnicity, age, religion, or gender.[25] It is seen as actions that limit the social, political, or economic opportunities of a particular person or group.

Openly segregated schools once served as a form of institutional discrimination, but today other forms of institutional discrimination can be seen in curriculum content, school financing, and quality of teachers and facilities. This is the focus of Jonathan Kozol in his *Savage Inequalities: Children in America's Schools*.[26]

Ethnocentrism

This is the tendency of individuals or a group to perceive reality exclusively from a personal or cultural point of view. Other cultures and practices are judged by the standards of one's own culture and often despised and looked upon as inferior. My culture becomes the standard by which every other culture is judged. My own cultural etiquette becomes binding on others who may not necessarily value them.

QUESTIONS AND APPLICATION

Case Study: Handling Racial Slurs among Students

Background

You are a white fourth-grade female teacher in a suburban school with a student population of about 80 percent white, 10 percent Hispanic, 8 percent Asian, and 2 percent African American. Your class has no African American student in it. Mr. Becks, a fellow fourth-grade teacher is an African American man. He has one African American student in his class-room. Mr. Becks is your team teacher. You work together on a number of projects, including PE.

The Problem

One day during PE, Stanley, the one African American student in Mr. Beck's class, comes to you to complain that Andrew, a white student in your class, used the "N" word to him. Andrew's parents are known racists. They believe in the superiority of the white race, and they have often said openly that they can use whatever racial slur they choose to use; it is their civil right.

The Challenge

1. What will you say to Stanley in response to the complaint he lodged to you?
2. How would you address Andrew on this matter? What will you tell him? What would you require him to do in order to placate Stanley?
3. Would you involve the rest of your students in this matter? Why? Why not?
4. Would you involve Mr. Becks in this matter? If yes, what would you want him to do?
5. Would you involve Andrew's parents in this matter? What would you expect them to do? Why would you choose to involve them or not to involve them?
6. What possible volatile issues must be avoided in handling this matter?

Activity

The United States of America reached a significant landmark in 2008 when Barak Obama was elected the first African American president of the United States. Discuss the level of racism and prejudice against blacks in the United States today. Using journal and newspaper resources, identify the different ways racism, prejudice, and bias against blacks and Hispanics still happen in the school systems. Discuss what you can do as a K–12 teacher to mitigate these for your black and Hispanic students.

Strategies for Application in the K–12 Classrooms

1. Grades K–6: Read the story of Ruby Bridges. Ask students to write personal journals on discrimination. Journals should focus on personal experiences or things they have read or heard about. Journals should be posted on a bulletin board accessible to the whole school community.

2. Grades K–12: Ask students to reflect on the circle of their friendship and determine how many friends they have outside of their ethnic/cultural circles. Encourage them to identify someone from a different ethnic or cultural background and spend the week trying to befriend that individual. Allow students to share their experiences openly at the end of the week.

Chapter Four

Educational Inequalities in American Schools

Chapter Objectives:

The goal of this chapter is to discuss the constitutional and legal basis for the struggle for educational equality in the United States of America. At the end of this chapter, readers will be able to:

1. discuss the constitutional basis for the struggle for equal educational opportunities in the United States
2. name and discuss the various landmark legal rulings on which the struggle for equal educational opportunities is anchored in the United States
3. identify and discuss the various areas where the struggle for equal educational opportunity continues

WHAT IS EDUCATIONAL INEQUALITY?

James Banks, in an attempt to define multicultural education, stated, "Multicultural education incorporates the idea that all students—regardless of their gender and social class and their ethnic, racial, or cultural characteristics—should have an equal opportunity to learn."[1] The problem that arises from this concept of multicultural education is how to understand what an equal educational opportunity really means. How can we define equity to make sure that there is no ambiguity about it?

In order to understand what is meant by equity in the educational systems, we will need to review some historical cases in the American educational history that are anchored on the struggle for equality. These landmark cases were brought by groups and individuals who felt that their right to fair and equal educational opportunities were being denied them.[2]

Plessy v. Fergusson—Separate but Equal Doctrine

One of the foremost judicial rulings that set the stage for the unending battle for equality in America is *Plessy v. Ferguson*.[3] Critics have argued that prior to the ruling in 1896, the gap between the races was not as wide as this ruling drove it in the years that followed. During the Reconstruction era, the Southern States had adopted Jim Crow laws requiring separate facilities (toilets, water fountains, recreational facilities, seating in public transportation and other places) for whites and "colored" Americans.[4] The U.S. Civil Rights Act of 1875[5] promised common civil rights to all Americans. An 1878 U.S. Supreme Court ruled that states could not prohibit segregation on common carriers such as railroads, streetcars, or steamboats. In 1890, the General Assembly of the State of Louisiana passed a law providing for separate railway carriages for the white and colored races.[6]

The petitioner was a U.S. citizen residing in the state of Louisiana, of mixed blood in the proportion of seven-eighths white and one-eighth African blood. He argued that the colored blood was virtually indiscernible in him and that he was entitled to every recognition and privilege that other U.S. white citizens were entitled to. He had paid for a first-class ticket on the East Louisiana Railway from New Orleans to Covington. He entered the train and took a seat in the section where the white passengers were seated. Even though there was no previous law authorizing the trains to segregate the passengers on the grounds of race, the conductor required him to vacate the seat or face ejection from the train as well as possible imprisonment He refused to comply, and with the aid of police officers, he was ejected from the train and thrown into a jail. In filing this case, the plaintiff argued that the state of Louisiana's segregation law violated the Thirteenth and Fourteenth Amendments,[7] laws prohibiting slavery and prohibiting the states from restricting the rights of freed slaves. In delivering the U.S. Supreme Court ruling on this case, Mr. Justice Brown read,

> We cannot say that a law which authorizes or even requires the separation of the two races in public conveyances is unreasonable, or more obnoxious to the Fourteenth Amendment than the acts of Congress requiring separate schools for colored children in the District of Columbia, the constitutionality of which does not seem to have been questioned, or the corresponding acts of state legislatures. We consider the underlying fallacy of the plaintiff's argument to consist in the assumption that the enforced separation of the two races stamps the colored race with a badge of inferiority. If it is so, it is not by reason of anything found in the act, but solely because the colored race chooses to put that construction upon it.[8]

In this ruling, the courts accused the U.S. Congress of initiating the very first act of institutional segregation as they chose to approve the segregation of white and colored students in the District of Columbia, where they lived and worked. The ruling upheld a law that compelled under penalties, the separation of the two races in every form of public and social life. Based on this precedence and the judicial provisions of the Supreme Court ruling of 1878, the State of Louisiana had a solid basis for enacting its own law, which in this ruling, the U.S. Supreme court upheld. This was the official ground upon which American schools were segregated for the next seven to eight decades. Dissenting on this ruling, Justice Harlan stated,

> The Caucasian race deems itself to be the dominant race in this country. And so it is, in prestige, in achievements, in education, in wealth and in power. So, I doubt not, it will continue to be for all time, if it remains true to its great heritage and holds fast to the principles of constitutional liberty. But in view of the Constitution, in the eye of the law, there is in this country no superior, dominant, ruling class of citizens. There is no caste here. Our constitution is color-blind, and neither knows nor tolerates classes among citizens. In respect of civil rights, all citizens are equal before the law. The humblest is the peer of the most powerful. The law regards man as man, and takes no account of his surroundings or of his color when his civil rights as guaranteed by the Supreme law of the land are involved. . . . In my opinion, the judgment this day rendered will, in time, prove to be quite as pernicious as the decision made by this tribunal in the Dred Scott case."[9]

What this case represents to us as we study the topic of social and educational inequality in America's public schools is the fact that our history has indelible records of social and educational inequalities that have been institutionally implemented, and if left unchallenged could still be going on today. We live in a society where the concept of equality is not a generally agreed-upon term. Some citizens believe that equality does not mean they are equal with certain sections of the populace, and the governments and the legal institutions have often taken sides with such persons in the past.

Brown v. Board of Education of Topeka

This court ruling in 1954 is regarded as the final blow on the separate but equal doctrine of *Plessy v. Ferguson*.[10] The major contention in *Brown v. Board of Education of Topeka* is that segregated schools are not equal and cannot be made equal, and that they deprive nonwhite children of their rights under the law. The Reverend Oliver Brown of Topeka, Kansas, had an eight-year-old daughter named Linda. Linda was forced, on account of her race, to travel long distances to attend Monroe Elementary school (an all–African American school) when close to her home was Sumner Elementary School, an all-white school. With the Support of the National Association for the Advancement of Colored People (NAACP), Reverend Brown attempted to enroll his daughter into the neighborhood school in the fall of 1950. She was denied admission, and on behalf of this family and thirteen other families, the NAACP filed a lawsuit against the board of education in February 1951, which eventually reached the U.S. Supreme Court.[11]

The plaintiffs argued that the separate but equal doctrine of *Plessy v. Ferguson* has no place in the educational setting.[12] The plaintiffs, through their attorneys, sought the aid of the courts to gain admission into public schools in their communities on a nonsegregated basis. In rendering the opinion of the court on this matter, Mr. Chief Justice Warren said, among other things,

> Today, education is perhaps the most important function of the state and local governments. Compulsory school attendance laws and the great expenditures for education both demonstrate our recognition of the importance of education to our democratic society. . . . It is the very foundation of good citizenship. Today it is a primary instrument in awakening the child to cultural values, in preparing him for later professional training, and in helping him to adjust normally to his environment. . . . Such an opportunity, where the state has undertaken to provide it, is a right, which must be made available to all on equal terms.[13]

This court went further to state that separating the African American students from their peers on the basis of race "generates a feeling of inferiority as to their status in the community that may affect their hearts and minds in a way unlikely ever to be undone. . . . Segregation of White and colored children in public schools has a detrimental effect upon the colored children."[14] The court consequently ruled that the doctrine of separate but equal has no place in the educational system.

This landmark case broke the back of institutional segregation in the United States and opened the door for a fight for equality, which has continued till today. Sadly enough, some people think the fight is over. If the fight is over, we will not be discussing this issue any more. The next two cases are two significant indicators that the fight for equality has not really ended.

San Antonio Independent School District v. Rodriguez

This landmark case was argued October 12, 1972. A group of Mexican American parents brought a suit against this school district of Texas in the summer of 1968 alleging that the school finance system of Texas, which was based on property tax, was unconstitutional, as it violated the provisions of the Equal Protection Clause of the Fourteenth Amendment. The background was that the Edgewood Independent School District, from which these students came, was situated in the core-city section of San Antonio with little or no commercial property. The residents were predominantly Mexican Americans (about 90 percent) with only 6 percent African American students.

The average assessed value for homes in this community was $5,960, the lowest in the state. The district contributed $26 to the education of each child in the year 1967–1968, while the state foundation program contributed $222 per student, and the federal government contributed $108 per child, bringing the total amount of money spent on each child per year to $356. When compared to Alamo Heights, the most affluent school district in San Antonio, with a population distribution of predominantly Anglo, 18 percent Mexican American, and less than 1 percent African American, spending $594 per pupil as a result of strong property tax base, these plaintiffs argued that: (1) the school financing in Texas discriminated against "poor" persons; (2) against people who were relatively poorer than others; and (3) against people who happen to reside in relatively poorer school districts, regardless of their personal income.[15] In deciding this case, the lower court ruled that the Texas school finance system was unconstitutional, as it violated the provisions of the Fourteenth Amendment. The Supreme Court of the United States, however, ruled that the financing method employed (by the State of Texas) did not infringe upon any fundamental human right so as to call for the application of strict judicial scrutiny. In addition, the court did not view education as a fundamental right that was afforded explicit or implicit protection under the Constitution.

The initial ruling was consequently reversed and the state was cleared of the charges. It is significant to note the subtle but clear divergent views on the constitutional provisions for educational rights as perceived by the judges in *Brown v. Board of Education* and in *San Antonio v. Rodriguez*. Even the courts have a difficulty defining what constitutes equal educational rights. Individual biases and prejudices play into every situation.

Lau v. Nichols

In this case, the court discovered about 2,856 Chinese students in the San Francisco public school system that did not speak English. Of this number, only 1,000 were given supplemental courses in English language. The remaining 1,856 students did not receive such support. The school district even required English-language skills before children could participate in educational programs. The parents of these students felt their children were receiving unequal educational opportunities. The Supreme Court upheld that despite the fact that the Chinese American students had the same caliber of teachers, textbooks, curriculum and school facilities, they were being denied equal education because their unique language and cultural needs were not being met. Part of the court ruling stated as follows,

> Discrimination among students on account of race or national origin that is prohibited includes "discrimination . . . in the availability or use of any academic . . . or other facilities of the grantee or other recipient." Discrimination is barred which has that effect even though no purposeful design is present. . . . It seems obvious that the Chinese-speaking minority receive fewer benefits than the English-speaking majority from respondents' school system which denies them a meaningful opportunity in the educational program.[16]

The Supreme Court reversed a previous appeals court ruling, to agree with the plaintiffs that their children had not been provided equal educational opportunity as provided by the law, especially as provided under the Thirteenth Amendment. To conclude our thoughts on these court landmarks, we will need to take a look at the Fourteenth Amendment to examine what it says about equal rights.

The Fourteenth Amendment

The Fourteenth Amendment to the Constitution has five different sections, each dealing with issues that relate to the rights of individual citizens in a participatory government, as well as the duties and obligations of the states and the nation to naturalized or native-born citizens. The part of this amendment that has direct implications for the discussion in this section reads,

> All persons born or naturalized in the United States, and subject to the jurisdiction thereof, are citizens of the United States and of the State wherein they re-

side. No State shall make or enforce any law, which shall abridge the privileges or immunities of citizens of the United States; nor shall any State deprive any person of life, liberty, or property, without due process of law; nor deny to any person within its jurisdiction the equal protection of the laws.[17]

This amendment forbids any state to make a law or enforce one that abridges the privileges or immunities of citizens of the United States. It further prevents them from depriving any citizen of "life, liberty, or property" rights without due process of law. If the statement in the Supreme Court ruling on *Brown v. Board of Education of Topeka*, which says that educational opportunity, "where the state has undertaken to provide it, is a right which must be made available to all on equal terms"[18] is taken to be true, it implies that a fair and equal education is no longer a privilege but a constitutional right. Once a mandate is placed on citizens to send their children to school until they reach a certain age, with the threat of punitive action, then the government also places on itself the mandate of providing all children an equal-quality educational experience. Equal educational opportunity, therefore, can be defined as the provision of equal educational facilities, personnel, resources, and learning experiences to every child, enabling all children to reach their maximum potential within the society.

The assumption of multicultural education is that the educational programs we have in place today fall short of this standard. American children do not enjoy equal educational facilities, personnel, resources, and learning experiences. More than a decade ago, Jonathan Kozol went around many big American cities and studied the quality of education being provided to America's children. This research was published under the title, *Savage Inequalities: Children in America's Schools*.[19] He opened our eyes to the sad reality that equality still does not exist in our educational systems. The schools in affluent neighborhoods have the money to buy the resources necessary for student success. They have better and newer buildings, air conditioning, science laboratories, gyms, and so on, while their counterparts in the inner cities have to make do with structures that are on active toxic dumps, hundreds of years old, lacking heating, air conditioning, science texts, libraries, and practically everything else the affluent schools have. In many cases they are handed down textbooks that have been used by students in the richer neighborhoods decades after the official end of separate but equal doctrine. Stories from all the cities sounded so much alike. The problems in New York were the same as in Chicago, San Antonio, New Jersey, and Los Angeles. In

East St. Louis, Missouri, students went to school on an active toxic dump. It all comes down to the haves and have-nots. For the most part, the haves are the whites living in suburban America and the have-nots are the African Americans and Hispanics living in the inner cities. When structured this way, the schools fail to fulfill their role as instruments for the propagation of knowledge and responsible citizenry. "It becomes striking how closely these schools reflect their communities, as if the duty of the schools were to prepare a child for the life he's born to. . . . It hardly seems fair."[20]

Kozol's book was written in the 1990s, and one would expect that, given all the publicity it received and the educational reforms we have seen in the last decade, things would have changed dramatically. Sadly enough, a current look at the state of those schools still does not indicate equal educational opportunity. Multicultural education calls for a time and environment where America's children, whether rich or poor, African American or white, can learn in a clean classroom, use current textbooks, and enjoy the privilege of learning from qualified teachers who care about their welfare and learning. All our children need to grow up in an environment where they know that their only limitation is their own personal aspiration, not the opportunities out there. This is not utopian thinking for a nation that enjoys political, economic, and military strength matched by no other on the planet.

THE SPECTRUM OF INEQUITY IN EDUCATION

This section attempts to isolate the areas where we have continued to experience inequality in our educational system.

Curriculum Content

Over the years many battles have been fought over our curriculum content. The war has been waged from the gender angle, the racial/ethnic angle, and the ability/disability angle. For the most part, America's educational curriculum has been essentially Eurocentric, male-dominant, and insensitive to disabilities. Recently, school districts are beginning to respond to some of these challenges by requiring the writers of textbooks to become more balanced. There still remains a problem. The idea of inclusiveness with regard to ethnicity, gender, and ability in the content of our textbooks remains an area we can make improvements in.

Teacher Quality and Ethnic Makeup

Inner-city schools have always been laden with the burden of short-term, inexperienced teachers who come there to start their careers only to transfer out as soon as they begin to get a handle on what they are doing. These schools have the endemic problem of inexperienced unqualified teachers teaching the sciences and mathematics. The quality of instruction going on in such schools is persistently below average, yet in this era of testing and accountability, these students are held to the same standards and expectations as the more successful suburban schools. Even amid the current requirements of the No Child Left Behind (NCLB) act,[21] inner-city schools are still struggling with the problem of depending on a pool of inexperienced, underqualified teachers.

Another issue is better articulated by Geneva Gay, who said that "most graduates of typical teacher education programs know little about the cultural traits, behaviors, values, and attitudes that different children of color bring to the classroom, and how they affect students' responses to instructional situations."[22] Many inner-city schools are predominantly minority, while their teacher population has remained predominantly white, with little or no multicultural training. Unfortunately, a lot of these teachers still resist multicultural education.

Buildings, Facilities, and Funds Allocation

The reforms of the last decade have led to many education bonds that have resulted in facilities' restorations, construction, and modernization, yet many schools remain deprived of these face-lifts. Schools still lack heating and air conditioning while their richer neighbors have no lack. Many states are taking a second look at how education is funded, and there is hope that more improvement is on the horizon, but we still have a long way to go.

Special Programs

Minority children, especially African American boys, remain the highest population in special education programs, while the white students remain predominant in gifted and talented (GATE) programs. Misinterpretation of cultural behaviors and perspectives remains a major issue in placements. According to James Banks, "Many African American and Latino students who are labeled mentally retarded function normally and are considered normal in their homes and communities."[23]

Assessments and Testing

Standardized testing has emerged as the only way the politicians can determine whether a school is doing well or not. Under the provisions of the NCLB act, schools that are not doing well risk getting shut down, while their more successful counterparts stand the chance of financial rewards from the state. The sad reality is that every child does not come into the classroom with the same amount of capital, and given the sociocultural differences that we have referred to, it is simply unjust to hold them to the same standard when they are not all receiving equal education.

FACTORS THAT INFRINGE ON EQUITY IN SCHOOLS

Social Class

More than race, social status has emerged as the leading variable in student achievement today. Children from more affluent families have a tendency to do better than children from lower-income homes. Ironically, however, there is a racial dimension to it, as most people at the lower end of the socioeconomic structure are minorities and single mothers. Family status, therefore, as a social issue, has its own impact on the students, making equal educational opportunity more difficult as some students bring more to the classroom than others.

Parents Education Level

Children of parents who have a college education tend to do better at school than children whose parents are less educated. The support children get from home has a very definitive impact on how they do generally at school. Many schools are operating a scripted curriculum today and much of the instructional activities are one-directional: driven by tests. Children whose parents are educated have the benefit of their parents discovering what is lacking in their education and working with them to bridge the gap. Parents with lower education would not know when their children are being deprived of meaningful learning experiences. How would they be in a position to provide remediation outside of the classroom?

Racism

Racism remains a problem to contend with in today's schools. Institutional racism may be on the decline given the possibility of lawsuits and social isolation that accompanies such activities, but people's perspectives and mindsets don't change easily. Some individuals still go out of their way to give preferential treatment to particular students in academic situations. Tracking is one vehicle that racists have used to marginalize minority students over the years, and its residue remains.

School Culture

Every school has its own culture. Some school cultures encourage equity and social justice, while others perpetuate inequality. Sometimes, inaction becomes an action. When school leadership fails to do something proactive to facilitate equity and social justice, it often becomes an unwritten approval for inequality. Schools must establish a climate that is empowering to all and make clear their disapproval of social inequity and injustice.

~

QUESTIONS AND APPLICATION

Case Study: Hispanics against Blacks

Background

You are the new principal of Jackson High School in South Central Los Angeles. Your school population is evenly split between the African American and Hispanic population, with a negligible number of whites and other minority groups. Jackson is known for its end-of-year gang warfare between African American and Hispanic gangs. Last year the situation was so bad that the police had to come and shut down the school on the last day of classes. This disrupted end-of-year programs that had been organized by many arms of the school. Many teachers and parents protested that action, and consequently it led to the removal of the last principal. You have been brought in to straighten up things. You are known as a no-nonsense administrator. The district superintendent brought you here with a clear job description: the end of the gang rivalry at Jackson and improved academic achievement.

The Problem

You are African American. Upon arrival at Jackson, the Hispanic students and their parents immediately raised a protest. They saw your coming to replace the white principal as a victory for the African American students and their parents. They vowed to make sure you are removed. They began a petition drive immediately, and many openly expressed to you their disapproval of your appointment.

The Challenge

1. The district superintendent is aware of the resentment from the Hispanic community, but has decided he would not replace you, counting very much on your ability to turn things around. Why would you want to convince him otherwise?
2. What action(s) would you take to gain the confidence of the Hispanic parents that you are not there as an advocate for the African American students?
3. How would you work with the Hispanic students to gain their trust and confidence?
4. How can you build a bridge with the Hispanic community without at the same time burning the bridge that already exists with the African American community due to common ethnicity? What would you do to ensure that the African American community does not see you as a "sell out"?
5. What would be your school-wide plan for reducing racial tensions? Present your first-, second-, and third-year plans.
6. What community activities would you undertake to further reduce ethnic tension among the parents?
7. Facilities, special programs, and testing are among the factors that continue to perpetuate inequality in schools. Discuss ways the local schools and the school districts can work around these challenges and still be able to meet the needs of their diverse student populations.

Strategies for Application in the K–12 classrooms

1. Grades K–12: Work with your students to examine the main textbooks you use and determine the extent to which the various populations represented in your class are portrayed in the text being used. Brainstorm with your students how to secure resources to balance the curriculum so that every group's contribution to that field is well represented.

2. Grades K–12: Lead your students to discuss the issue of discrimination. Let them create dioramas depicting their individual interpretations of discrimination. The dioramas can be displayed at the school library for the school community to view.

3. Grades 7–12: Research and discuss migrant field workers and their issues, treatment, and abuse in the United States. Write reports, news briefs, and letters addressing your concerns for these workers and send to newspapers and legislators.

Chapter Five

Historical Foundations of Multicultural Education in the United States

Chapter Objectives:

This chapter explores the history of the development of multicultural education in the United States. It explores social and political developments, legal and legislative actions, educational developments, and the impacts of significant individuals toward this movement. Readers will be able to:

1. define multicultural education and trace its historical foundations
2. discuss the impacts of the civil rights movement on the development of multicultural education
3. discuss various legislations that impacted the development of multicultural education movement in the United States
4. identify the historical contributions of individuals such as John Ogbu, James Banks, and Jane Elliot, toward the multicultural education movement

WHAT IS MULTICULTURAL EDUCATION?

Multicultural education has been defined in many ways along anthropological, sociological, philosophical, and psychological lines. Whereas the term *multicultural education* may suggest a narrow focus on culture and cultural differences, it has been expanded over the years to include a vast array of diversity issues that span beyond culture to include gender, disability, and other diversity issues, thereby rendering the validity of the term itself questionable in its ability to encompass the vast array of issues that it addresses. Whereas most educators and sociologists have continued to use the term because of its historical significance, it is the opinion of this writer that the term "diversity" may be more embracing. Nagai defined multicultural education as "an educational process or strategy involving more than one culture, as defined by national, linguistic, ethnic, or racial criteria."[1] It is seen as an attempt to create awareness and tolerance between cultures and related worldviews.

James Banks presents a more technical definition when he defines multicultural education as an idea, a process, and a reform movement.[2] According to him, multicultural education as an idea holds that all students—regardless of their gender, social class, ethnic, racial, or cultural characteristics—should have an equal opportunity to learn. The argument is that some students, because of race, gender, or social class, have a better chance to learn in schools as they are currently structured than do students who belong to other groups or who have different cultural characteristics. Multicultural education as a process implies that it is not a one-shot activity. It is expected that it be an ongoing process that becomes an intrinsic part of the educational program, not just a program or activity carried out at one point or the other. As a reform movement, it targets schools and educational systems with the intent of transforming them to the point where social class, gender, ethnicity, and languages no longer pose a hindrance to any child in attaining his or her best in the schools. It calls for curricular changes as well as ideological changes.

This definition of multicultural education is significant as we begin to explore its history and development. The question we are attempting to address here is: "When and why did it become necessary to require the educational system to cater to the needs of all students represented in the school systems, and how has that attempt progressed over the years?"

HISTORICAL FOUNDATIONS OF MULTICULTURAL EDUCATION

The history of multicultural education in the United States does not enjoy the same deep roots that bilingual education can claim since the early days of the nation. Whereas U.S. society has been multicultural from its earliest days, education and educational institutions have been essentially Western in their structures and curricula. At its beginning, U.S. society did not see education as a civil right; instead it was seen as a privilege reserved for a select few. Even among people from Western Europe, education (at least formal education) was not seen as a civil right; rather it was a privilege for those who could afford it. White women were denied equal access to formal education for many decades.[3] Since community schools were originally constituted along ethnic lines, the idea of multicultural education, which involved a heterogeneous student population and diverse curricula content, was unthinkable. The only visible diversity that the educational system enjoyed from the early days was a diversity of Eurocentric curricula that included the study of German, Latin, French, and other European languages in English schools.

Exception, however, must be made for education pioneers like Horace Mann,[4] who in 1847 introduced the notion of universal public education as a worthy enterprise. Due to Mann's influence and a number of other factors such as the need to stem the growing child labor that was endemic among immigrant populations, legislation for compulsory education came into effect in many states between 1852 and 1914.[5] Reed Ueda makes reference to the existence of an "intercultural education"[6] program in the early 1920s.[7] He further writes about a 1956 book by Jack Allen and Clarence Stegmeir, titled *Civics*, which reflected the trend toward endorsement of cultural pluralism in America. In this book they made the point that America is not a melting pot in which people of different origins mix and become one new and different people, but a place where good citizens live and work together in many groups. They advocated that the idea of a melting pot be discarded, since America is a country where a variety of people have something of value to contribute.

Even though the U.S. Congress passed the Fourteenth and Fifteenth Amendments to the Constitution in 1870, guaranteeing civil rights and the right to vote to African Americans, the idea of education as a civil right did not actually become a popular opinion until the end of the Jim Crow laws in the Southern states.[8] Before the Emancipation Declaration, it was illegal to teach African Americans to read and write. Long after that law was rescinded, African Americans who got any education whatsoever got them at the hands of fellow African Americans and a few white abolitionists. Whereas the years between 1865 and 1876 are regarded as the Reconstruction era—the period during which federal laws provided civil rights protection for African Americans in the Southern states—the Jim Crow laws were in effect between 1876 and 1964. During this era, it was required by law in many states to provide separate educational and public facilities for whites and African Americans in the United States. In the state of Florida, for example, an 1895 education statute stated a penal offense for any person or school conducting public or private education where whites and "colored" people are taught in the same building or classroom. This statute had a penalty of between $150 and $500 or three to six months of imprisonment. In the state of Mississippi, a similar law went as far as dictating that textbooks could not be used interchangeably between white and black schools. This was one of the worst states for discriminatory practices.[9] Even with the *Brown v. Board of Education* ruling of 1954, which upheld the rights of every child (white or African American) to attend their neighborhood schools, laws were made by state and local school districts to circumvent this mandate, and up until 1964 many court cases were filed, tried, and ruled upon in response to *Brown*.

The movement toward multicultural education cannot claim a coordinated development that brought it about, yet many of the recent movements that have contributed to make it a reality can trace back to the civil rights era. James Banks articulates the development of multicultural education in the United States under five dimensions: content integration, knowledge construction, equity pedagogy, prejudice reduction, and empowering school culture and social structure.[10] According to Banks, the roots of content integration trace far back to the works of an African American scholar, George Washington Williams,[11] whose historical works date as far back as between 1882 and 1883. Banks traced knowledge construction to as far back as the 1960s in the works of revisionist social scientists who were primarily people of color. Gary Nash,[12] while not disputing the 1960s historical roots of the knowledge construction movements, indicates that in the 1990s the battle for cultural parity would be fought in the classrooms as African American and other minority parents sought to alter what their children were being taught in schools, a prediction that has proved to be true.

Banks traced prejudice reduction to the 1920s researches on children's racial attitudes and traced equity pedagogy to the cultural deprivation paradigms of the 1960s.[13] Empowering school culture was traced to more recent works that focused on the needs of students from diverse ethnic, language, and racial groups and social classes.[14] Equity is identified as the basic concept of the 1960s, and it provided the basis for both the integrationist movements and the movement toward gender equality in the United States.[15] Regardless of the effects of the ideological elements identified by Banks, much of the 1970s and 1980s focused on desegregation and physical integration of African American and white students in schools through busing, school choice, magnet schools, ratios, redrawing boundaries, intra- and interdistrict transfers, and many other similar activities.[16] Banks's *Handbook of Research on Multicultural Education* has a detailed discussion of these five dimensions and their significance to understanding multicultural education today.

The scope of this work would not allow a detailed engagement with those varied dimensions, but suffice it to say that whereas those dimensions focused on the ideological trends that provide foundational principles upon which we can build, there were a number of other radical and more obvious developments that made multicultural education what it is in our time. These are laws, movements, and initiatives that brought about radical revolutions that propelled us to where we are today in the push toward equality and equity pedagogy.

In the sections below we will investigate the various movements, laws, and individuals who have influenced the development of multicultural education as "an idea, a process, and a reform movement" in the United States.

U.S. SOCIOPOLITICAL MOVEMENTS

The Civil Rights Movement—Legal Foundations

Most historians place the birth of the civil rights movement on May 17, 1954, when the U.S. Supreme Court ruled that an African American girl had the right to attend her neighborhood white school. This ruling practically killed an 1896 court ruling, *Plessy v. Ferguson*,[17] which held that it was lawful to provide separate but equal educational facilities for whites and African Americans. The significance of the *Brown v. Board Education*[18] ruling lies in the fact that for the first time, the constitutional provisions of civil and voting rights given to African Americans under the law carried significance, as the law now gave them equal access to educational facilities and resources. As indicated earlier, this landmark ruling did not go unchallenged, as many states and local school districts sought for ways to circumvent it. While this battle was still raging, Rosa Parks, an African American woman refused to give up her seat at the front of the bus to a white passenger in Montgomery, Alabama, on December 1, 1955.[19] She was arrested, as the law ordained, and this sparked an immediate reaction from the African American community in the form of bus boycotts, which continued until December 21, 1956, when it ended with desegregation in buses.[20] This was the incident that propelled Dr. Martin Luther King Jr. to the limelight of the civil rights movement. As the newly elected president of the Montgomery Improvement Association (MIA), he spearheaded the boycott and soon joined with a number of other African American leaders to found the Southern Christian Leadership Conference (SCLC), and was made its president. His organization became one of many such African American movements advocating equal rights across the Southern states. Such movements as the Student Nonviolent Coordinating Committee (SNCC), the Congress of Racial Equality (CORE), and the National Association for the Advancement of Colored People (NAACP) all played significant roles in the civil rights movement.[21]

Students' actions during the civil rights movement may be of greater significance for the history of multicultural education. In September 1957, nine African American students showed up at all-white Central High School in Little Rock, Arkansas, where they were blocked from entering the school grounds by the order of the governor of the state. This attracted national attention, and the U.S. president, Dwight Eisenhower, had to send the National Guard to intervene on behalf of those students. In Greensboro, North Carolina, four African American students from the North Carolina Agricultural and Technical College launched a sit-in at a segregated lunch counter in Woolworth's, where they were refused service. This triggered similar sit-ins across the South. A large number of protesters and freedom riders of the civil rights movement were students.[22] On October 1, 1961, James Meredith, an African American student, became the first person of African descent to enroll into the University of Mississippi. The violence and protest attracted by this from the white segregationists compelled President Kennedy to send 5,000 federal troops to restore calm.

These series of students-involved events, protests, acts of civil disobedience, and demands for fair treatment culminated in the 1964 Civil Rights Act, which was signed into law by President Lyndon Johnson on July 2, 1964, prohibiting discrimination on the basis or race, color, religion, or national origin. The impacts of the civil rights movement and the laws that followed it are more evident when you consider the fact that from the 1800s to 1968 African Americans were practically invisible in the major newspapers of Los Angeles,[23] but the movement propelled them to the front pages.

Ethnic Studies Movements

James Banks traces the roots of ethnic studies programs to the works of a number of African American scholars[24] such as G. W. William (1882–1883), Woodson and Wesley,[25] and W.E.B. Du Bois.[26] Du Bois's work titled *African American Reconstruction* may be one of the major catalysts that sensitized American historians to begin to look at American history from a more objective perspective, thus providing a strong basis for multicultural education.[27] Ethnic studies programs as we know them today, however, can be regarded as a by-product of the civil rights movement. In the years following the Civil Rights Act (mostly 1970s), educators began to advocate the inclusion of the history and accomplishments of ethnic minorities in the school curriculum. Up until 1970, much of the U.S. educational curriculum had been essentially Eurocentric. Stories of most American peoples were omitted, and even the earliest Americans (Native Americans) were absent in the pages of many history books.

As minority students got more and more involved in the mainstream educational structures of the United States, they saw the need for the schools to speak to their own stories and struggles. The 1970s saw a wave of ethnic studies programs across U.S. colleges and universities: African American Studies, Asian Studies, and Hispanic Studies programs, even the story of Native Americans began to find its way into the mainstream educational curriculum. Whereas these ethnic studies programs catered to the needs of the ethnic populations in colleges and universities, they were mostly sidelined, as often only ethnic minority people took these courses. So in effect, even though it brought in a divergent cultural view to the educational curriculum, these programs did not effectively infuse multiculturalism into the curriculum, student life, and culture. In many places, these programs were isolated. The Reagan years of the late 1980s can be seen as an era in which ethnic studies programs suffered even further setbacks because the administration and its secretary of education did not see much usefulness in these programs.[28]

A number of other kinds of movements played roles in establishing the grounds on which multicultural education has now flourished. Such movements include the founding of various associations that have influenced educational policies and practices. Some of the organizations include the American Council on Education (ACE), the Anti-Defamation League (ADL), the National Education Association (NEA), and many others.[29] These organizations are known to have often challenged the complex sociopolitical factors that have perpetuated inequality, prejudice, and discrimination.

GOVERNMENT LEGISLATION

Whereas laws do not change minds, laws and other government actions have remained the primary instruments that have provided protection for minorities in the United States. It is sad to note that every one of the civil liberties enjoyed by minorities in the United States today came about as a result of decades of struggles and battles in law courts, the Congress, or in the White House. This proves the assertion that those with power are never willing to share it. In this section, therefore, we will discuss landmark legal and congressional actions that have influenced the development of multicultural education in the United States.

Brown v. Board of Education of Topeka

This court case may be the most significant turning point in the fight for civil rights in U.S. history. The plaintiffs argued as follows:

> Segregation of white and Negro children in the public schools of a state solely on the basis of race, pursuant to state laws permitting or requiring such segregation, denies the Negro children the equal protection of the laws guaranteed by the Fourteenth Amendment . . . even though physical facilities and other "tangible" factors of white and Negro schools may be equal. . . . Where a State has undertaken to provide an opportunity for an education in its public schools, such an opportunity is a right, which must be made available to all on equal terms. Segregation of children in public schools solely on the basis of race deprives children of the minority group equal educational opportunities, even though the physical facilities and other "tangible" factors may be equal.[30]

Thurgood Marshall, an African American attorney, and a team of other highly qualified lawyers argued this case before the U.S. Supreme Court. In deciding this case, the Court ruled that in the field of public education, the doctrine of "separate but equal" has no rightful place, as segregated schools are inherently unequal. The court further stated, "We have now announced that such segregation is a denial of the equal protection of the laws."

This ruling initiated sweeping educational and social reforms across the United States, and arguably it can be stated that on this day, multicultural education was born. For the first time, the U.S. courts placed their seal of approval on the Fourteenth Amendment to the Constitution, thereby laying a strong foundation for multicultural education.

The Civil Rights Act of 1964 (Title VI)

The general provisions of the Civil Rights Act of 1964 defines it as an act

> To enforce the constitutional right to vote, to confer jurisdiction upon the district courts of the United States to provide injunctive relief against discrimina-

tion in public accommodations, to authorize the Attorney General to institute suits to protect constitutional rights in public facilities and public education, to extend the commission on Civil Rights, to prevent discrimination in federally assisted programs, to establish a Commission on Equal Employment Opportunity and for other purposes.[31]

The term "federally assisted programs" includes, but is not limited to, college, university, and other postsecondary institutions; secondary and elementary schools; and any other school system receiving any kind of federal funding. This act, and its sister, the 1965 Civil Rights Bill provided minorities a legal basis to demand equality with the white population. They outlawed discriminatory practices that had gone on for decades under the protection of the law, thereby setting the stage for minorities to demand equal treatment in educational settings as well as in the other public arenas that the legislation provided for such.

Equal Education Act of 1974

This act says that no state shall deny equal educational opportunity to any individual on the account of "race, color, sex, or national origin." The act provided a broad protection from many discriminatory practices among which are

- the deliberate segregation by an educational agency of students on the basis of race, color, or national origin among or within schools;
- the failure of an educational agency which has formerly practiced such deliberate segregation to take affirmative steps, consistent with part 4 of this subchapter, to remove the vestiges of a dual school system;
- the assignment by an educational agency of a student to a school, other than the one closest to his or her place of residence within the school district in which he or she resides, if the assignment results in a greater degree of segregation of students on the basis of race, color, sex, or national origin among the schools of such agency than would result if such student were assigned to the school closest to his or her place of residence within the school district of such agency providing the appropriate grade level and type of education for such students;
- the failure by an educational agency to take appropriate action to overcome language barriers that impede equal participation by its students in its instructional programs.[32]

This act was preceded by a 1972 Title IX Education Amendment, which among other things, outlawed discrimination in educational opportunities on the basis of gender. Women in the United States gained legal rights to attend schools of their choices and pursue educational programs of choice without discrimination.

Such law suits as *Lau v. Nichols* in California, and *San Antonio Independent School District v. Rodriguez* projected the damaging effects of discriminatory practices and legal prohibitions that lead to inequity in educational opportunities as well as the resistance struggles that accompanied them. The proximity of these two landmark cases to this law makes clear the law's timeliness for reducing the tension that was already mounting in many parts of the nation. Equal educational opportunity now became a legal right, and for some years the debate centered on a definition of equal educational opportunities, a debate that is still ongoing.

SCHOLARS AND EDUCATORS— INTELLECTUAL FOUNDATIONS

Laws do not change minds, neither do they reduce prejudices, but they are necessary parameters that sensor actions in a civilized society. Whereas laws have made the general provisions for the pursuit of equality and multicultural education, multiple scholars and academicians have produced research insights that are changing minds, attitudes, and behaviors, making the provisions of law more acceptable to people in such a pluralistic democracy as the United States. In the time period following the 1970s, scholars and academicians have championed the journey toward implementation of equal educational opportunities, and multicultural education. A cursory glance reveals certain names whose contributions have been significant. James Banks identified a number of these people, himself being one, with others such as L. D. Delpit, J. Ogbu, B. J. Shade, Michael Harrington, Jane Elliott, and many others.[33]

From outside of the United States, Paulo Freire published his *Pedagogy of the Oppressed* in 1970, and *Education for Critical Consciousness* in 1973. These two works had a radical impact on education and the social climate of schools. It became obvious that educational structures that do not have liberating effects fall short of the ideal. In a way, other Latin American liberation movements, some of which found expression in liberation theology, black liberation, and black theology movements in the United States and South Africa, and other similar influences, may have had their own impacts. By the late 1970s it was becoming clear that the purpose of education was not only to provide learning and skills development, but empowerment, which allow the recipients of educational programs to critique their environment, question issues, and actively engage in social and civic life.

We will outline a brief summary of the contributions of some of these individuals as we conclude this chapter.

James Banks

James Banks is the Kerry and Linda Killinger Professor of Diversity Studies and Director of the Center for Multicultural Education at the University of Washington, in Seattle. His areas of specialization are multicultural education and social studies education. One of his significant contributions to the field of multicultural education is his "approaches to curriculum reform," in which he gives four levels of multicultural education: the Contributions approach, the Additive approach, the Transformation approach, and the Social Action approach. He articulated levels three and four as the most effective ways to implement multicultural education curriculum.[34] Banks is probably the most published scholar in the United States in the field of multicultural education. A chronological list of some of his significant works is as follows:

1969—"A Content Analysis of the African American in Textbooks"
1970—*Teaching the African American Experience: Methods and Materials*
1973—*Teaching Ethnic Studies: Concepts and Strategies*
1984—"African American Youths in Predominantly White Suburbs: An Exploratory Study of Their Attitudes and Self-Concepts"
1988—"Ethnicity, Class, Cognitive, and Motivational Styles: Research and Teaching Implications
1991—"The Dimensions of Multicultural Education"
1991—"Multicultural Education: Its Effects on Students' Ethnic and Gender Role Attitudes"
1992—"Multicultural Education: Approaches, Developments, and Dimensions"

1993—"The Canon Debate, Knowledge Construction, and Multicultural Education"

1993—"Multicultural Education for Young Children: Racial and Ethnic Attitudes and Their Modification"

1996—*Multicultural Education, Transformative Knowledge, and Action: Historical and Contemporary Perspectives*

1998—"The Lives and Values of Researchers: Implications for Educating Citizens in a Multicultural society"

2001—*Cultural Diversity and Education: Foundations, Curriculum and Teaching*

2003—"Approaches to Multicultural Curricular Reform"

2003—"Multicultural Education: Characteristics and Goals"

2003—*Teaching Strategies for Ethnic Studies*

2003—*Multicultural Education: Issues and Perspectives* (ed. with Cherry A. McGee Banks)

2004—*Handbook of Research on Multicultural Education* (ed. with Cherry A. McGee Banks)

John Ogbu

John Ogbu, a Nigeria-born scholar and professor of anthropology at the University of California at Berkeley, who passed away in 2003, is described as "a path-breaking scholar in the fields of minority education and identity."[35] Ogbu attempted to understand and explain how racial and ethnic diversity influenced achievement educationally and economically. He focused primarily on differential educational achievement of minority students in the United States. As an anthropologist he undertook a series of primary research that targeted minority groups. Some of his works include the following:

1993—"Differences in Cultural Frame of Reference"

1994—"Culture and Intelligence"

1996—"Educational Anthropology"

1997—"Speech Community, Language Identity, and Language Boundaries"

1997—"Racial Stratification in the United States: Why Inequality Persists"

1997—"Understanding the School Performance of Urban African Americans: Some Essential Background Knowledge"

1997—Foreword to *Reconstructing "Dropout": A Critical Ethnography of the Dynamics of African American Students' Disengagement from School* by G. J. S. Dei, J. Mazzuca, E. McIsaac, and J. Zine

1998—"Voluntary and Involuntary Minorities: A Cultural-Ecological Theory of School Performance with Some Implications for Education" (with H. D. Simons)

1999—"Beyond Language: Ebonics, Proper English, and Identity in an African American-America Speech Community"

1999—"Cultural Context of Children's Development"

2000—"Collective Identity and Schooling" (in Japanese)

2001—"Cultural Amplifiers of Intelligence" (with P. Stern)

2001—"Caste Status and Intellectual Development" (with P. Stern)

2002—"African American-American Students and the Academic Achievement Gap: What Else You Need to Know"

2003—*African American Students in an Affluent Suburb: A Study of Academic Disengagement*

Jane Elliott

A mother of four children and a third-grade teacher at the Riceville, Iowa, Community Elementary School, Elliott was not a household name until 1968, when she began to take a radical step to address the issues of racial discrimination and inequality within the four walls of her own classroom. It was on the day following the death of Dr. Martin Luther King, Jr., that she began to carry out an exercise that was soon to revolutionize her classroom, raise protests from some whites in her community, and bring her lots of insults, abuse, attacks, and ostracism. This activity, which she called "Blue Eye Brown Eye," addressed racial discrimination based on skin color, eye color, and hair texture and color.

The activity turned the tables of discrimination on the light-skinned blue-eyed kids in her classroom, and she gave them a one-day taste of what it feels like to be discriminated against. Both the controversies and rejections she attracted as a result of this activity propelled her to public view when in 1970 her classroom activity of "Blue Eye Brown Eye" was featured on ABC News under the title, "Eye of the Storm." Since that time, Elliott has spent her time teaching and lecturing on the impact of racial discrimination, and her videos and lecture materials are used across the nation in many classrooms. She has

taken her lectures and activities beyond the shores of the United States, and
has continued to change people's perspectives as she confronts people with
the harmful reality of discrimination.[36]

Elliott's works have been produced in videos to spread her one-person
campaign for racial tolerance.

Her radical approach to multicultural education has penetrated unusual
places in the United States, such as police academies, the public service
arena, and institutions of higher learning.

$\sim$

QUESTIONS AND APPLICATION

Case Study: Teaching at Abbot High

Background

You are the new history teacher at Abbot High School. Abbot High is one of
the most reputable high schools in the nation. Known for its high academic
standards and a history of highly successful alumni, you are expected to
carry on in a 100-year-old tradition of high academic excellence and uncompromising commitment to a high level of integrity. Most teachers at Abbot
have been there for twenty years or more. People hardly leave Abbot to go
to another school, as it would be seen as a demotion. Abbot is meticulous in
its selection of teachers and always hires the cream of the crop. Coming into
Abbot at your youthful age, people see you as highly privileged and specially
favored. The older teachers continually remind you of how lucky you are to
join them and how happy they are to have you. Parents tell you that you are
privileged to be hired at Abbot and that they know you will prove worthy of
the honor. The school, while mostly white, with a very insignificant number
of blacks and Asians and no Hispanics, espouses to be color-blind in their
policy toward racial and cultural integration. People are supposed to be seen
as people and not as racial groups or cultural groups.

The Problem

During your first week at Abbot, you took time to go through the adopted
textbooks that you are required to teach from. You were shocked to realize
that most of the texts, while new, follow an old tradition of male-dominated

curriculum. The female gender and minority figures are conspicuously absent in the pages of the history books. The curriculum is a very dominant white male curriculum. The culture of the school is a dominant Anglo-Saxon male culture. The minority students are often called names, but they cannot protest for fear of raising issues and being kicked out of this highly respected high school. You have been thoroughly immersed in multicultural education and you strongly believe that curricula should be balanced ethnically and gender-wise.

Your Challenge

1. What modifications would you make in your text selection, curriculum content, and instructional strategies?
2. Would you confront the school authorities with your impression of the adopted texts? Why? Why not?
3. Should you choose to confront them with the problems with the adopted texts, how would you describe the problems to them? What would be your rationale for requiring a review of the adopted texts? What compromises are you willing to make concerning the texts and your convictions and beliefs in a balanced curriculum?
4. Should you fail to convince them to change the adopted texts, what would you do to make up for the lack of balance in the curriculum? What risks do you run when you include materials that are not part of the adopted texts?
5. Would you choose to engage the school with the racial insensitivity that you are observing? If you choose to address it, how would you start? What risks do you run as you choose to engage this topic?
6. What convincing arguments can you put across to the school authorities on the major weakness of the color-blind approach to cultural integration?

Review Questions

1. What would you consider the foundational developments that gave birth to multicultural education in the United States?
2. In what unique ways was the civil rights movement a catalyst toward the development of multicultural education?
3. In what ways did sociopolitical movements help to advance multicultural education?

4. Who would you consider the intellectual forerunners of the multicultural education movement? What were their unique contributions to this movement?

5. What landmark pieces of legislation had the most profound impact on the advancement of multicultural education in the United States? How did they advance multicultural education?

Strategies for Application

1. Grades K–6: Read the stories of Linda Brown and Harriet Tubman and discuss with class how these individuals helped to change our society into a better place. Discuss problems of discrimination and oppression that still exist in our society today and even at the school and let students brainstorm ways they can make a difference.

2. Grades 7–12: Provide students with or ask them to go on the Internet and research different versions of Jim Crow laws. Create opportunities for students to read, analyze, and discuss these laws in the context of civil rights. Allow them to identify and discuss factors that would lead to such laws in any given society and what is wrong about those laws.

3. Grades 7–12: Allow students to research the history and controversies surrounding affirmative action. Structure an informed debate on the pros and cons of the affirmative action for the twenty-first century. Allow students to come up with what could be a reasonable alternative to affirmative action for the twenty-first century.

Chapter Six

Title I Categorical Fund

A Sample Federal Government Attempt at Educational Equity

Chapter Objectives:

This chapter discusses the Title I Categorical fund as an example of the federal government's attempt at equal educational opportunities. It discusses its history, scope, and impact. Readers will be able to:

1. explain the purpose of Title I Categorical fund
2. access resources for exploring and understanding the scope and impact of the Title 1 fund on their local U.S. school district
3. develop a curiosity to become more knowledgeable on how funds are received and spent at their local U.S. school districts

The full title of this fund is Title I—Improving the Academic Achievement of the Disadvantaged. This is one of the few funds that target educational equity. The public school system is often accused of gross inequalities resulting from the way governments (federal and state) fund education. There is not much, however, said about some of the attempts that have been made by the states and the federal government toward equalizing the playing field in educational opportunities. In studying this fund, therefore, we will engage the purpose of this fund, its history, and its impact on public school funding. We will also take time to look at some studies that have evaluated the effects it is having on the educational system.

PURPOSE

The primary purpose of the Title I fund is "to ensure that all children have a fair, equal, and significant opportunity to obtain a high-quality education and reach, at a minimum, proficiency on challenging State academic achieve-ment standards and state academic assessments."[1] In order to achieve the stated purposes, a number of steps must be taken. The steps are as follows.

First, ensure that high-quality academic assessments, accountability sys-tems, teacher preparation and training, curriculum, and instructional materi-als are aligned with challenging state or national academic standards so that students, teachers, parents, and administrators can measure progress against common expectations for student academic achievement.

On the issues of assessment and accountability, the assumption here is that by ensuring high-quality academic assessment and accountability sys-tems across the board, all students will benefit. Some believe that once the standard is raised, all students will be challenged to perform better. Sadly though, this may be idealistic thinking, especially when the standards are raised by high-quality assessments alone, without raising the quality of instruction. This objective, however, addresses the need for high-quality curriculum, teacher preparation, and standards-based instructional materials. The central goal is to measure progress against central expectations. This means that this is a fund that requires accountability in the form of data-based academic records.

Second, this fund also ensures that educational needs of low-achieving children, migratory children, children with disabilities, Native American children, neglected or delinquent children, and young children in need of reading assistance are met. This objective targets children who are outside the bell curve and often the most neglected in the educational systems. The government, through this fund, demands that their needs be met.

This fund is used to meet a number of needs, including purchasing specific learning materials that target these low-achieving students. It could be used to buy learning tools, and lower-level books than the grade levels the chil-dren are at (but at their reading level). More often than not, the fund is used to hire teaching assistants so that these children can get one-to-one attention during instruction and be provided after-school support.

Third, it targets closing the achievement gap between high-achieving and low-achieving students, especially the achievement gap between minority and nonminority students and disadvantaged and more advantaged students. In the course of this study it was discovered that some schools have difficulty demonstrating how this is done, especially schools with large populations of both minorities and nonminorities.

In segregated schools, it is easy to account for this kind of money, but in mixed schools, it seems to be a challenge. Granted the fact that this fund represents only a negligible proportion of every state's educational expenses, it falls far short in achieving the goal of bridging the gap between the minority and nonminority students. In a case decided in early 2001, Justice Leland DeGrasse of the New York State Supreme Court in Manhattan declared that the State of New York's funding system violated the state constitution and fell short in providing for a "sound basic education" across the board. The ruling also found the state in violation of federal civil rights laws because it "harms" students of color disproportionately.[2]

During this trial, the plaintiffs argued that the state's funding system routinely shortchanged students in the large New York City district, which was educating more than 70 percent of all the minority students in the state. The state was accused of failing to ensure that these schools had all the resources they needed to meet the new learning standards.[3] This is where inequity is perpetuated using the contemporary tools of standardized instruction and assessment. When the low-achieving, low-income, and minority schools are not adequately equipped, and yet are being held to the same rigorous standards that other better-equipped schools are held to, the state is shortchanging those low-income students and using the governmental structures to perpetuate inequality. Unfortunately, the State of New York was pushing a rigorous set of standardized exams across the board at the same time that these allegations were being made, hence the ruling.

Fourth, this fund is used to hold schools and local and state educational agencies accountable for improving academic achievement across the board. It is used to identify and turn around low-performing schools. Using this fund, the school is able to target low-performing students and provide them alternative learning experiences that can help them improve. Some of those alternatives can be special field trips.

The idea of field trips sounds weak as a tool for improving academic achievement. Although field trips alone cannot do much in closing achievement gaps among students, they do provide students access to life experiences and a knowledge base they would otherwise not have. Sadly though, some schools are unable to come up with more dynamic programs that can better close these achievement gaps. They seem more concerned with using the funds within the limits of the specified provisions rather than with the actual outcome of the funds used. One year, a site administrator at a school district in Southern California used this fund in a uniquely positive way. She purchased a computerized accelerated reading program, which was loaded into about twenty-four computers in the library. This is a program that students at all reading levels could enter into with relative ease, begin at their ability level, work independently through the course, and progress at their own pace, until they graduate out of it. The program was exciting and engaging enough for students to want to come back to it every day. The target students had a three-hour window every school day to work on this resource until their reading skills improved. They were not pressured by any timeline; they worked at their own pace under the supervision of a reading teacher. It made a significant difference that year as the school's Academic Performance Index (API) shot up the second year after this program was introduced.

For lack of space to continue to analyze each goal separately, let's go ahead and list the remaining goals of this fund, which requires:

1. distributing and targeting resources sufficiently to make a difference to local educational agencies and schools where needs are the greatest
2. improving and strengthening accountability, teaching, and learning by using state assessment systems designed to ensure that students are meeting challenging state academic achievement and content standards, and increasing achievement overall, but especially for the disadvantaged
3. providing greater decision-making authority and flexibility to schools, and responsibility for student achievement
4. providing children an enriched and accelerated educational program, including the use of schoolwide programs or additional services that increase the amount and quality of instructional time
5. promoting schoolwide reform and ensuring the access of children to effective, scientifically based instructional strategies and challenging academic content
6. significantly elevating the quality of instruction by providing staff, in participating schools, with substantial opportunities for professional development
7. coordinating services under all parts of this title with each other, with other educational services, and to the extent feasible, with other agencies providing services to youth, children, and families
8. affording parents substantial and meaningful opportunities to participate in the education of their children[4]

SOURCE AND SIZE OF THE FUND

The Title I fund is a federal government fund that goes through the states to the local school districts and schools. It is a large fund covering many programs, which will not be discussed here due to brevity of space, scope, and time. There are many parts to the fund. Part A deals with improving basic programs operated by the local educational agencies (LEAs) from pre-school to high schools. Part B focuses on student reading skills, especially from kindergarten to third grade. Part C focuses on the education of migrant children. Part D deals with prevention and intervention programs for children and youth who are neglected, delinquent, or at risk. Part E focuses on a national assessment of Title I—a kind of federal audit to assess the effectiveness of the program itself in improving student achievement at state, local, and school levels. Part F deals with comprehensive school reforms, exploring factors that will enable students to meet the challenging state academic standards. Part G focuses on advanced placement programs for high school students. Part H deals with school dropout prevention. Finally, Part I deals with the general regulations concerning this fund.[5]

The funds involved in Title I programs are large, despite the fact that at the end of the day they represent a small proportion of local school funding. For carrying out part A alone, the following amounts were authorized to be appropriated from the federal government from year 2002 to 2007:

Year	Amount
2002	$13.5 billion
2003	$16 billion
2004	$18 billion
2005	$20.5 billion
2006	$22.75 billion
2007	$25 billion

For the Los Angeles Unified School District, the categorical funds from the federal government under this program totaled $591,319,373 for the fiscal year 2002–2003. This represents 10 percent of the total budget of $5,919,185,613. The state funds provided 68.8 percent of the total budget. Local property tax provided 19.1 percent of the budget, while other local revenue provided another 2.1 percent. The Title I fund, therefore, represents the lowest source of educational funding, though it comes with the most rigorous accountability demands and compliance issues. As a result of the stimulus from the Obama administration, however, LAUSD is estimated to get $180.5 million for Title I funding in the 2009–2010 school year and the same amount for the 2010–2011 school year.

HISTORY OF TITLE I FUND

Geoffrey Borman, in an article titled "How Can Title I Improve Achievement?"[6] traced the history of this fund. The goal of the Elementary Education Act of 1965 at the time it was enacted was to improve schooling in high-poverty contexts and to advance equality in education. Borman cites research evidence that makes the case that in the 1970s and 1980s this program made tremendous progress in closing the persistent achievement gaps between low- and high-income students, African American and white students, more privileged and less privileged students.[7]

According to Borman's study, the achievement gap between African American and white students shrank by about two grades. He cites other studies that involved a comprehensive meta-analysis of seventeen federal evaluations and more than 40 million Title I students' test scores from 1966 to 1993, which indicated that the 1970s and 1980s recorded the greatest improvement in Title I students' reading and math achievements.[8]

According to Borman, beginning in the 1980s, the gains made by African American students began to erode due to the fact that some federal lawmakers had started to nurse the opinion that Title I was "largely ineffective." Some lawmakers called for total elimination of the program in the 1990s, while others asked for its modification.

The life of this fund, however, has not only been extended, but President George W. Bush's No Child Left Behind Act (NCLB) rejuvenated it. The NCLB act came to life with the goal of "transforming the Federal role in education so that no child is left behind."[9] Part of the summary statement for this act reads as follows:

> As America enters the 21st Century full of hope and promise, too many of our neediest students are being left behind. Today, nearly 70 percent of inner city fourth graders are unable to read at a basic level on national reading tests.

Our high school seniors trail students in Cyprus and South Africa on international math tests. And nearly a third of our college freshmen find they must take a remedial course before they are able to even begin regular college level courses. . . . The academic achievement gap between rich and poor, Anglo and minority is not only wide, but in some cases is growing wider still.[10]

In order to attempt to address these problems, this act places certain mandates on the school systems as prerequisites for them to continue to receive the federal funds for Title I programs. The demands are as follows:

- Increased accountability for student performance: Increased academic achievement will be rewarded to states, districts, and schools, while failure will be sanctioned.
- Focus on what works: Federal funds will be spent on effective, research-based programs and practices.
- Reduced bureaucracy and increased flexibility: Flexible funding will be increased at local levels, with increased flexibility also at state and district levels.
- Empower Parents: Parents are to be provided more information on the quality of their children's schools. They will have a choice to pull their children out of persistently low-performing schools.

Under NCLB, Title I program remains the largest federal program aimed at supporting elementary and secondary education. A set of four parameters has been established for distributing this fund to schools. The first category is the Basic Grant, which provides funding to any school district with at least ten poor children. This program makes the fund available to virtually all school districts. The second is the Concentrated Grant Formula, which provides funding to schools based on the number of poor children they serve. This program requires that the district have at least 15 percent of its students in poverty to qualify or have 6,500 poor children enrolled in the district. The third is the Targeted Assistance Grant, which provides more funding to the district as the number of children in poverty enrolled in the district increases. This limits the process by which the same amount of money is given per child, but actually raises the amount of money based on the increase in the number of poor children. The last is the Education Finance Incentive Grant. This grant rewards schools for spending more state money on public education. The more state and local funding that goes into education, the more federal money that goes into education for that state, thus encouraging local effort.

In the year 2009 $6.6 billion of the Title 1 fund was distributed through the Basic Grant, $1.4 billion on Concentrated Grant, $3.3 billion on Targeted Assistance Grant, and $3.3 billion through the Education Finance Incentive Grant program. This brings the total spending under these four grants to $14.4 billion.[11]

BUDGET CONSTRAINTS AND LIMITATIONS OF THE TITLE I FUND

The Title I fund is a categorical aid. That is, this money is intended for school districts and local schools to meet specific needs. Since much of this money is based on the characteristics of the children and families being served—gifted and talented, special education, English-language learners, low-income, migrant—and specific activities or expenses such as school improvement, urban impact aid, educational technology, mentor teachers, professional development, and instructional materials, it is oftentimes very limiting.[12] Administrators' hands are often tied as they cannot freely put this money into other areas they may consider more important and more productive. The fund leaves little or no room for discretionary spending.

There is a growing trend in educational spending to allow greater discretion in budget decisions at the local level. This has been imbedded into NCLB, so there is hope that more and more discretion will be allowed at the local levels so that these funds can be channeled to their maximum use.

ASSESSMENT OF TITLE I FUNDS' EFFECTIVENESS

Reading through the study done by Borman and its findings, it is encouraging to discover that in the 1970s and 1980s this fund actually made a significant impact on the educational opportunities of minority students. There is a concern that part of the failures we have noticed from the 1990s on may be a result of a lowered accountability system. Although schools, districts, and the states made their annual reports to the federal government on the management of the funds, a critical study of the direct effect on achievement did not necessarily accompany them. This writer once worked in a school where one day the principal called teachers together and told them that they had about $50,000 in categorical funds money that had not been used and that it must be used before the end of the school year or they might lose it and consequently face the likelihood of a reduced allocation for the next school year. Many teachers of Title I students went around ordering materials and texts that they had no well-thought-out plan for and no idea as to what the impact would be on the population that needed those funds, the Title I students. Teachers saw it as an opportunity to acquire more classroom materials. The academic objective was not clear, and the needs of the Title I students were practically out of the picture.

The above perspective does not in any way imply that all schools are approaching this need the same way. A study done at an elementary school in the Midwest describes a situation where teachers work together with Title I students in grades K–3. The program is structured to provide pullout programs four times a week, individualized programs, literacy booster clubs, and literacy teams.[13] Another school, Williams Elementary School in Williams, Oregon, used the Title I criteria to identify homeless children, and special programs spanning from before-school to after-school programs were designed to meet these students' specific needs.[14] This means that a number of schools are working hard on utilizing this fund to effect changes in achievement, but some others may need to improve the way the funds are used.

There is need for a clearer and more comprehensive way to tie the use of these funds to the services that directly benefit these low-achieving students. This fund is a good gesture on the part of the federal government toward facilitating equity in educational opportunities, but we need a better implementation and supervision modality, as schools, districts, and states are asking for the funds to be enlarged. Title I funds should be enlarged in view of the additional mandates of NCLB. It has worked in the past; it can work again.

Added to the concerns expressed above is the finding from a U.S. Department of Education study that the distribution method for this fund still creates inequality, as high-poverty schools end up receiving less money per student when compared to low-poverty school districts. The difference is said to be $558 per student in high-poverty schools compared to $763 in low-poverty schools. There is also the concern that the funding is not evenly distributed in its support across grade levels.[15] Further critique of these funding formulas reveals the system unfairly favors large districts even when they have low poverty rates. [16]

~

QUESTIONS AND APPLICATION

Case Study: School Funding

Background

You are the site administrator at Jones Elementary School in downtown Los Angeles. Your school site received the sum of $150,000 from the Title I fund this school year. The previous year your school site received money from the school district for new text adoption for mathematics, language arts, and science across all grade levels. You also received a grant from Microsoft Corporation for putting computers in every classroom.

The Problem

You have asked your teachers to submit a list of items and resources they would need to buy to enhance what they do for the Title I students this year, and after supplying those needs you still have about $122,000 left from the fund.

Your Challenge

1. Identify programs and resources you can develop for your school site to provide additional support for the Title I students.
2. Develop a plan of action on how the programs will be implemented, clearly articulating measurable objectives for each program or resource.
3. Develop an instrument or benchmarks for measuring the success of the programs and resources.
4. Develop a timeline for measuring success of the new programs and resources.

Review Questions

1. Explain the purpose of Title I funds.
2. Research the local school district in your area and find out how much Title I money they are receiving this year.

3. Interview some teachers at your local school on what they are doing with the Title I money their school received this year.

Strategies for Application in the K–12 Classrooms

More than 90 percent of the students who are categorized as Title I, or at risk, are not aware of this label. They do not know the implications of the label "at-risk," and the fact that their socioeconomic, health, and other conditions predispose them for failure unless they work hard to combat these forces. Some of the following activities can be used to educate and motivate these students to accept and utilize the resources being provided to them.

1. Grades K–4: Read and discuss stories like "Jack and the Bean Stalk," "The Woodcutter," and "Hansel and Gretel." These and other stories that discuss the problem of poverty will provide an excellent context to engage the classroom in a discussion of poverty and other forms of lack and their possible effects on a child's future. During this kind of discussion the teacher can bring home to the students that education is the great equalizer, which can actually bridge the gap between poverty and disabilities and a good future for kids.
2. Grades 5–12: Teachers can engage their students in researching the demographic of their city or county, focusing on the economic index and its implications for personal and community advancements. U.S. census data will be an excellent resource for this. Classes will discuss the findings and their implications on school funding, individual upward mobility for children and families affected by poverty, and the role of schooling in bridging that gap.

Chapter Seven

American Multilingualism and the Challenge of English Language Learners in the American Educational System

Chapter Objectives:

This chapter addresses the historical and pedagogical factors that affect the way the needs of English-language learners (ELLs) are met in the United States. History reveals that America, from the time of the earliest settlers, has been and will always be a multilingual society, yet it has continuously failed to come to terms with its multilingual character. Readers will be able to:

1. trace the multilingual history of the United States from precolonial days to the present
2. describe the strengths and weaknesses of the English-Only movements
3. explain the impact of immigration on American's multilingualism

From generation to generation, the educational and sociocultural landscape of the United States has seen recurring movements for a monocultural and monolingual society, organizing themselves often in the form of "English-only" movements. The thrust of their arguments has always been the fear that the English language is under threat amid increasing numbers of immigrants who do not speak English and that this popular and dominant language faces the likelihood of extinction as a result of these competing interests. Yet, English has remained the dominant language in America from decade to decade, consistently proving the extinction theory as unfounded.

The United States has historically been a multilingual society, a character that it has maintained over the centuries. The dominance of the English language as America's popular language was established as far back as 1790, yet a national census that same year established the plurality of languages that make up what is known as America.[1] In order to appreciate the historicity of America's multilingualism we must first explore historical time periods and appreciate the extent to which diverse languages have characterized the American peoples from time immemorial.

LANGUAGE IN COLONIAL AMERICA

Precolonial America as we have come to know it was a land of free peoples, Native Americans. These original Americans were made up of different ethnic groups, different languages, and different cultures and worldviews. The land was vast and open, and each ethnicity chose for itself a way of life that suited its culture and geographical location. It is estimated that more than 150 ethnic and language groups existed here before the advent of the first European settlers.

The first phase of immigration to America attracted Western Europeans, who were mostly English speaking. The colonization of the New England territories by Britain, however, did not imply that Britons were the only settlers in a land as vast and open as America. Some other non-English Western Europeans and Europeans from other regions followed quickly, and before long Anglo-Saxon English-speaking people were living alongside people from German-speaking countries, Ireland, Sweden, and Switzerland. Given the fact that the number of non-English speaking immigrants was relatively low at the early stage, they were easily assimilated into the Anglo-Saxon sociopolitical, economic, and language structures that dominated that era.

Education during the colonial years first started as household affairs. Mothers taught their children how to read and write at home. Then came the era of the dame schools, when young boys and girls, mostly white, were educated in their parents' homes by a visiting tutor or in the homes of women who had both the time and desire to teach.[2] This educational structure evolved into organized school houses. The Records of the Governor and Company of Massachusetts Bay notes that a time came in Massachusetts when an order was issued for every township to appoint someone to teach the children to read and write in their community once the population of the township got to fifty households. The wages of such teachers were to be paid by the parents of the children or their masters. Townships that reached 100 households were required to set up a grammar school to prepare the young ones for university education.[3] Schools operated smoothly as community affairs for a long time. After the Civil War, as immigration into the United States increased, the challenge of education intensified, and the need for government oversight gradually increased.

POST-COLONIAL AMERICA

As non-English speaking peoples entered the United States in large numbers, the dominant language of English was immediately threatened, or so it seemed. Noah Webster, in his *Dissertation on English Language*, which was published in 1789, titled a section "The Call for a National Culture." He stated categorically that English was an inheritance that Americans had received from their British parents and the task to cultivate and adorn it was unquestionable. He advocated the annihilation of the differences that existed in the spoken languages in America by establishing schools and a uniform language and text for the schools.[4] His effort was geared more toward a co-ordinated English language that was conventional across the land, as a way to establish cultural homogeneity.

Marion Brown, in an article titled "Is There a Nationality Problem in Our Schools?" published in the *National Education Association Proceedings* in 1900,[5] approached the same problem differently. He wrote that a glance at the American population showed that every nation under the sun had representatives in America in numbers proportionate to its distance from the American shores; that,

> every town has its German, its Italian, or its Irish colony. In the West there are Scandinavian villages; in the Southwest, perfect reproductions of old Spain. The census of 1890 reports 32 percent of our entire population of foreign parentage. The native-born White population of native parents has diminished in percentage, swamped by the foreign-born influx. . . . As long as there is unused territory or demand for cheap labour, the children of these people with different political creed and national ideal will constitute a large part of our public-school attendance.[6]

His essay engaged the overwhelming demographic changes taking place in postcolonial America. He mentioned a school in New York that reported 98 percent of its students unable to speak English. He talked about an instance in which a ship unloaded 1,100 Italians at New Orleans whose 250 children went to register for school a few days later unable to speak English.

Unlike Noah Webster, he did not call for a forceful immersion into English, rather he pointed to the Roman Empire as an example America should follow. In addressing this topic he wrote,

> The Roman Empire was a collection of national units held together by a strong centralized power, while claiming the privileges of "Romanus sum," the individual retained his language and national life untouched by the political rule of the seven-hilled city. With us the aggregation of nationalities is in the community, in the individual, making temperaments that combination of spiritual and mental qualities—character. . . . As Rome brought order, peace, and personal freedom to the various nationalities in her borders, so today must the teacher endeavour for each of the ethical microcosms that we call American children.[7]

While not advocating that they be immersed into the English language and dispossessed of the language and heritage of their non-Anglo ancestors, Brown adjured the teachers to bring the children up to the Anglo-Saxon standards of self-control, freedom, love of country, and justice. The question American educational institutions and policy makers must engage today, in the wake of the new revival of English-only movements, is whether these ideals of the American civilization, of order, peace, justice, freedom, and patriotism, can be taught to the new immigrants and lived out by them without dispossessing them of their ancestral languages. The fact that more than thirty thousand noncitizens living in this country are willing to lay down their lives in military service to this nation should be a clear indication that language is not the primary cohesive factor in this country, but rather its ideals of freedom, justice, and love for country.

Brown, however, must have been among the earliest educators to address the challenge of educating English-language learners (ELLs) in postcolonial America. Given the fact that schooling was a community-based affair, dual-language instruction was not a problem in postcolonial America. Most communities educated their young ones in their own languages and taught them the dominant language of English at the same time. Dual-language instruction is evidenced in the 1840 Ohio policy, which resulted in about 17,584 students being taught in English and German. It is further reported that out of fifty-seven public schools in St. Louis by 1880, fifty-two had dual-language programs that centered mostly on German and English languages and that Anglo students were often required to learn German.[8]

Cultural and linguistic diversity was not only due to the influx of Western Europeans. The colonists had begun early to import slaves from Africa, bringing in a more global diversity that went beyond multiple European groups. By the late nineteenth and early twentieth centuries, more immigrants flowed in from other parts of Europe.[9] According to the 1790 census figures, roughly half of the U.S. population at that time were of English origin, about 19 percent of African origin, 12 percent Scottish or Scotch Irish, 3 percent Irish, with another 14 percent representing Dutch-, French-, and Spanish-speaking peoples.[10] America was a cultural and language mosaic from as early as history can remember. So whereas a handful of English-speaking peoples saw a linguistic threat, about half of America's population saw bilingualism as a way of life.

The Twentieth Century

Between 1900 and 1920 much of the ground gained in dual-language instruction in America was lost as a result of two major factors, namely: the influx of many Irish Catholic immigrants, whose presence was highly resented by Anglo-Saxon Protestant Americans, and the anti-German sentiments that came as a result of the World War I. By this time, newcomers were expected to forget and let go of their past ways and adopt the Anglo-Saxon language and culture.[11] This was the era characterized by the metaphoric melting-pot ideology. During this period, most American schools were being persuaded to eradicate dual-language instruction and conform to the Anglo-Saxon culture and language. The goal of many leading educators became the eradication of all ethnic traits in order for immigrants to become real Americans. One of the leading educational minds of that age, Ellwood Patterson Cubberly, stated the major goal of common school thus:

> Our task is to break up these groups or settlements, to assimilate and amalgamate these people as part of our American race, and to implant in their children, as far as can be done, the Anglo-Saxon conception of righteousness, law and order, and popular government, and to awaken in them a reverence for our democratic institutions and for those things in our national life which we as a people hold to be of abiding worth.[12]

The passage of the 1917 and 1924 Immigration Acts further illustrate the desire to ensure a monocultural and monolingual America. Europeans from all parts of Eastern and Southern Europe were required to pass a reading test in English language to enter the United States. As a result of these laws, the number of immigrants from these parts of the world dropped drastically by 1924.[13] Similarly, the anti-immigration sentiments and anti-German sentiments of this era brought the number of America's forty-eight states with English-only policies from fourteen before the World War I to thirty-four in 1923.[14] Nothing significant happened to turn the tide in favor of dual-language instruction until the 1950s, when a series of events began to unfold.

In 1954, the Supreme Court of the United States ruled on *Brown v. Board of Education*, establishing the right of every child to attend its neighborhood school regardless of race or ethnicity. This was the first time a minority group gained any significant victory in the American courtroom for challenging denial of the rights of the minority to a fair and equal education. The National Defense Education Act of 1958, which was necessitated by the Soviet launch of Sputnik, acknowledged the possession of national language as necessary for our national defense. It went a step further, providing funding for foreign-language studies. By 1961, the Cuban revolution of 1958 had brought in a flood of immigrants who were non-English speakers. The challenge posed by these immigrants led to the establishment of many private bilingual schools and later in 1963 the Coral Way Elementary School of Dade County, Florida, was established to offer dual-language instruction to mostly Cuban children.[15]

The civil rights movement of the early 1960s further intensified the need to address the learning opportunities for non-English-speaking minority children of this nation as fair and equal education began to be seen as a civil right. By 1964, President Johnson pushed Kennedy's Civil Rights Act to its final stage, thereby outlawing discrimination against immigrant Americans based on national origin. This law soon opened the door for supporting bilingual education programs in many states, especially the southwestern states. By 1968, the U.S. Congress passed the Bilingual Education Act, which gives federal funding to school districts to incorporate second-language instruction to meet the needs of English-language learners.

The next significant landmark in the history of second-language instruction after the civil rights era was the Supreme Court ruling on *Lau v. Nichols* in 1974. This was a case in which Chinese parents sued the San Francisco Unified School District for failure to provide their children with equal educational opportunities as were provided native English speakers. The Supreme Court ruled that providing students with the same teachers, textbooks, curriculum, and facilities does not mean equal education, as students who do not speak English may not be receiving meaningful education despite that level of equality. That same year, Congress passed the Equal Educational Opportunity Act (EEOA),[16] stating that schools with second-language learners are required by law to provide them with meaningful education by taking appropriate measures to overcome barriers that impede equal educational opportunities. The next year, 1975, the National Association for Bilingual Education was founded.

The late 1990s and the early 2000s have seen a resurgence in anti-immigration and anti-bilingual education tendencies that can find roots in earlier cases like the Michigan Supreme Court ruling of 1897 that declared English the official language of this nation.[17] Some states are once again enacting legislations to eradicate bilingual education in public schools. California and Arizona, among others, have successfully done this. This resurgence may be blamed on the increasing Mexican immigration and the demand for teachers and public workers to be knowledgeable in Spanish in order to meet the needs of this growing population.[18] The latter part of the twentieth century also opened a wide door to Asian immigration, which is another factor that has led to anti-immigration feelings. It is sad to conclude that into the third century of its existence, the United States still has not resolved the dynamics of her plurality as it affects the education of children who are recent immigrants as well as the fact of the permanence of multilingualism and multiculturalism as an intrinsic part of the American identity. The English language development (ELD) program, however, has emerged as a more acceptable approach, in lieu of full bilingual instruction, toward meeting the needs of these new Americans, whose desire for freedom and justice and their love for country may not weigh any less than most native-born Americans.

Table 7.1 is a historical time line of the progression of bilingual instruction and the crises of educating the English-language learner, for a bird's-eye view of how far we have come. This time line attempts to integrate a national trend with California's trends in bilingual education.[19]

On January 2, 1968, President Lyndon B. Johnson signed into law the Bilingual Education Act, which signalled the first attempt on the part of the U.S. government to address the needs of English-language learners in the schools.[20] In 1968, when President Johnson signed the Bilingual Education Act, it was a compensatory civil rights action aimed at poor and educationally disadvantaged immigrant children whom language barriers prevented from getting a good education. The argument put forward by the

Table 7.1. Historical Time Line for Second-Language/Bilingual Education in the United States

Time Period	Event
	1700s
1703	**Equal Opportunity Act:** No state shall deny equal Educational opportunity to an individual on account of his or her race, color, sex, or national origin, by . . . the failure by an educational agency to take appropriate action to overcome language barriers that impede equal participation by its students in its instructional programs.
1749	**Latin School:** Benjamin Franklin initiated the idea of an English Language School in Philadelphia, but some of the friends he expected would help with funding pressured for the inclusion of foreign languages. The school ended up establishing a Latin School and an English School. In the English school content materials were taught in English and the English tongue was taught grammatically and as a language. But in the Latin school, the Latin Master taught Latin and Greek as well as the content areas. This school gave the foreign languages a more exalted place in the curriculum above the English language, being established academic languages.
1780	John Adams made a proposal for an American Language Academy, whose goal would be to improve, refine, and ascertain English as America's language.
1782	**Statutes at Large of Pennsylvania, Chapter 1109:** This was an act establishing and incorporating a public school at Germantown in the county of Philadelphia. This academy was established to instruct the youth in the foreign languages, reading and writing English, the mathematics, and other useful branches of literature.
	1800s
1828	**Cherokee Treaty:** Treaty with the U.S. government recognized language rights of the Cherokee Indians. Their educational system was later to achieve a 91 percent literacy in Cherokee language.
1830s	**Immigrant wave:** Bilingual education was accepted in places where minorities had influence and rejected where there was none; no official language policy adopted.
1839	**Native Language Instruction law:** Ohio law authorized instruction in English, German, or both in areas where the parents request it, making it the first state to adopt bilingual education.
1847	**Wisconsin Multilingual Law:** The Wisconsin state legislature passed a resolution authorizing the use of German, Swiss, Dutch, and Norwegian for instruction in those communities. **California Construction:** California required the publication of all laws in both English and Spanish; practice was soon abandoned.
1850	**New Mexico Bilingualism:** New Mexico territory authorized Spanish-English bilingual education.
1860	**Plains Indians Ledger Act:** The plains Indians were driven out and forced to attend schools on reservations.
1884	**New Mexico Literacy law:** The State of New Mexico passed a law authorizing the setup of a school district for teaching literacy in either English or Spanish, depending on the need of a given community.

Time Period	Event
1864	Congress declared it illegal to teach Native Americans in their own languages.
Mid-1880s	Bilingualism was a socially accepted and politically protected activity as many official documents of the Continental Congress were published in French, German, and English.

1900s

1906	Congress passed the first law requiring English-language ability for naturalization as U.S. citizens. This was a reactionary law against a wave of Italian, Jewish, and Slavic immigration, as well as people from southern France.
1917	**The United States entered WWI:** A wave of language restrictions resulted from the opposition to Germany. Many states enacted English-only laws.
1923–1934	States had outlawed instruction in languages other than English. In *Meyer v. Nebraska*, a parochial school teacher was charged with the crime of reading a Bible story in German to a ten-year-old child. This led to a Supreme Court ruling that declared unconstitutional any law prohibiting the use of foreign languages in schools.
1963	**Coral Way Elementary School:** This school was established in Dade County, Florida, to offer dual-language instruction to Cuban and non-Hispanic children.
1965	**Elementary and Secondary Education Act:** The ESEA is the first and largest comprehensive federal education law that provides substantial monetary funds for kindergarten through twelfth grade education. As mandated in the act, the funds were authorized for educators' professional development, instructional materials, and resources to support educational programs and parental involvement promotion.
1965	**Elementary Education Act:** This act was passed, mandating elementary education for all children. **Coral Way High School:** This school received recognition for its dual-language immersion program.
1967	**California Senate bill 53:** This bill ended a ninety-five-year-old state education mandate that required all schools to carry out all instruction in English.
1968	**Bilingual Act:** Congress passed the Bilingual Education Act of 1968 in order to mandate schools to provide bilingual education programs. This was the first time Congress had endorsed funding for bilingual education. The Bilingual Program was a federally funded program through Title VII of the Elementary and Secondary Education Act, with the revision of Improving America's Schools Act of 1994.
1972	**California AB 2284:** This was the first piece of state legislation that pertained to funding school districts for services provided for English-language learners (ELLs).
1974	***Keyes v. School District* (Denver, Colorado):** The courts argued for special remedy above and beyond district's desegregation efforts. **Equal Opportunity Act:** No state shall deny equal educational opportunity to an individual on account of his or her race, color, sex, or national origin, by the failure by an educational agency to take appropriate action to overcome language barriers that impede equal participation by its students in its instructional programs.

(continued)

Table 7.1. (*continued*)

Time Period	Event
1975	***Lau* Remedies:** Terence Bell, the U.S. commissioner for education issued remedies that went beyond the *Lau* decision to require bilingual education to students who are non-English-language speakers.
1980	**The *Lau* Regulations:** Jimmy Carter's administration instituted this regulation to mandate bilingual education in schools with at least twenty-five English-language learners of the same language group. **California AB 507:** This legislation was called Bilingual Education Improvement and Reform Act. It updated AB 1329 of 1976, mandating that school districts provide bilingual education for every student in California who is an English-language learner.
1981	**The Bilingual Education Act** was strengthened, spelling out the obligations of school districts to English-language learners.
1986	**California Proposition 63:** This proposition aimed at amending the Bilingual Education Act. It declared English as the official language of California without necessarily preventing first-language instruction for English-language learners in California.
1994	**California Proposition 187:** Proposition 187 banned illegal immigrants from public social services, nonemergency health care, and public education. Various state and local agencies would be required to report anyone suspected of being an illegal immigrant to the state attorney general and U.S. Immigration and Naturalization Service (INS).
1995	**California ABC Bills:** Assembly Bill 170, Chapter 765, Statutes of 1995, and Assembly Bill 1504, Chapter 764, Statutes of 1995, which require, in part, that the State Board of Education adopt materials in grades one through eight that include "systematic, explicit phonics, spelling, and basic computational skills."

2000s

2000	**Promotion Retention Bills California AB 1626, Pupil Promotion and Retention** requires all school districts to establish a promotion and retention policy, based on the student's achievement of grade level standards (skills) for students between grades two and three, three and four, and four and five, as well as between elementary and middle school, and between middle school and high school. **California AB1639 Intervention Program** requires school districts to offer supplemental instruction to students in grades two through eight with low reading, writing, or math achievement. **Goal 2000: Educate America Act:** George W. Bush's educational initiative, which did not provide much aid to second-language learners. The act does not mention or have any resources for second-language acquisition. Some of its objectives are that (i) all children will have access to high-quality and developmentally appropriate preschool programs that help prepare children for school;(ii) every parent in the United States will be a child's first teacher and devote time each day to helping such parents' preschool child learn, and parents will have access to the training and support parents need.
2001	**2001 Federal "No Child Left Behind" Act:** This Act is the most sweeping reform of the Elementary and Secondary Education Act

Time Period	Event
	(ESEA) since ESEA was enacted in 1965. It redefines the federal role in K–12 education and aims at closing the achievement gap between disadvantaged and minority students and their peers. It is based on four basic principles: stronger accountability for results, increased flexibility and local control, expanded options for parents, and an emphasis on teaching methods that have been proven to work.
2002	**2002 Federal "No Child Left Behind" Act** required schools to show adequate progress in at least 95 percent of the various subgroups of students, including English-language learners. It required special accommodations to meet the needs of these students.

main sponsor of this bill, Senator Ralph Yarborough,[21] was that, "It is not the purpose of the bill to create pockets of different languages throughout the country. . . . Not to stamp out the mother tongue, and not to make their mother tongue the dominant language, but just to try to make those children fully literate in English."[22]

Yarborough actually wanted the bill to aid only Hispanic children because he argued that they are the only immigrant population that did not actually leave their homeland to come to America; instead, America came to them. This argument was not popular among most people who had anything to do with bilingual education, including Hispanic leaders, who feared a major backlash should the bill target Hispanics exclusively.

By 1974, when the Bilingual Education Act came up for reauthorization, Congress linked bilingual education to equal educational opportunity.[23]

This act suffered a major setback during the Reagan years (1981–1988) because William Bennett, Reagan's secretary of education, was not only too critical of the implementation of the Act, he saw little value in it.

The Bilingual Education Act has undergone many revisions and criticisms, yet it remains the primary legal ground for advocating equal educational rights for children who are English-language learners.

PLANNING, TEACHING, AND LEARNING IN BILINGUAL CLASSROOMS

Certain languages and terms have been used over time to describe the group of students we are focusing on: English-language learners (ELL), limited-English-proficient students (LEP), nonnative English speakers, and second-language learners. The programs for assisting these groups of students to learn and speak the English language have been referred to either as English for speakers of other languages (ESOL) or English as a second language (ESL). English language development (ELD) has become the most contemporary term for the process of assisting English learners to acquire English language in U.S. schools.

In the school systems, there are large numbers of immigrant children who have migrated to the United States from different countries of the world. These students are going through a process of acculturation, trying to establish a foothold in the American system. Another group that constitutes part of this special population is children born in the United States to parents who are non-English speakers. Most of these are immigrant parents, while some are Native American parents who can trace their American history to long before the coming of the English speakers, who continue to deal with issues of cultural identity, if not linguistic issues.

When these children come as new immigrants, they bring with them their cultures, languages, customs, and ways of life, which often differ significantly from American ways.

The process for teaching English to English-language learners is called English language development. The most current and popular strategy for teaching academic content areas such as mathematics, sciences, and even history and social studies to English-language learners is Specially Designed Academic Instruction in English (SDAIE).

English Language Development Programs

There are two major approaches to English-language development, namely: Basic Interpersonal Communications Skills (BICS) and Cognitive Academic Language Development (CALP). Basic Interpersonal Communication Skills is a nonacademic-based approach for teaching second language, in which learners are immersed in the second language and learn through everyday communication and interaction. Cognitive Academic Language Proficiency refers to the learning approach, which involves academic instruction and cognitive development in a more structured setting.

Another important concept is Sheltered Instruction, which is the means by which grade-level content such as science, social studies, and math is made more accessible to English-language learners. The idea of "sheltered" suggests that the instruction is provided in a context where learners are protected from rigorous language demands, which may interfere with learning. Features of Sheltered Instruction include:

- Wait time: Teacher allows a wait time before eliciting a response from them.
- Key vocabulary: These are identified, explained, illustrated, and made comprehensible.
- Adapted content: Supplementary materials are used to clarify the content information.
- Language objectives: Teacher identifies specific language objectives to be achieved in the lesson.
- Clarification in first language: During sheltered instruction, teachers make clarifications on the content material in the learners' first language.
- Appropriate speech for proficiency level: Teacher uses speech and language that is appropriate to the level of the students.
- Supplementary materials: A lot of supplementary materials are used.
- Students' background experiences: These inform the structure and development of the learning experience.

Specially Designed Academic Instruction in English (SDAIE)

Under SDAIE, students are taught the subject matter in English language. Special skills and strategies are used to assist students to understand content information in English despite the fact that they are still limited in English-language skills.

Scholars believe that this is more effective when used with students who have already achieved an intermediate level of English-language proficiency. In the middle and high schools, the ELD teachers focuses exclusively on language development, while the content materials are taught to this group by teachers who are trained in SDAIE methods.

TEMPLATES FOR PLANNING AND TEACHING ELD AND SDAIE LESSONS

In this section we will use the seven-step lesson plan to provide a structure for planning and teaching English language and content area materials to

English-language learners. Each template contains specific directions and pointers as to what teachers can do to make special accommodations for their ELD students. (See also table 7.2.)

ELD Lesson Plan Template

Grade Level:

Lesson Topic:

ELD Standards: Here you indicate all the state ELD standards that you are planning to address.

Language Objectives/Outcomes: Here you indicate the speaking, listening, reading, and/or writing objectives you want to achieve as a result of this lesson, in keeping with all the different ELD levels in your classroom (preproduction, early production, intermediate fluency, advanced fluency).

Entry/Anticipatory: In this section you indicate the activity you will use to excite your students about this lesson. The KWL (Know, Want to Know, Learned) chart is a common tool teachers use here. You could also read a short but interesting story/book about the topic you are about to teach. You could plan a skit, a song, a chant, etc., just to get them excited about the topic. For most ELD lessons from the Hampton Brown resource kit, this activity is already provided for you.

Instructional Input: In this section you write down everything you will teach in this lesson. You write down the steps you will take to teach them. You specify the vocabulary words you will use in teaching the lesson and how you will develop those vocabulary words (poems, chants, visuals, songs, etc.). You indicate instructional strategies you will utilize in teaching the lesson, as well as groupings.

Guided Practice: A vital part of guided practice is teacher modeling. You model for the students what you want them to be able to do, and you walk them through the process of doing it, and in so doing you see them complete the process under your guidance. If you want them to chant, you chant and they repeat, or you can have an audio, visual, or written instruction for them to follow. You provide the cue and they carry out the action.

Independent Practice: This is the place where students are required to complete the process on their own, without your help. However, the ELD

Table 7.2. English Language Development (ELD) Strategies

Steps	Meta-cognitive Activities	Cognitive Activities	Social/Affective Activities
Pre-instructional Assessment/ Knowing about your students	Apply multiple strategies to access information on students' skills and abilities relevant to the topic. Place your topic in meaningful context.	Pose questions, administer tests and performance-based assessment; evaluate oral and written responses relevant to the topic.	Be excited about the new topic and find ways to activate students' interest on the topic. Reduce anxiety level.
Entry/Anticipatory Set	Read a story; do hands-on activity; dance, sing, chant, tell a story.	Preview/review materials; do a discussion; make and revise predictions.	Listen to music on tape, show a short video slide, walk around the campus and make connections with real objects relevant to the topic.
Instructional Input	Be intentional in teaching reading, writing, speaking, and listening. Use TPR, brain storming, cooperative activities, hands-on, jigsaw, etc.	Review key vocabulary. Use appropriately modified speech, body language, gestures, and facial expressions. Provide information and ask questions at students' language proficiency levels. Model good speaking and listening.	Expect students to perform well. Create interactive activities. Teach and model positive use of language. Show respect to students and encourage them to do the same to each other.
Guided Practice	Provide a nurturing and supportive learning environment that allows risk taking.	Allow wait time for students' response. Provide students with multiple opportunities to demonstrate learning. Use activities such as labelling, matching, pointing at, sorting, grouping.	Do not force response from students. Ensure a low anxiety level. Avoid overt oral corrections.

(continued)

Table 7.2. (continued)

Steps	Meta-cognitive Activities	Cognitive Activities	Social/Affective Activities
Independent Practice	Provide clear and specific guidelines for completing activity. Make clear the expected outcome and competencies. Provide varieties of activities and provide choices and options.	Ensure that the language demands in the activities are at students' language-proficiency level. Instructions and guidelines should be in simple and clear language. Provide activities that require higher-order thinking skills.	Allocate time for task completion with due consideration to students' skills and abilities. Provide language support materials that would enhance students' performance and lead to success. Provide built-in incentives for successful task completion
Assessment/Evaluation	Monitor the learning process from beginning to end. Take note of students' challenges and successes along the way. Pose lots of clarifying questions along the way.	Assessment must utilize performance-based activities. Scoring criteria must be clear and understandable to students. It must be an objective instrument like rubrics.	Celebrate the least accomplishments and prompt students to aim higher. Reward task completion even when finished product does not meet your expectation. Reward openly, but correct privately.
Closure	Question yourself openly on the success of strategies and materials used. Model reflective practice through self-evaluation and critique.	Develop clear and predictable ways to measure and assess personal success on lesson planning and delivery.	Openly congratulate yourself on successful strategies and practices, and openly reprimand yourself on errors and mistakes, and disclose what you will do differently the next time.

students need modifications such as reduced workload and/or activities according to their ELD levels and in keeping with your already identified objectives above.

Assessment/Evaluation: This is where you tell how you will score the activity or grade student performance. Again you will need to use different assessment and evaluation standards, since the objectives vary according to the variations in ELD levels.

Closure: Make summary statements about how you will assess your personal success on teaching this lesson.

SDAIE Lesson Plan Template

Subject:

Grade Level:

Lesson Topic:

Academic Content Standards: Here you indicate all the state academic content standards that you are planning to address.

Learning Objectives/Outcomes: Here you indicate the measurable academic objectives you have for your students in this lesson.

Language Objectives/Outcomes: Here you indicate the speaking, listening, reading, or writing objectives you would want to achieve as a result of this lesson.

Into Activities:

1. Background/Summary. Here you can summarize the lesson and give background as to its place in a larger unit, what came before it, and what would follow after this lesson?

2. Entry/Anticipatory. In this section you indicate the activity you will use to excite your students about this lesson. The KWL (Know, Want to Know, Learned) chart is a common tool teachers use here; you could also read a short but interesting story/book about the topic you are about to teach. To meet the requirement to infuse student-friendly technology into your lesson, visit www.songsforteaching.com. Identify ideas and activities from this or other websites you can integrate into your lesson. For the entry, you could plan a skit, a song, a chant, etc., just to get them excited about the topic.

Through Activities:

1. Instructional input. In this section you write down everything you will teach in this lesson. You write down the steps you will take to teach them. You specify the vocabulary words you will use in teaching the lesson, and how you will develop those vocabulary words. You should visit the website, www.flachcardexchange.com and www .unitedstreaming.com. Identify activities from these or other websites you want to infuse into this lesson. You indicate instructional strategies you will utilize in teaching the lesson, as well as groupings and scaffolds: visuals, multimedia activities, video streaming, and so on. In short, this is the place where the bulk of your SDAIE strategies and scaffolds need to be stated clearly, and how they will be used.

2. Guided practice. A vital part of guided practice is teacher modeling. You model for the students what you want them to be able to do, and you walk them through the process of doing it, and in so doing you see them complete the process under your guidance. This place also needs SDAIE strategies, as you will need to make modifications in how you will assist the ELD student through the process.

Beyond Activities:

1. Independent practice. This is the place where students are required to complete the process on their own, without your help. To meet technology requirement create or identify a technology activity students will perform as part of this lesson. Make modifications for students who may not have access to a computer either because they do not have one at home, or due to disability (e.g., blindness). The ELD students, however, need modifications such as reduced workload, extended time for work completion, pairing, L1 language resources, teacher assistance, etc., to help them successfully complete the process. In your planning you indicate the nature of modifications you will make.

2. Assessment/Evaluation. This is where you tell us how you will score the activity or grade student performance. Again you will need to indicate whether you are going to use a different rubric for ELD students from the general class rubric. Will their passing cut-off point be lower than the English speakers? What modifications will you make for them here?

3. Closure. Make summary statements about how you will assess your personal success on teaching this lesson.

~

QUESTIONS AND APPLICATION

Case Study: Proposition 227

Background

You are a trained bilingual educator in California. You know that research has established that the most effective way to meet the needs of students who are English-language learners is to teach them the content areas in their native languages, if possible, and to provide English-language instruction using sheltered instruction.

The Problem

Your state, California, has just passed proposition 227, which effectively ended bilingual education with very minimum exceptions. Your school site principal has instructed you that she wants all bilingual teachers to effectively cease to teach in two languages. She wants English immersion for all students, because she wants to see an increase in their test scores over the next three years. Your fifth-grade classroom of thirty-one students is made up of twenty-one English-language learners, mostly Hispanic, who have been in the United States for less than three years. They are all at the beginning level of English language development.

Follow-Up Questions

1. How would you react to the principal's instruction?
2. What strategies can you apply to assist you in meeting the needs of these English language learners in your classroom in the absence of the use of their primary language?
3. What social action, if any, do you think you as a teacher and a citizen can embark on to challenge the validity and constitutionality of this law?

Review Questions

1. What is the official language of the United States?
2. How has immigration shaped American multilingualism?

3. ~~How~~ has the United States embraced multilingualism over the decades?

4. What government policies have influenced the ways the needs of English-language learners have been addressed in the United States over the years, and how have these policies influenced education?

Strategies for Application in the K–12 Classrooms

1. Grades K–12: Allow your students to share their memories of times when they have traveled with their parents to a place where they do not know anyone or to a foreign country whose language they could not speak. Let them share how they felt and how people responded to them. Allow them to use their experiences to imagine how people who are nonnative speakers of English feel when they arrive in the United States.

2. Grades 7–12: Lead your students to research and present biographical reports on Horace Mann, Noah Webster, Benjamin Franklin, and many other historical figures who made positive impacts on the American educational system.

3. Grades 7–12: Class should research the treaty of Guadalupe Hidalgo, Sputnik, and the 1917 and 1924 U.S. Immigration Acts and present reports on their impacts on second-language learning in the United States.

4. Grades 7–12: Students should research the Coral Way Elementary School in Dade County, Florida. Study should focus on history, forms of bilingual education, and academic performance index compared to nonbilingual education schools in the same county. Discuss the unique benefits of the bilingual education programs in this school.

Chapter Eight

Religious Diversity and the Public School Systems

Chapter Objectives:

This chapter engages the place of religion in the public school system. It addresses constitutional arguments relating to religion in schools, and attempts a timeline depicting the struggles for freedom of religious expression on school grounds dating back to the colonial days. Readers will be able to:

1. Distinguish between the Establishment Clause and the Free Exercise Clause in the First Amendment to the U.S. Constitution, and analyze their implications for religious freedom in America.
2. Become familiar with presidential position statements on Religious freedom and their implications from religious expression in schools for students and teachers alike

A fundamental question that has plagued the American educational system in the last few decades has to do with the place of religion in the school systems, especially the public school system. The "religious right" in America is always claiming a right to religious expression within the school grounds, while the secular left is always arguing against it. Individuals from each faction often cross over in sympathy with one view or the other. Probably the most reliable statement that can be made about the place of religion in the American public schools is that Americans are confused about the place of religion in the public school system. In order to engage this topic, we need to begin by addressing the question, "What place does religion have in the American public school?

131

WHAT PLACE DOES RELIGION HAVE
IN THE AMERICAN PUBLIC SCHOOL?

"Congress shall make no law respecting an establishment of religion, or prohibiting the free exercise thereof; or abridging the freedom of speech, or of the press; or the right of the people peaceably to assemble, and to petition the government for a redress of grievances."[1]

The article above, the First Amendment in the U.S. Bill of Rights, has generated all kinds of controversies surrounding the practice of religion in American public schools today. Individuals and interest groups across the nation have interpreted these statements differently, each group strongly favoring their own interpretation over their opponents'. Interest groups who wish to exercise their religious rights as well as groups and individuals who see it as their duty to ensure a school climate free of any kind of religious dominance have appealed to law courts from time to time to interpret this statement and determine whether certain expressions of religious beliefs and/or practices are protected under this law.

A fundamental argument that must be given serious consideration appeals to an understanding of the contextual meaning of the legislation when it was made more than two centuries ago, as well as its contemporary significance for the United States of the twenty-first century. When the founding fathers made the declaration that Congress shall make no law respecting an establishment of religion, what did they mean? What was "religion" as it was practiced among the settlers on the American frontiers? Chief Justice Waite, delivering the opinion of the Supreme Court of the United States in *Reynolds v. United States* in 1878, stated categorically that "the word 'religion' is not defined in the Constitution," and therefore, we must look to other sources for its meaning, "no where more appropriately, we think, than to the history of the times in the midst of which the provision was adopted."[2]

Study shows that religion at that time was more of a diverse expression of Christianity than a multiplicity of religions as we have today. The spirit of this amendment derives from the desire of the founding fathers, whose forebears had escaped Europe as a result of religious persecution, to create a place where they could worship their Christian God with no governmental interruption. The spirit of this amendment, therefore, was a desire to protect the rights of the various factions of the Christian church of that age, rather than to limit it. By implication, they provided for the rights of people, who may wish to depart from the Christian experience of faith in search of other forms of religious expression, since the call to the Christian faith itself requires an individual decision and response to God rather than a collective societal (peoples) movement. The spirit of this amendment takes a stand against an official state religion, while focusing on the rights of individuals to religious expression anywhere in society.

It should be pointed out that the crisis of how to regulate religious activities in the public school system was not an issue for the earlier generation of Americans. Education was not a state program, but private and religious organizations ran the schools. Schools were community based, and most communities enjoyed religious homogeneity, so religion was very much a part of the educational programs.

In the twentieth and twenty-first centuries, however, not only has the American religious landscape shifted, but educational programs have also transitioned from being overwhelmingly private and religious to public and secular. Communities have also become more diverse, both ethnically and religiously, making diversity an issue to contend with in the school systems. America is no longer religiously homogeneous (if it ever was, considering the various religious practices of Native Americans and African slaves). One must also submit to the fact that even among the settlers, the concept of religious and cultural homogeneity was practically impossible. The question then arises as to what place religion would have in our government-controlled public school systems.

Some courts have interpreted the First Amendment more rigorously, making a clear distinction between the first (establishment clause) and the second (free-exercise clause) parts, the latter of which addresses religious rights. The general interpretation is that whereas the government cannot establish a religion or favor an established religion, the government cannot limit the rights of citizens to practice religion. In *Reynolds v. United States*, one of the earliest judicial interpretations of the First Amendment is given with very strong historical backing. According to Justice Waite and his colleagues,

Before the adoption of the constitution, attempts were made in some of the colonies and states to legislate not only in respect to the establishment of religion, but in respect to its doctrines and precepts as well. The people were taxed, against their will, for the support of religion, and sometimes for the support of particular sects to whose tenets they could not subscribe. Punishments were prescribed for a failure to attend upon public worship, and sometimes for entertaining heretical opinions. . . . At the first session of the Congress the amendment now under consideration was proposed with others by Mr. Madison. It met the views of the advocates of religious freedom, and was adopted. Mr. Jefferson afterwards, in reply to an address to him by a committee of the Danbury Baptist Association, took occasion to say: "Believing with you that religion is a matter which lies solely between man and his god; that he owes account to none other for his faith or his worship; that the legislative powers of the government reach actions only, and not opinion,—I contemplate with sovereign reverence that act of the whole American people which declared that their legislature should "make no law respecting an establishment of religion or prohibiting the free exercise thereof," thus building a wall of separation between church and state.[3]

The implications these statements bear on our understanding of the First Amendment is that it aimed at preserving individuals' right to religious expression as well as precluding the government from favoring one religious expression over another. This makes valid the judicial interpretation of the establishment clause and the free-exercise clause. They are separate but closely related entities.

It appears that the crises of interpreting the First Amendment have been primarily due to the tendency of some government officials to part ways with the manner in which certain courts interpret that law. As the U.S. Constitution empowers the judicial branch of the government to interpret the laws, there often arises a conflict between their interpretation and the way that some state and federal executives, whose function is the execution of the laws, see it. This may be the reason why every government in power wants to fill the courts with justices who share their own views on most issues.

The 1963 case of *Abington School District v. Schempp*[4] is a classic example of this dichotomy. The case centered on the fact that the Commonwealth of Pennsylvania instituted a law (24Pa. Stat.15-1516) that was further amended in December 1959 to require the following: "At least ten verses from the Holy Bible Shall be read, without comment, at the opening of each public school on each day. Any child shall be excused from such Bible reading, or attending such Bible reading, upon the written request of his parent or guardian" (Pub. Law 1928, Supp. 1960). Mr. Edward Kemp, his wife, and two children filed a suit against the state arguing that such a law violated their First Amendment rights since they were practicing Unitarians. The trial courts ruled to their favor, and the case made its way to the U.S. Supreme Court. The Supreme Court in its interpretation of the First Amendment in the context of this case stated that this court has rejected unequivocally the contention that the Establishment Clause forbids only governmental preferences of one religion over another. Almost 20 years ago in Everson, supra, at 15, the court said that "[n]either a state nor the Federal Government can set up a church. Neither can pass laws, which aid one religion, aid all religions, or prefer one religion over another."[5]

This interpretation of the Constitution is as far-reaching as can be. Should this interpretation be accepted, attempts to provide government funding to religious organizations involved in charity activities would be deemed unconstitutional and illegal since, in a way, it aids all religions who are involved in charity work. In this and other similar cases, the Supreme Court and other trial courts have tried to hold on to a neutrality stance as far as governmental involvement in religion is concerned. The timeline in table 8.1 is developed from various sources to give us a visual picture of where we are coming from in the separation of Church and state.

As part of the No Child Left Behind Act, The U.S. Department of Education, under the president's mandate, issued guidelines for constitutionally protected prayer in schools. A copy of the guideline is obtainable from the U.S. Department of Education's website. Complete texts of both Bush's and Clinton's guidance on constitutionally protected prayer are attached to this work as appendixes B and C. A section of the Bush guideline addresses the government's interpretation of the establishment clause as well as the free-exercise clause:

Accordingly, the First Amendment forbids religious activity that is sponsored by the government but protects religious activity that is initiated by private individuals, and the line between government-sponsored and privately initiated religious expression is vital to a proper understanding of the First Amendment's scope. As the Court has explained in several cases, "there is a crucial difference between *government* speech endorsing religion, which the Establishment Clause forbids, and *private* speech endorsing religion, which the Free Speech and Free Exercise Clauses protect."[6]

Whereas some courts see the role of the government as that of complete neutrality, other courts and government officials see their role as that of protection of religious rights. The government position also argues that the First Amendment does not forbid religious activities initiated by private citizens whether in public or private, thus making the case that whereas the government may not sponsor religion, religion has a place in the American

Table 8.1.   Time Line of the Battle for Separation of Church and State in the United States

Time Period	Event
	1700s
September 25, 1789	**The First Amendment** was adopted as part of the U.S. constitution: "Congress shall make no law respecting an establishment of religion, or prohibiting the free exercise thereof; or abridging the freedom of speech, or of the press; or the right of the people peaceably to assemble, and to petition the Government for a redress of grievances."
	1800s
October 1878	*Reynolds v. United States:* U.S. Supreme Court refused to find George Reynolds not guilty, having been indicted with the crime of bigamy, even though he had argued that he did it in keeping with his religious faith and tenet.
1899	*Bradfield v. Robert:* This ruling established that religious organizations could receive direct government aid for support of secular social-welfare needs.
	1900s
1908	Committee on Coinage, Weights, and Measures' report providing for the restoration of the motto "In God We Trust" on some denominations of the gold and silver coins of the United States was passed by Congress.
1912	A law was passed by Congress establishing that U.S. post offices (of the first and second classes) should not be opened on Sundays for the purpose of delivering mail to the public.
1944	Congress passed a law designating the period from Thanksgiving Day to Christmas of every year as nationwide Bible-reading time.
1947	*Everson v. Board of Education:* The U.S. Supreme Court first reviewed a challenge to state law regarding educational policy. "Pursuant to a New Jersey statute authorizing district boards of education to make rules and contracts for the transportation of children to and from schools other than private schools operated for profit, a board of education by resolution authorized the reimbursement of parents for fares paid for the transportation by public carrier of children attending public and Catholic schools" (*Everson v. Board of Education of the Township of Ewing* [No. 52] 133 N.J.L. 350, 44 A.2d 333).
1948	*McCollum v. Board of Education:* U.S. Supreme Court found the practice of inviting religious instructors into public schools to give optional religious instruction in violation of the establishment clause.
1952	*Zorach v. Clauson:* The court ruled the practice of giving public school students "release time" for religious activities as constitutional.
1962	*Engel v. Vitale:* The Supreme Court ruled that the practice in the state of New York whereby the school day began with a prayer drafted by school officials violated the establishment clause.
1963	*Abington School District v. Schempp:* The Commonwealth of Pennsylvania by a 1928 law required that "At least ten verses

Time Period	Event
	from the Holt Bible shall be read, without comment, at the opening of each public school on each school day. Any child shall be excused from such Bible reading, or attending such Bible reading, upon the written request of his parent or guardian." The Schempp family, husband, wife, and two of their three children challenged the law's constitutionality under the provisions of the First Amendment. The Supreme Court decision was that "the practices at issue and the laws requiring them are unconstitutional under the establishment clause, as applied to the States through the Fourteenth Amendment."
1968	**Board of Education v. Allen:** A group of New York school boards filed a suit against the New York commissioner for education, challenging the educational laws requiring the state to provide textbooks to all students in grades seven through twelve who attended both private and public schools violated the establishment clause. The U.S. Supreme court ruled that the New York law in question furthered a secular objective by increasing educational opportunities to students, and so does not violate the establishment clause.
1970	**Walz v. Tax Commission:** Walz, a real estate owner in Richmond county of New York filed a law suit challenging the tax exemption granted to religious worship buildings, which he argued made non-worship properties to be taxed higher than they should. The Supreme Court upheld tax exemption for worship centers by a vote of eight to one.
1971	**Tilton v. Richardson:** This lawsuit challenged a Federal Higher Education Facility Act of 1963 that made money available to church-sponsored higher education institutes. The money had to be used in constructing nonreligious school facilities, but after twenty years the group could use the building for whatever purpose they chose. The Court ruled that the grant did not violate the establishment clause, but by an eight-to-one vote ruled that the twenty-year limit was unconstitutional.
1973	**Hunt v. McNair:** This case was filed to challenge a South Carolina Educational Facilities Act that issued bonds that benefited a Baptist-controlled college. It was accused of violating the establishment clause. The Supreme Court ruled that the specific provisions of the act, the rules and regulations of the authority, and the college proposal do not demonstrate an excessive entanglement between religion and the state. So the court held that the act was constitutional and did not violate the establishment clause. **Levitt v. Committee for Public Education and Religious Liberty:** In this case, the court was asked to decide whether chapter 138 of New York State's Laws of 1970, which required the state to reimburse private schools (including religious) throughout the state for costs of certain tests and recordkeeping, violated the establishment clause. The Supreme Court upheld a lower court ruling that deemed this unconstitutional.
1977	**New York v. Cathedral Academy:** The court struck down a new statutory program that would entitle private schools to obtain reimbursement for expenses incurred the same year that the program was voided.
1980	**Stone v. Graham:** The U.S. Supreme Court held unconstitutional, and in direct violation of the establishment clause, a Kentucky state statute that required the posting of a copy of the Ten Commandments purchased with private funds on the wall of every public school classroom in the state.

(continued)

Table 8.1. (*continued*)

Time Period	Event
1982	**Larson v. Valente:** A law in Minnesota that required charitable organizations to register with the state's Department of Commerce and to file annual reports of their income and expenditures placed a condition that if more than 30 percent of their annual expenditure was spent on administration, the organization would cease to solicit funds from within the state. A law suit was filed by members of the Unification Church arguing that the law violated the establishment clause. The Supreme Court ruled the law unconstitutional.
1985	**Aguilar v. Felton:** New York city under the Title I program of the Elementary and Secondary Education Act of 1965 reimbursed the salaries of public employees who taught in parochial schools to assist low-income children with special needs. A group of taxpayers filed a suit claiming that it violated the establishment clause. The Court ruled that though the aid to the parochial schools may not have a primary effect of advancing religion, the closeness of the interaction was deemed to result in the act of promoting the advancement of religion, so the court ruled against the reimbursement.
1987	**Edwards v. Aguillard:** This case came to the Supreme Court as a challenge to a Louisiana "Creationism Act" which required that creation science be taught alongside evolution in public elementary and secondary schools, forbidding that none be taught without the other. The Supreme Court upheld a lower court ruling that held that the act violated the establishment clause.
1990	**Westside Community Board of Education v. Mergens:** A group of students who wanted to form a Christian club in their school were denied the permission to do so by the Westside Community Schools Board of Education in Nebraska. They denied the students the right to have a faculty sponsor as other clubs have the privilege of doing, stating it would imply an endorsement. The students filed a suit alleging that their rights under the Equal Access Act had been violated. The Supreme Court ruled in their favor, stating that they had the right to form their Christian club.
1992	**Lee v. Weisman:** This case centered on the practice in Providence, Rhode Island, where principals of public schools invited the clergy to pray in school graduation ceremonies. A student, Deborah Weismann, and her father filed a suit asking for a restraining order on a rabbi who had been invited to say a prayer at Deborah's school graduation. The district court later ruled the practice unconstitutional and in violation of the establishment clause, and the U.S. Supreme Court upheld the decision on June 24, 1992.
1999	The U.S. Supreme Court upheld a Ninth Circuit Court of Appeals decision that a school district was within its rights to abolish a program of paid advertisement signs on school grounds rather than accept a sign promoting the Ten Commandments.
	2000s
2000	**Mitchell et al. v. Helms:** This case deemed constitutional chapter 2 of the Educational Consolidation and Improvement Act of 1981, in which funds from the federal government are channeled through the state educational agencies (SEAs) to the local educational agencies (LEAs) and are in turn channeled to private and public elementary and secondary

schools through the lending of educational materials like library and media materials and computer software and hardware. ***Hood v. Medford Board of Education***: A Federal Third Circuit Court was evenly divided on the case of a boy in New Jersey who was prevented from reading his favorite Bible story to his first-grade class, letting stand a lower-court ruling that the school district did not violate the boy's free-speech rights. ***Books v. City of Elkhart, Indiana***: The Seventh Circuit Court of Appeals ruled that a monument inscribed with the Ten Commandments, which was displayed on the lawn of the municipal building, violated the establishment clause, as plaintiffs who were exercising their rights or duties to be at the government building were compelled to view a religious object that they would rather avoid.

2001   ***American Civil Liberties Union of Ohio v. Capitol Square Review and Advisory Board***: The Sixth Circuit Court of Appeals ruled that the state's adoption of the motto: "With God, All Things Are Possible" under Ohio Rev. Code 5.06 did not violate the establishment clause, as its sentiments has been part of the country's long and deeply entrenched tradition of civility, piety, or "ceremonial deism." ***Columbia Union College v. Oliver***: The Fourth Circuit Court of Appeals ruled that it does not matter whether an institution of higher learning is "pervasively sectarian" in determining whether financial assistance would violate the establishment clause, as long as the assistance has a secular purpose and uses neutral criteria. ***Brown v. Gilmore***: The U.S. Fourth Circuit Court of Appeals ruled that a Virginia law that mandates a moment of silence in the public school violates the establishment clause because it accommodates religious exercise but does not mandate it. ***Linnemeir v. Board of Trustees of Purdue University***: The Seventh Circuit Court of Appeals ruled that the First Amendment does not forbid a state university from providing a venue for the expression of views antagonistic to conventional Christian beliefs. ***Henderson v. Kennedy***: This is a ruling by the District of Columbia Circuit Court of Appeals, stating that the amendments to the Religious Freedom Restoration Act 42 USC 2000cc-5(7)(A), which extended the protections to any exercises of religion whether or not it is compelled by or central to a system of religious belief, did not change the propriety of inquiring into the importance of a religious practice when assessing whether a substantial burden exists. ***Knight v. State of Connecticut Dept. of Public Health***: The Second Circuit Court of Appeals ruled that public employees do not have the right to discuss and promote their religious beliefs while working with clients receiving government services. ***Gernetzke v. Kenosha Unified School District No 1***: The Seventh Circuit Court of Appeals ruled that 20 USC 4071 (f) of the Equal Access Act allows a school principal to prohibit a student religious group from painting a religious mural on school property where the principal has also prohibited other nonreligious murals.

2002   ***Mellen & Knick v. Bunting***: A federal judge at a U.S. district court for the Western District of Virginia in Lynchburg ruled that school-sponsored prayer at the Virginia Military Institute was unconstitutional as it allowed government to "become entangled with religion." ***O'Bannon v. Indiana Civil Liberties Union et al.***: U.S. Supreme Court upheld a lower-court

(*continued*)

Table 8.1. (*continued*)

Time Period	Event
	injunction on Frank O'Bannon, governor of Indiana, from erecting a limestone monument with the Ten Commandments on the statehouse lawn in Indianapolis. *Sally E. Flynn v. West Chester County Philadelphia*: A U.S. district judge ruled that the Ten Commandments plaque that was posted outside the Chester County Courthouse is unconstitutional and must be removed. *Gallwey v. Grimm*: The Supreme Court of the State of Washington overruled a trial court and held that the state's Educational Opportunity Grant (EOG) program does not violate the state constitution by allowing college students to use their tuition grants at religious or religiously affiliated institutions of higher learning. *Logiodice v. Trustees of Maine Central Institute*: This law suit charged that a school district had improperly delegated to a private school that receives government funds to provide services for public school students the power to discipline publicly funded students without adequately assuring that it followed federal due-process safeguards. The U.S. First Circuit Court of Appeals in Maine ruled that for the purposes of due process, this private school did not engage in a traditionally public function and was not intertwined with the government. *Newdow v. U.S. Congress*: The U.S. Ninth Circuit Court of Appeals left standing a district court ruling that the addition of the words "under God" in the Pledge of Allegiance, which a school district in California has a policy of teacher-led daily recitation, violated the First Amendment. *Prince v. Jacoby*: The U.S. Ninth Circuit Court of Appeals held that a school district violated either the Equal Access Act or a student's First Amendment rights in denying the Bible club she belonged to rights and benefits that other school clubs enjoyed. This was in relation to a school authority's refusal that the Bible club use the school's facilities.
2003	*Doe v. School District of the City of Norfolk*: A student and his parents filed a suit challenging what they called "unwelcome recitation of the Lord's Prayer" at graduation ceremonies. The court ruled that since the recitation was a private act, there was no affirmative sponsorship from the school, and therefore there was no constitutional violation.
2004	*Newdow v. U.S. Congress*: The U.S. Ninth Circuit Court of Appeals ruled that Michael Newdow's claim that his daughter is injured when compelled to "watch and listen" as a state-employed teacher leads her classmates through a ritual recitation that affirms that there is a God (one nation under God) was "not sufficiently concrete" and lacking in specific injury. *Doe v. Porter*: The U.S. Sixth Circuit Court of Appeals affirmed a lower court ruling that stated that Sue Porter, superintendent, and the Rhea County School system violated the First Amendment's establishment clause by allowing a religious organization, Bible Education Ministry (BEM), run by a Christian college, Bryan College, into a public school. This program taught the Christian Bible as religious truth, and the court deemed it a violation of the establishment clause. *Pierce v. Sullivan West Central School District*: The U.S. Second Circuit Court of Appeals ruled that school regulations that allowed "public school student release time" to attend religious instruction is not in violation of the establishment clause. *Wiggs v. Sioux Falls School*: The U.S. Eighth Circuit Court of Appeals ruled that the participation of a teacher in a Christian club's after-school activity was private speech and did not present the school with any risk of violating the establishment clause.

public life if the citizens choose to execute such rights. Under President Bill Clinton, a guideline was issued to the public schools that stated: "The Establishment Clause of the First Amendment does not prohibit religious speech by students. Students, therefore, have the same right to engage in individual or group prayer and religious discussion during the school day as they do to engage in other comparable activity."[7]

When Clinton's position is compared to George Bush's stand, it is significant to note that two ideologically opposed administrations seem to agree on this one issue. This means that, depending on who is in the oval office, the executive branch of the government is inclined to reject any interpretation of the First Amendment that defines neutrality as staying away from the realm of religion. In this light, therefore, religion will continue to be an intrinsic part of American government and the American public school system.

Where in the Public School Curriculum Does Religion Belong?

For most educators and politicians, as well as parents and students, the fact that religion has a place in the public school system raises another question, namely: Where specifically in the school system does religion belong? The documents on constitutionally protected prayer in schools from both the Clinton and Bush administrations provided detailed guidelines on the nature of religious programs students could carry out while in school. Their definition of government neutrality is seen in the need for government officials while acting in their official capacity to refrain from leading, initiating, or participating in any religious activity. They cannot, however, prevent students from religious activity during school hours. Students are empowered to use school facilities to hold prayer services, worship exercises, or Bible study to the same degree that nonreligious clubs in the schools use these facilities to hold their prayer services, worship exercises, or Bible Study. Students are free to distribute religious flyers in the schools to the same extent that nonreligious clubs have rights to do. They are entitled to use school public address systems to advertise their events to the same extent that nonreligious clubs are allowed to. Students can be excused from class to engage in a religious activity over a brief period of time, such as Muslim students needing to pray during Ramadan.

Some significant issues are addressed in Bush's document but not addressed in Clinton's. The Bush document addressed the need to allow for moments of silence if the school chooses to implement one. It discourages teachers and school administrators from encouraging or discouraging prayers during this time. The two documents each address the right of the student to express a religious belief in homework, artwork, and other written or oral assignments. The work is to be judged on the basis of its academic content not its religious merit. Students are allowed to distribute religious literature to their fellow students to the degree that they could distribute other materials. The Bush document emphasizes the neutral role of teachers and administrators in leading or participating in a religious activity with students and provides for teachers and administrators to be able to "take part in religious activities where the overall context makes clear that they are not participating in their official capacities. Before school or during lunch, for example, teachers may meet with other teachers for prayer or Bible study to the same extent that they may engage in other conversation or nonreligious activities." It also suggests that "teachers may participate in their personal capacities in privately sponsored baccalaureate ceremonies."[8]

The Clinton document addresses, in addition, the issue of teaching about religion in the school curriculum. It stipulates that public schools may not provide religious instruction, but may teach about religion, "including the Bible or other scriptures: the history of religion, comparative religion, the Bible (or other scripture)—as literature and the role of religion in the history of the United States and other countries."[9]

Evolution is one topic that is conspicuously absent in both documents, yet it remains one of the most controversial topics when Americans discuss the place of religion in the public school curriculum.

What Provisions Do Students and Teachers Have for Religious Expression in Schools?

- Morning Prayers: School administrators and teachers cannot mandate a morning prayer. Such would be an attempt to advance religion and significantly departs from the neutrality stance of government. A moment of silence may, however, be observed, and students may choose to pray during this time or not pray.
- Prayers in Athletic Events: The government position states that students reserve the right to initiate such prayers, but they cannot be mandated to do so by the school leadership. A school will also be violating the neutrality stance if it chooses the event leader based on the likelihood to pray or not to pray.

- Prayers at Graduation Ceremonies: Prayers are acceptable if initiated by students and not faculty. There is ambiguity as to what teachers should do when in an official school activity like games or graduation a student initiates a prayer and people join in. The most popular position is that teachers should not participate. They are to never join the students in religious activities during their official work hours. After official hours, they can join.

∼

QUESTIONS AND ACTIVITIES

Case Study: Religion in Schools

You are a retired public school teacher who spent your life teaching American history and heritage in high school. After your retirement, some of your students decided to set up a history social studies foundation in your honor. You were invited to chair the foundation, thus providing you an opportunity to continue to make personal contributions toward the study of American history and heritage. In pursuit of one of your passions, the religious heritage of America, you decided to create a competitive essay project on America's religious heritage. High school students were to research issues on America's religious heritage and write essays and/or build projects to illustrate those significant religious aspects of America's heritage. The awards would include monetary compensations, trophies, and certificates.

Challenge

You have approached every school district around you, including the very district where you spent thirty-four years of your life, and none of the districts is willing to participate in the competition. School superintendents and principals see the activity as an endorsement of the Christian religion, the backlash from which they are not willing to deal with.

Follow-Up Questions

1. Explain why this activity would or would not amount to an undue attention to the Christian faith?

2. What structures within the school systems can you legally harness to implement your project, if any?
3. What previous court cases and constitutional insights can you appeal to in defense of your project?
4. What legal or political recourse do you have should the superintendents prevent you from tapping into the already existing structures you believe you can safely work with to implement your program?

Review Questions

1. Explain the differences between the establishment clause and the free-exercise clause in the First Amendment. Cite some court cases that have dealt with the issues addressed by the two.
2. Read the court case *Abington School District v. Schempp*. Discuss its merits and demerits based on your own religious convictions.

Strategies for Application in the K–12 Classrooms

1. Grades 7–12: Research Catholicism, Protestantism, Evangelicalism, Judaism, and Islam. Discuss their histories and the scope of their influences on American social, political, and religious life over the centuries.
2. Research anti-Catholic sentiments, anti-Semitism, anti-Muslim sentiments, and anti-Christian sentiments in the United States, tracing their history and sociopolitical impacts on America today.
3. Grades K–12: Visit the U.S. Department of Education website and download copies of the president's position statement on Constitutional Protected Prayer in Schools. Discuss the provisions of these statements with students to educate them on their constitutional rights to freedom of religious expression in the school grounds.

Chapter Nine

Gender and Women's Rights in American Educational History

Chapter Objectives:

Most books on multicultural education approach the question of gender equity from the point of view of advocacy and sometimes a militant advocacy for gender rights without necessarily giving the background that makes that advocacy necessary. This chapter presents the history and development of the battle for gender equality in the United States. Readers will be able to:

1. describe what rights, if any, women had in the colonial, postcolonial, and modern-day United States
2. discuss the history and development of the suffragist movement
3. identify and describe such prominent pioneer feminists as Ann Hutchinson, Sarah Grimke, Sojourner Truth, and other leading figures of the suffrage movement

The twenty-first-century American teacher must see himself/herself as an active participant in the struggle to level the playing field between males and females in American society. The struggle for gender equity in the United States dates back to the colonial days. Sadly enough, the length of this struggle has not eradicated the inequity that still exists in today's educational settings.

In order to fully appreciate this struggle, we need to undertake a historical overview of this struggle, and place our role as twenty-first-century educators within its appropriate context.

Figure 9.1. Wordle Display of Women's Rights Issues

GENDER AND WOMEN'S RIGHTS
IN COLONIAL AMERICA

American colonies based their laws on English common law, which was summarized in the Blackstone Commentaries. This legal system defined marriage as follows: "By marriage, the husband and wife are one person in the law. The very being and legal existence of the woman is suspended during the marriage, or at least is incorporated into that of her husband under whose wing and protection she performs everything."[1] This imported legal system entrenched within the American social atmosphere an ideology that regarded women as second-class, dependent upon males, and unable to assert their own individuality. David H. Fischer, in his *Liberty and Freedom: A Visual History of America's Founding Ideas*, states, "From the start of English settlement in America, women asserted their rights to liberty and freedom."[2] Colonial girls grew up to become mothers and wives, and society offered them no other alternatives. Yet, colonial women did not sit back and accept the second-class position handed to them by men.

Around 1637–1638, Anne Hutchinson, a separatist freelance preacher, was banished from Boston for asserting her God-given right to teach God's word to colonial males, whom she regarded as "living examples of depravity."[3] The education of girls in colonial America was very limited. The formal and organized educational systems that we are familiar with today were unimaginable in the colonial days. Children were viewed as economic help to the family, and formal education was not available. Children helped in the kitchens, gardens, fields, and orchards. The educational structure was such that girls learned how to cook, spin, and weave, while boys learned how to provide food and shelter. Less than one-third of the women in colonial America could sign their name. Those who received any kind of education got their schooling at home in nonformal settings.[4] As community-based schools emerged, they generally excluded girls. The education provided to Puritan girls aimed at equipping them to be able to read the scriptures, and nothing beyond that. Women were seen as weak and were consequently not encouraged to pursue academic achievements.[5] Even though a woman donated the first school ground in New England, girls were not allowed to attend that same school.

The very English common law that defined marriage in the language stated above prevented women from ownership of land and landed properties. The only condition under which a woman could own landed property was if she was widowed. In that situation she could serve as the custodian of her husband's properties. Should she choose to marry, however, her properties automatically turn over to her new husband, who was legally empowered to exercise up to 100 percent control over the property in some cases.

Profile: Anne Hutchinson, Preacher, Teacher, and Dissident

Widely regarded as the earliest feminist of the New World, Anne Hutchinson was born in Alford, Lincolnshire, England. Her father was Francis Marbury, a minister of the Church of England. Anne learned theology from her father and later married a wealthy merchant named William Hutchinson. Her family bought into the Puritan teachings and was among the group who left England in 1633 to escape persecution and arrest.

Anne Hutchinson was the mother of fifteen children, and unlike the majority of women of her time who lost half of their babies before the children reached the age of three, she lost only three of her children. Michael Winship describes her time in these words: "Married women had few privileges. They could not buy or sell property, make contracts, or sue or be sued. If they earned money, it legally belonged to their husbands. When possible, they were expected to focus on the arduous tasks of being wives, mothers, and household managers. The Bible commanded them to submit to their husbands."[6]

While in England, Anne had undergone such a deep spiritual experience that she began to question the spiritual fervor of the Puritans as well as the Church of England. Through a habit of self-seclusion and immersion in prayer and study of the scriptures Anne began to receive some revelations. Upon arriving in the New World, Anne did not shy away from making public her prophetic gifts and ministry, serving God in quiet but public ways. There soon arose a controversy among the Puritans of the colony on whether divine grace required human cooperation or whether the covenant of grace depended totally on God. Anne Hutchinson took sides with the position of total reliance on the goodness and grace of God, instead of human personal good. This was a position endorsed by one of her spiritual mentors, John Cotton. She soon became a stubborn defender of this position, holding meetings at her home to teach and convince people on this position. The attendance soon grew, and even the governor of Massachusetts, Sir Henry Vane, attended her meetings.[7]

As the controversy heated up, Hutchinson compared the ministers who preached grace plus works with the Christ's disciples before the resurrection and ascension of Christ. She accused them of being unable to function as ministers of the New Testament. She soon faced major resistance from the ministers in the colony. Nevertheless, she "asserted her superior right and duty as one of God's elect to teach His word to unregenerate males whom she regarded as living examples of depravity."[8] Anne and her followers were soon accused of antinomianism, which means going against custom. Hutchinson led a movement that almost turned all Bostonians against their ministers, until she finally had to be stopped.[9] In her trials and exile, Anne Hutchinson established herself as the first feminist of record in the New World.

GENDER AND WOMEN'S RIGHTS DURING AND AFTER THE AMERICAN REVOLUTION

The fact that the society restricted women's rights and opportunities does not mean that women generally settled with the assigned roles and accepted them. There were women who dared to challenge the system and question the assumptions underlying the restrictions imposed on them. There were also men who stood up for women and challenged the status quo. In 1745, a frontierswoman and poet in Pennsylvania by the name of Susanna Wright became the first woman to provide notary services in the colony. She became the legal counselor to her illiterate neighbors, preparing their wills, deeds, and other legal contracts. More than one hundred of Wright's manuscripts were preserved.[10] The Great Awakening, with Jonathan Edwards as its most prominent minister, had confronted Americans with a sense of sinfulness that did not have gender or racial limitations. Men and women were equally damned before God, so it awoke within American women and well-meaning American men, the consciousness of gender equality before God, and thereby opened a crack in the wall for the pursuit of gender equality on temporal grounds.[11]

In 1764, James Otis, an American patriot and writer compared the legal requirements of the colonies' submission to the British government to the legal submission of women to men, and raised the question whether women were not born as free as men. He argued that the subjection of women to men implies that women are also slaves by nature. In 1775, Thomas Paine, in the spirit of the American Revolution, published an article in *Pennsylvania Magazine*, in which he made a proposal for women's rights in the colonies.[12]

Profile: Abigail Adams, Wife, Mother, and Political Activist

Abigail Adams may well stand for all the women of the revolutionary era. Born Abigail Smith, daughter of a Congregational minister, Abigail did not have the privilege of formal schooling. What education she received was at home, yet she learned how to read, write, and add and subtract. She immersed herself in her father's library and took advantage of the tutorial skills of family members and friends. Abigail and her two sisters emerged among the most educated women of their time. Her husband, John Adams, considered her an intellectual equal, choosing to discuss politics with her without requiring her to yield to his male prerogatives. This enabled Abigail to become a major influence that shaped the political views of both her husband and son. Abigail's political influence is said to have propelled her to becoming the nation's best-informed woman on public affairs during her time.[13] Her letters to her husband during the Revolutionary years have become invaluable resources for looking at the sentiments and feelings of the average American during that time. In one of her correspondences to her husband she wrote concerning the British,

> I could not join today, in the petitions of our worthy pastor, for reconciliation between our no longer parent state, but tyrant state, and these colonies. Let us separate; they are unworthy to be our brethren. Let us renounce them; and instead of supplications as formerly, for their prosperity and happiness, let us beseech the Almighty to blast their counsels, and bring to naught all their devices (12 November, 1775).[14]

Abigail not only entertained lofty thoughts of separation from Britain, she reflected upon the political and social consequences of such. Fifteen days after this letter, she wrote yet another one to her husband in which she wondered,

> The reins of government have been so long slackened, that I fear the people will not quietly submit to those restraints, which are necessary for peace and security of the community. If we separate from Britain, what code of laws will be established? How shall we be governed, so as to retain our liberties? Can any government be free, which is not administered by general state laws? Who shall frame these laws? Who will give them force and energy (27 November, 1775)? [15]

Abigail's letters continued to flow to her husband through the Continental Congress. Some of these letters addressed matters relating to taxation, foreign policies, and all matters of government. In one letter she wrote,

> I suppose in Congress, you think of every thing relative to trade and commerce, as well as other things; but as I have been desired to mention to you some things, I shall not omit them. One is, that there may be something done, in a Continental way, with regard to excise upon spirituous liquors, that each of the New England colonies may be upon the same footing. . . . That excise is necessary, though it may be objected to by the mercantile interest, as a too frequent use of spirits endangers the wellbeing of society. Another article is that some method may be devised to keep among us our gold and silver, which are now every day shipped off to the West Indies for molasses, coffee, and sugar (10 December 1775). [16]

In 1776 the Continental Congress in Philadelphia passed the Declaration of Independence declaring that "all men are created equal," a gender exclusive language, which did not seem to pose any problem to the "all-male" Continental Congress. In 1777 all states passed laws that denied a woman's right to vote. It was not until 1789 that the United States Constitution was ratified and the terms "persons," "people" and "electors" were used, allowing an interpretation that included women.

GENDER AND WOMEN'S RIGHTS DURING
THE ABOLITION MOVEMENT

One of the unique by-products of the American Revolution was the thirst for freedom, which spread like wildfire across the colonies. As the colonists sought for the means to break the English stronghold, both female colonists and African slaves sought a crack through which their own freedom could be obtained. The years following the birth of the nation were busy with abolitionist and women's rights activities. In 1790 the colony of New Jersey granted "all free inhabitants" the right to vote, thus extending voting rights to women. This right was quickly rescinded, however, when in 1807 a male politician who came close to losing an election to a female contestant sponsored a bill to repeal the voting rights of women. In 1821, the Troy Female Seminary was established in New York. This was founded by a female, Emma Hart Willard, as the first endowed school for girls in the nation.[17]

Sarah Margaret Fuller (1810–1850) was a woman whose ideas and writings challenged and threatened the male claim to superiority. She was said to have possessed one of the most powerful and creative minds of her generation. Her book *Women in the Nineteenth Century*, encapsulated her idea of freedom, which goes beyond feminism to address what has been described as "a larger transcendental vision of liberty and freedom."[18]

In 1836, a female abolitionist, Sarah Grimke, began a speaking career on slave abolition and women's rights. She was quickly silenced by male abolitionists, who were very uncomfortable with her role as a woman in the movement. By the following year, the first female Anti-Slavery Society Convention was held in New York City, with eighty-one delegates from twelve states attending. In 1839, the state of Mississippi became the first state to grant women the right to hold property in their own name, with their husbands' permission.

In 1844, female textile workers in Massachusetts organized themselves into the Lowell Female Labor Reform Association (LFLRA), demanding a ten-hour workday and birthing the first permanent labor association for women in U.S. history. Four years later, 1848, 300 women and men gathered at Seneca Falls, New York, to sign the Declaration of Sentiments, a plea for the end of discrimination against women in all spheres of society. This declaration followed the structure and logic of what has been called its literary progenitor, the Declaration of Independence.[19] It highlighted the wrongs committed against women through gross misappropriation of male authority. This declaration resolved that woman is man's equal as was intended by the creator, and demanded that she be recognized as such. It questioned the intellectual superiority of men, as well as their moral superiority over woman. It asserted the sacred rights of women to secure for themselves their "sacred rights to elective franchise."[20] This declaration not only attracted criticisms, it sparked a major debate over the rights of women. In 1855, in *Missouri v. Celia*, a black female slave was declared to be property without a right to defend herself against a master's act of rape. This depicts the deeper predicaments confronting women of color, especially blacks, in this male-dominated society.

Whereas the Quakers may not be known as being women's rights oriented, they extended educational rights to women equal to those of men. Abby Kelley Foster, a Quaker woman from Massachusetts, earned herself a reputation for being antislavery and pro-women's rights. She thrilled her audience in 1853 with her speech at the Fourth National Woman's Rights Convention in Cleveland, Ohio. By the time the American Civil War broke out in 1861, there was a temporary setback to the activities of the suffragists until the war's end in 1865.

Other occurrences in this time period that have significance for women's right to education included the founding in 1837 of Mount Holyoke College in Massachusetts, the first four-year college for women in the United States. A number of other colleges for women followed this, and in 1873, the first college for Catholic women was founded in Baltimore, Maryland.

Profile: Sojourner Truth, Preacher, Abolitionist, and Feminist

Sojourner Truth, born Isabella in 1797, was a slave girl whose life experiences and personal struggles are significant not only for women of color but for all women. Her life was typical of a slave girl's in the early 1800s. Sold at different times to different slave owners, Sojourner lived with her last slave master for eighteen years. When John Dumont, her slave master, failed to honor his promise of meritorious emancipation, Isabella left Dumont at her own will. Religion and spirituality soon became the focus of her life upon leaving her slave life. A series of spiritual experiences led her to the conclusion that God had chosen her to be a sanctified instrument of his use. She spent some time with the African Methodist Episcopal Church, but soon found her calling as a camp meeting revivalist, preaching among the poor, prostitutes, and the down and out. In 1843, she dropped the name Isabella and took up the name Sojourner Truth. She made her way to the western Massachusetts, where she joined up with a radical abolitionist group that worked with the Underground Railroad. It is said about Sojourner Truth, who never went to school, that she "rubbed elbows, traded barbs, argued the Bible, and talked politics with the nation's most uncompromising reformers, including William Lloyd Garrison, Abby Kelley Foster, Frederick Douglass, Rev. Samuel J. May, Charles Lenox Remond, and Olive Gilbert."[21]

Truth distinguished herself among the women of her time in different ways. After her emancipation from slavery, a member of her former slave master's family sold one of Truth's sons into slavery in Alabama. Truth went to court and sued successfully for the recovery of her son. Around 1835, a member of an unorthodox spiritual group to which she belonged accused her of attempted poisoning. Truth sued him for libel and cleared her name. She dictated her autobiography to Olive Gilbert, and it was published in 1850 under the title *The Narrative of Sojourner Truth*. From the proceeds of this book she earned enough money to buy a home for herself on Park Street in New York City. The proceeds from the many different editions of this book and other publications of Truth, an illiterate woman, enabled her to establish herself as a woman of measurable means. She built a house on College Street in Battle Creek, Michigan, in 1867 that was big enough to house her daughters and their families.

Truth was a very active feminist, present at the 1851 Woman's Rights convention in Akron, Ohio. It got to the point when she could no longer hold her peace, since, being a woman of African descent, the other feminists did not seem to treat her as an equal. She demanded to speak and the convention president could not refuse her request, though many in the audience opposed the idea of a black woman speaking in public. She rose to her feet and demanded that the poor working women of color be counted as women, posing a rhetorical question, "And aren't I a woman?" This question encapsulated her feminist argument for the years to come.[22]

Her political activism extended beyond her abolitionist and feminist activities to meetings with President Lincoln to work out ways to assist black refugees of the Civil War. She petitioned the Congress to allocate government land in the west for resettling free black people. Congress never granted the petition, but her petition spurred a massive migration of freed slaves out of Texas, Louisiana, Mississippi, and Tennessee to Kansas in 1879. One writer sums her story as follows: "In modern time, she has come to stand for the conjunction of race, class, and gender in American liberal reform and symbolizes the un-intimidated, articulate black woman . . . intelligent although totally unschooled, Truth represents a type of inspired, naïve witness that has long appealed to Americans suspicious of over-education."[23]

It is said that Truth refused to define herself by her enslavement, rather she challenged the kind of racial stereotypes utilized by Harriet Beecher Stowe in her *Uncle Tom's Cabin*.[24] Though a gospel preacher, she took a stand against preachers of her day who used the Bible to silence women, and she insisted on the right of women to appear at the podium, to think, and to say what they think.[25]

GENDER AND WOMEN'S RIGHTS
AFTER THE AMERICAN CIVIL WAR

A number of American women were engaged in philanthropic activities during the Civil War. This was one way they continued to advance women's rights during these unsettling times. By 1869 Elizabeth Cady Stanton and Susan B. Anthony formed the American Equal Rights Association, a radical organization that included both black and white women, while Lucy Stone, Henry Blackwell, and Julia Ward Howe organized a more conservative group called American Woman Suffrage Association (AWSA) based in Boston, Massachusetts.[26] Let us also note that Margaret Fuller, whose ideas and writings were noted earlier, directly influenced Elizabeth Stanton in her early years.

By the end of the Civil War, a number of colleges and universities compelled by need for money opened their doors to female students. These women did not come in as equals but faced hostilities from the male students as well as a differentiated curriculum that made sure their chances did not equal those of men at graduation.[27]

In 1868, the Fourteenth Amendment to the U.S. Constitution was ratified, extending constitutional rights and protections to all citizens. This amendment, however, defined citizens and voters as "male."

In 1869, the first woman suffrage law in the United States was passed in the territory of Wyoming, and by 1890 Wyoming was admitted into the union with the suffrage provision intact. By 1870, the Fifteenth Amendment received its final ratification, stating, "The right of citizens of the United States to vote shall not be denied or abridged by the United States or by any State on account of race, color, or previous condition of servitude." By its text, women are not specifically excluded from the vote. The first sexually integrated grand jury heard cases in Cheyenne, Wyoming, in 1870.[28]

In 1872 Susan B. Anthony was arrested and tried in Rochester, New York, for attempting to vote in the presidential election. During the same election, Sojourner Truth appeared at a polling booth in Michigan and demanded a ballot. She was turned away. In 1873, in *Bradwell v. Illinois*, the U.S. Supreme Court ruled that a state had the right to exclude a married woman (Myra Colby Bradwell) from practicing law. In 1875, in *Minor v. Happersett*, the Supreme Court ruled that despite the privileges and immunities clause, a state could prohibit a woman from voting. It defined women as "persons," but held that they constituted a "special category of nonvoting citizens."

By 1895, Elizabeth Cady Stanton, pioneer member of the National American Woman Suffrage Association (NAWSA), published *The Woman's Bible*. This publication caused many conservative suffragists to distance themselves from her. She resigned as NAWSA president and was never invited to sit on the stage at their conventions from that time forward. In 1896, the National Association of Colored Women (NACW) was founded in Washington, D.C., by Harriet Tubman, Fanny Jackson Coppin, Frances Ellen Watkins Harper, Mary Church Terrell, Margaret Murray Washington, Ida B. Wells-Barnett, and Charlotte Forteen Grimke.

Women have been at the forefront of providing educational opportunities to both men and women in the United States. The educational accomplishments of women during the 1800s have been summarized as follows:

> Emma Hat Willard began a boarding school for girls in her home in 1814 and Mary Lyon opened Mount Holyoke Seminary in 1837. Elizabeth Blackwell became the first American woman to earn the Doctor of Medicine degree, and astronomer Maria Mitchell was appointed the first female science professor at Vassar in 1862. Florence Bascome became a geologist with the U.S. Geological Survey in 1896 and a fellow of the Geological Society of America in 1894.[29]

It is evident that despite the institutional structures that prevented women from advancement in U.S. society, and the opposition women faced on their road to equal rights, women continued to make major advances throughout the 1800s.

It is evident that not only did women play a significant role in the education of both boys and girls in the early period of American educational history, but an annual report of the School Committee of Concord, Massachusetts, from the early 1800s to 1855, stated that students made more academic improvements when taught by female teachers than male teachers.[30] Despite the accomplishments by women in education, many people in American society still considered it a risk to allow women to pursue higher education. Edward Clark, a member of Harvard University Medical School, wrote a book titled *Sex in Education; Or, a Fair Chance for Girls* published in 1873, in which he listed among the dangers of female education: monstrous brains, puny bodies, flowing thought, and constipated bowels.[31]

GENDER AND WOMEN'S RIGHTS IN THE TWENTIETH AND TWENTY-FIRST CENTURIES

The twentieth century was the most progressive era in woman's rights. Many educational and social advances were made that enhanced women's place in society. An organization of middle-class and working-class women was formed in 1903 under the leadership of Mary Drier, Rheta Child Dorr, and Leonora O'Reilly for unionizing working women. This group, which was originally called Women's Trade Union League of New York, later became the International Ladies' Garment Workers' Union (ILGWU).

The seminaries were the first in higher institutes to admit women. Since seminaries emphasized self-denial and strict discipline, they became important avenues for molding devout wives and Christian mothers. As much as these seminaries were offering superior education, they were training women for a world that was not prepared to accept educated women. Female seminary students were allowed to become teachers until they were prepared to marry.[32]

By 1911, the National Association Opposed to Woman Suffrage (NAOWS) was formed by mostly wealthy influential women and some Roman Catholic clergymen. The following year Theodore Roosevelt's Progressive Party (Bull Moose/Republican) became the first major political party in the nation to take a stance in favor of woman suffrage.

In 1916, Montana became the first state to elect a woman, Jeannette Rankin, to the U.S. House of Representatives. Two years later (1918) she opened the debate on a suffrage amendment in the House of Representatives. The amendment passed, but failed to win the required two-thirds majority in the senate to become law. On August 26, 1920, the Nineteenth Amendment was ratified, granting American women full rights to vote. The amendment declared: "The right of citizens of the United States to vote shall be denied or abridged by the United States or by any state on account of sex." In 1938, the Fair Labor Standards Act established a federal minimum wage that prohibited discrimination on the basis of gender.

Beginning in 1941 and throughout the World War II years, women became a force to reckon with in the labor industries. With many men away fighting the war, massive government and industry campaigns were launched to persuade women to enter the labor forces. About 7 million responded and worked at various sectors, and 400,000 women joined the military. World War II gave women a significant measure of respect in the government and in industry, but these gains did not last long, as women began to lose those jobs to men returning from the war by 1945. About 80 percent of the women who were let go from the workforce wanted to continue to work.

The 1954 *Brown v. Board of Education of Topeka Kansas* decision is often linked exclusively to the civil rights movement, disregarding the fact that the main plaintiff, Linda Brown, was not only African American but also female. This landmark decision ended years of educational inequality that negatively affected many women of color. On December 1, 1955, at about 5:30 PM, Rosa Parks, a quiet, middle-aged working-class African American woman, refused to give up her seat for a white passenger. Her arrest sparked the Montgomery bus boycott, which lasted for more than one year, until the buses were desegregated in December of the following year. Her action ignited the fire that sparked what we have come to know as the civil rights movement of the late 1950s and early 1960s.[33]

In 1960, the Food and Drug Administration approved birth control pills for the first time. Abortion had been criminalized under the sponsorship of the American Medical Association since 1858.[34] The 1960 approval of contraceptives is a result of years of activism on the part of many women like Margaret Sanger, who in 1916 was arrested along with hundreds of other women who were actively working to establish the rights of women to control their own bodies. Sanger won a lawsuit against the State of New York in 1918 to allow doctors to advise their married patients on birth control for health reasons.

Beginning in 1955 there was a return of the widening gap between the wages of men and women in the work force. By 1960 white women earned sixty cents for every dollar earned by men. Minority women earned only forty-two cents for every dollar earned by a white male. In 1963, Congress passed an act establishing equal pay for men and women who performed the same duties. This was quickly followed the next year by the 1964 Civil Rights Act, which prohibited employment discrimination on the basis of race, color, religion, nation of origin, or gender.

In 1966, twenty women came together and founded the National Organization for Women, a civil rights organization that sought to enforce the Equal Employment Opportunities Act of 1964. Two years later, the first Women's Liberation Conference was held in Chicago, Illinois. That same year, 1968, the National Abortion Rights Action League was founded. It was also the same year that the first African American woman, Shirley Chisholm, a New York Democrat, was elected to the U.S. Congress.

While it seemed as if women's rights were enjoying success in the political arena, women's rights continued to struggle in many other areas. By 1970 the earning gap between men and women had widened, as white women earned fifty-nine cents for every dollar earned by white men. Wages for minority women were also going down. This may have had a role to play in the reintroduction of the Equal Rights Amendment into the U.S. Congress in 1970.

Educationally, gains were made for women in the 1970s. Title IX (Public Law 92-318) of the Education Amendments was passed in 1972 prohibiting sex discrimination in every educational program that receives federal funds. By the mid-1970s, many U.S. colleges and universities began to offer women's studies courses, and support services were provided for women on college campuses. However, there remained a glass ceiling for women's access to certain academic fields like medicine, engineering, law, and other reputable professions. Very few women gained admission into these fields. It was only in the 1970s through the 1980s and 1990s that women in the United States won the right to be admitted to previously all-male Ivy League colleges and universities. It was in the 1990s that the Citadel and the Virginia Military Institute were compelled to admit women for the first time, as such discrimination violated the Fourteenth Amendment.[35] By 1978, however, more women than men were enrolled in American colleges and universities. This is a trend that seems to have continued into the twenty-first century.

In 1981, President Jimmy Carter proclaimed the first "National Women's History Day," to coincide with the March 8 International Women's Day. The same year, Sandra Day O'Connor became the first female to serve on the U.S. Supreme Court. Geraldine Ferraro became the first woman vice-presidential candidate of a major political party in 1984 when she ran on the Democratic ticket with Walter Mondale. That same year, the state of Mississippi finally ratified the Nineteenth Amendment, which it had refused to do since 1920, granting women the right to vote in Mississippi.

By 1990 the number of black women elected into political office had increased from 131 in 1970 to 1,950. By 1992, white women's wages had risen to seventy-one cents for every dollar paid to men. Black women earned sixty-five cents for every male dollar, and Hispanic women earned fifty-four cents. By 1997 The Supreme Court ruled that college athletic programs must involve roughly an equal number of women and men in sports to qualify for federal support.

Just before the turn of the twenty-first century, women filed many lawsuits in different parts of the United States accusing corporations of employment discrimination. Two of the most prominent among those were the 1998 law suit against Mitsubishi Motor Corporation USA, in which the company agreed to pay $34 million to settle the case, and the 2000 CBS $8 million sex discrimination settlement with 200 women.

In 2002, Nancy Pelosi, Democrat of California, became the first female Speaker of the House of Representatives. The year 2008 recorded the most significant political landmark in women's rights into the twenty-first century. Senator Hilary Clinton (Democrat of New York) became the first woman to have her name appear on the nomination ballot of a major party for the office of the presidency. Clinton won 18 million votes in the Democratic primary election, losing the nomination by a very slim margin. The same year, the Republican Party nominated a woman (Sarah Palin) as a vice presidential candidate for the first time.

Challenges Facing Women in Twenty-First-Century America

The challenges facing women in twenty-first-century America remains the glass ceiling in career opportunities, educational opportunities, and wages.

The glass ceiling is the invisible barrier that confronts ethnic Americans and women in trying to reach the upper echelons of corporate America. These demographics can see the next level of professional attainment that they could ascend to, but an invisible obstacle is permanently placed on their way to attaining that height. It is further defined as when an individual's chances for upward social, economic, and educational mobility in the United States are highly related to social class, ethnic, gender, and other ascribed groups to which the individual belongs (Banks, 2004).

The glass ceiling allows an individual to see the top or preferred position, but he or she, regardless of proper qualifications, cannot reach the top because of barriers placed by those already on top. The barrier is based on some physical attribute of that person, which makes him or her a minority in American society. Such attributes include cultural or ethnic background, gender, religion, language, skin color, physical limitations or handicaps, and/or social or economic status.

This barrier continues to pose a hindrance to women's attempts toward upward mobility. In the United States, 95–97 percent of the senior managers of the *Fortune* 1,000 and the *Fortune* 500 companies are white males, while 57 percent of the workforce in these organizations is either ethnic minorities or women. Women's wages still lag behind those of their male counterparts by an average of 20 percent as of 2009. Women are also heavily underrepresented in the political arena.

The glass ceiling is evident in the field of education as well. Most teachers in elementary schools are women, while most of the administrators are males. Girls' test scores fall considerably behind boys as they move through the grades. Girls are less likely than boys to participate in class discussions and are less encouraged to do so. The glass ceiling continues to prevent college girls from accessing more lucrative careers.

Conclusion

The three areas of professional growth, educational opportunities, and fair wages remain major challenges in the battle for gender equity in the United States. It is a common saying that the purpose of history is to avoid a repeat of the mistakes of the past. The relevance of these historical facts in multicultural education is to enable the twenty-first-century teacher to appreciate the struggles and pains that are responsible for the gains that have been made in the battle for gender equity. Against that background, teachers must begin to see their roles within the classroom as crucial, requiring active engagement with, not passive tolerance of, gender rights. The twenty-first-century classroom is still plagued with different kinds of gender inequity: gender blindness, tokenism, cosmetic representation, and so on. It is important that we address each of these concerns and the roles teachers should be playing to address them in a multicultural classroom.

~

QUESTIONS AND APPLICATION

Case Study

Background

John is a young teacher who has recently graduated from a teacher preparation program. He had a thorough preparation in cultural diversity as part of the program, and he made a commitment to ensure that his classroom was an environment that respected gender and cultural diversity. John made sure that a girl was elected classroom president and another girl was made the mail runner, going to the office to receive and give out messages. These were the two valued class positions. The boys in John's classroom protested and cried out that it was unfair to have girls in those positions, giving them power over the boys.

Challenge

1. How would you advise John to respond to this protest from the boys in his classroom?
2. What, if anything, in John's appointment of girls to lead the class would you consider unfair?
3. How could John have done this differently to avoid the conflict?
4. How can a teacher successfully run a classroom that is free of gender bias?

Review Questions

1. Write a short essay on the positive and negative effects feminism has had on American society and its educational system.
2. What are some of the ways teachers can attain both equity and excellence for their students across gender lines?
3. What are some of the benefits of targeting both genders in our teaching practices?
4. Suggest resources that can be included in the curriculum to balance the gender ratio of the curriculum.

Strategies for Application for the K–12 Classroom

1. Grades K–12: Work with your students to review your class's primary texts to identify the degree to which female contributions have been represented in the textbooks. Identify concerns the class may have on underrepresentation, if any, and write a letter or letters to the publisher expressing your concerns.
2. Grades K–12: Invite a congresswoman from your district to visit the classroom and discuss the impact women have had on the legislative system, either at the state or federal level.

Organize a career day for your class and invite females in professional fields to come and address the students. Invite medical doctors, engineers, lawyers and judges, university professors, and women from other prominent professions.

Chapter Ten

The Learner and the Educational Process

Chapter Objectives:

This chapter introduces multicultural education as learner-centered pedagogy. It defines education, what it means to learn and to teach, and who a learner is. Readers will be able to:

1. articulate an understanding of the role of education in the larger society
2. define a learner, a teacher, and what it means to learn within the larger educational setting

A learner-centered pedagogy requires that we understand the meaning of education, define teaching and learning, and be able to fully grasp the nature of the interaction that takes place between the teacher, the learner, the content, and context of learning. It is the objective of this chapter to establish that the nature of this interaction makes multicultural education an inescapable reality in the American educational settings.

WHAT IS EDUCATION?

Education has been defined as "the process of training and developing the knowledge, skill, mind, character . . . , especially by formal schooling; teaching; training."[1]

Education as a process is often defined as the inculcation of knowledge. This definition first presupposes a source of knowledge; secondly, it presupposes a substance or material called knowledge; and lastly, a receptor.

163

The source is often called the teacher in the formal educational setting; the substance is often called information, ideas, or instructional content; and the receptor is the learner.

The dictionary definition above introduces a number of concepts, namely: training, developing knowledge, skills, mind, character, formal schooling, and teaching. This concept of knowledge development suggests a process of cultivating—planting and nurturing knowledge—as part of the educational process. This makes the teacher-versus-learner relationship indispensable in the educational process. It also suggests that education is both a matter of the "mind" as well as the "hand" when it talks about skills acquisition and the mind as a faculty undergoing development. The formal schooling process is necessary for meaningful education to take place. One essential ingredient that makes for a schooling system is the teacher-to-learner relationship. This relationship does not take place in a cultural vacuum. The teacher approaches teaching through his or her personal cultural lenses, while the student approaches learning through his or her own cultural lenses. When teachers are unable to connect with students and their cultural backgrounds, or students are unable to connect with teachers because of cultural divide, the educational process is shortchanged. This understanding of education suggests that it is a social contract, not necessarily an intellectual contract, as may seem to be the case in B. F. Skinner's definition of education as "the culture of the intellect."[2]

Skinner's definition means that education is something that happens within the realm of the intellect or the mind. His definition may stand critical inquiry if we can look at education as a process of the mind and skills acquisition as the end product of the educational process, or its fruit. It simply means that skills acquisition may be part of the educational process, but the practical application or use of the acquired skills is not education, instead it is called production. Skinner's definition, nevertheless, does not explain the whole educational process.

The Allegory of the Cave probably illustrates what education means in a nutshell. Plato talks about prisoners in an underground cave who are chained down so they cannot move around. They see the real world only in the form of shadows cast against the wall of the cave by burning fires. These images appear in disfigured and irregular forms so much that the images have no semblance to the realities outside. The prisoners get used to these images and are convinced that the images are realities in themselves. They have no knowledge of the realities outside, so they hold on to their half-baked ideas of reality as the one and only truth about reality. To convince them otherwise, Plato suggests unchaining them and taking them out to the world of reality. This allegory has a lot of implications for understanding the educational process.

Education is an enculturation process. The learner shares a lot of commonalities with Plato's prisoners. They are limited in their knowledge and ideas about the world of reality, and the educational process is supposed to unlock learners from that prison and release them into the world of reality. Education is supposed to be an empowering process, which transports one from the world of ignorance to knowledge. It's the process by which the prisoners are persuaded to engage the realities outside of the cave and the fact of the flaws of their perception. This is done either by unchaining them and taking them outside of the cave to confront reality face-to-face, or by attempting to persuade them by mere words to begin to look at reality differently. If the goal is to release the prisoners from the perceptual blindness created by their confinement, the ideal would be to release them from the chains and take them outside the cave. But if the goal is to create doubts in their minds that they have a full grasp of reality, or at least to provoke their thoughts to consider such a possibility, mere information may as well do it. It certainly takes one who has earned the trust and confidence of the prisoner to unchain him and persuade him to step outside of his phantom world to the world of reality.

Based on this interpretation of the allegory of the cave, one must question a definition of education that sees it exclusively as the transmission of information, as to whether this is fully representative of the meaning of education. The goal of education has to be to produce new and altered human persons significantly different from who they were before entering the educational process. This aims at social, intellectual, and skills transformation. The educated person must emerge a new and better person than he or she was before entering the educational process. For this reason, information transmission alone does not do it; rather, a restructuring and reorientating of the total person takes place in the educational process.

The educational context becomes, therefore, the best place to create and construct socially informed and civically responsible citizens. One of the fundamental flaws that developed in the American education system, which was not challenged until recently, has been the impartation of knowledge with no attempt to develop socially informed citizens who are committed to harmonious and respectful social coexistence in a diverse society like the United States. Most American children come to school ignorant of the world around them, and ignorant of the many different peoples that populate their communities. We educate them in the imprisonment of their minds and in small homogeneous communities and fail to expose them to the mosaic world of reality that makes America what it is. Whether raised in the white suburban communities of Iowa, or in the African American communities of Harlem and south-central Los Angeles, the world these students know is, exclusively, their own cultural world. The world outside of their communities is alien to them, and the educational settings work hard to keep it so, rather than unchain them from such imprisonments to expose them to the discomforting, yet necessary, world of reality beyond their comfort zones. This is a fundamental flaw with the American educational system, which must be challenged for the United States to produce world citizens, not the ethnocentric bigots that fill many American institutions. This is the place and purpose of multicultural education in the American educational system.

WHAT DOES IT MEAN TO TEACH?

It must be underscored here that the transmission or presentation of information is not synonymous with teaching. To teach involves a series of more complex processes, which are encountered in the everyday attempt to both influence students and transmit knowledge. The information being transmitted during a process of communication is one entity, the communicator is another entity, and the recipient of the information is another. The communicator must first of all understand and appropriate the information to the extent that he or she feels competent and comfortable enough to communicate it to another person with the intention of effecting some changes in the life or thinking of the recipient, the learner. An individual may take in a coded message without understanding what it means and relay the same message to another person without additions or distortions. That would not be teaching. Teaching, which imparts knowledge, must effect a change in personality and perspective for both teacher and student.

The allegory of the cave, once again, presents a classic case of what it means to teach. The teacher is like the first prisoner to be released from the chain. The first prisoner who is released and exposed to the world of reality faces the challenge of returning to the cave and convincing his friends that there is more to reality than they were beholding. For him to do that effectively he must not be reciting previously memorized texts, but speak about personal encounters. It takes a culturally and socially transformed teacher to impart life-transforming and culturally sensitive education. The prisoner must be persuasive enough to get other prisoners to take him seriously, to get them to begin to give some credibility to his ideas and thoughts. Such a development would only arise if there were physically convincing proofs that the teacher could employ to make his or her point. This introduces the idea of methodology. Possessing the information alone does not make for a good teacher, but possessing the right method for communicating the information and effecting changes in lives makes a difference.

In effect, therefore, to teach means both to model and to instruct. The teacher must be standing at the point where he or she wants to bring the students before attempting to get them to come on to that level of enlightenment. According to B. F. Skinner, the teacher instructs, informs, forms, and shapes the student. Teaching is the expediting of the learning process. He cautions that the teacher does not transmit his own behaviors to the student, instead he imparts knowledge, which could be meanings, concepts, facts, and propositions.[3] It must be stated here that it is practically impossible for the teacher to avoid imparting his behaviors to his students. The art of teaching is not just the transmission of information. Skinner says to teach means to "help the student learn," to "nourish or cultivate" the child.[4] The term *cultivate*, an agricultural term, presupposes planting and tending with the expectation of blossom and fruitfulness. To cultivate is to invest time and effort with an eager expectation for proceeds. Teaching as cultivation involves the investment of time and energy by the teacher into the student with the hope and expectation that the student will blossom and produce fruits that justify the energy that has been poured on her. A question every multicultural educator must ask is, "What kind of students do I want to produce?" You are planting and cultivating students who will grow up to represent your ideas, worldviews, and even your principles. How would you want to be represented?

We must concede to Skinner in a way, that teaching is not an attempt on the side of the teacher to reproduce himself; rather, it involves the task of helping the learner discover how to fully actualize himself or herself. To teach is to bring the learner to the point at which he or she can begin to ask the right questions, whose answers alone can place that learner on the road to self-realization and self-actualization.

WHAT DOES IT MEAN TO LEARN?

A major point B. F. Skinner makes about learning is that it can take place with or without the teacher, but that the degree of learning varies in each given situation. To learn is seen by Skinner as to acquire or receive education. He uses such verbs as *grasp, impress, drill,* and *inculcate* to describe what happens when concepts and ideas are transferred from the teacher to the student. To learn, therefore would mean to "absorb," as in soaking up something; "digest," as in chewing and swallowing; "conceive," as in impregnation by accepting from someone else the seminal fluid and conceiving of a child; or "contract," as in the medical process of getting an infection.[5]

Skinner's ideas suggest the transference of some concrete substance from the teacher to the learner. Once the learner accepts the substance, it becomes his or her own possession, no longer the teacher's. Learning goes beyond Skinner's thoughts. It is a process by which one's exposure to concepts and ideas in the educational context brings one to the point of both reflection and meditation. Education takes an individual beyond that point to discover what he is capable of being if he can rightly and adequately apply and utilize the resources around him. Abstract learning has no place in this definition of learning. Any learning that ends with the acquisition of ideas and concepts that are irrelevant to practical living and existence does not constitute full learning; instead it may constitute a waste of time and life resources.

To learn, therefore, is to accept modifications, intellectual or otherwise, that would bring one's life into contact with more enriching experiences and opportunities in the real life. It is to accept to change one's perspective or direction for the better. To learn is to grow richer and taller in quality of life as well as in intellectual capacity. Through education, therefore, we construct individuals and consequently a society. This is why multicultural education must take a central place in our educational practices. We do not only impart knowledge in the classrooms, we construct individuals and a social arrangement. Appreciation, respect, equality, and mutual coexistence, which are central to multicultural education, must be consciously constructed in the classrooms.

A learner, therefore, is one who is on a journey. The individual is on a journey to self-actualization and self-realization. A learner opens the self up to the intrusion of new and foreign ideas and concepts, with the hope that in sieving through them he or she will have access to some rules and resources that will increase the quality of his or her own life. A learner is not only motivated by the teacher and the presentation of the subject matter, but also by his or her own dreams and aspirations. The learner has clear goals and expectations along with the goals and expectations that the teacher has set, and the ones that are inherent in the subject of study. Learning is, therefore, a life-long undertaking. The journey does not end until one is dead.

If humanity is such a complex entity as we have described in this work, and if teaching and learning are such intricate undertakings, what then is possible in the classroom? Abraham Maslow saw human development in a unique way. According to him, the age of sixty and above is the age of self-actualization. If Maslow was right, that the self-actualizing age is sixty-plus, it means that most people in the classroom are on a journey.[6] Since many teachers retire by age sixty, the bulk of the teachers in the classrooms are still seeking. They are learners along with their students, on a journey to self-discovery and self-actualization. This gives reason to accept a view that the classroom is "an experiment in human possibilities."[7] This points to the possibilities of what a teacher can become as well as the students. How many teachers are open to these possibilities? Sadly there are not very many.

The young adult teacher is asking questions like "Where am I going from here?" "What else does life have for me apart from what I can see right now?" The senior adult is asking, "Is this all there is to life?" "Is there life after retirement?" The younger students are asking, "What does the future hold for me?" "Will I be a success or a failure?" The classroom nevertheless holds possibilities for each one of these individuals, as in it they can see their power to help in shaping tomorrow.

The hope, therefore, is that the teacher can find within the classroom walls answers to the questions both of the teacher and the students. This is why the teacher will more likely put in his best to be and become the best teacher there can be, since success in what the teacher is doing right now will very much impact his or her sense of validation as a human being or of frustration and worthlessness in the long run. One teacher may take the challenge and become the best teacher ever, while another may surrender to the worthlessness and futility of life and refuse to attempt to make much out of life. The teacher could say, "If all there is to life is work, live and die, why bother?" Students as well may see the classroom as the context in which they can take charge of their lives and launch out into a mission of self-actualization, and apply themselves to change the world. These ones will likely apply themselves to hard work and discipline, whereas others may see only their lack of opportunities and possibilities, and for that reason refuse to do anything to launch ahead.

The classroom presents us with a laboratory for viewing the possible demonstrations of the fullest extent of human potentials as well as the lowest depth of human failure. The variables that exist in each situation are the ways each individual involved perceives who they are and what their chances for success and failures are. One would wish that every teacher sees the classroom as the context where he or she must fully explore and utilize personal strengths and potentials, become a super teacher if there is any such thing and if it is attainable. One must learn patience for the weak, become a vehicle that must transmit respect, tolerance, life, and hope to all students. As a teacher, you must desire that your students become successful and self-actualized citizens, as you strive to become a successful and self-actualized citizen yourself.

$\sim$

QUESTIONS AND APPLICATION

Case Study: Dealing with Stereotypes

Background

You are a Chinese female teacher in a predominantly Hispanic neighborhood school. This is your first teaching assignment. During the teacher preparation program you developed a special passion for the inner-city schools. You wanted to work in these challenging neighborhoods to make a difference in the lives of students who rarely get the best of teachers and resources. You had an offer to work in a reputable suburban district, but you turned it down for this inner-city school job. You were looking forward to this new experience of doing something that would positively impact young lives.

The Problem

Your first week in the new school has been a major shock. The first day your car was broken into and valuables worth more than $800 were removed. On the second day upon arrival at school you entered your classroom and were shocked to see all kinds of graffiti written on the walls. There were some writings in plain English that stated, "This place is not for dog eaters." On the third day, one student raised his hand to ask a question, when you called on him, instead of addressing the lesson of the hour, his question was "How does dog meat taste?" This led to an outburst of laughter in the classroom. At this point you are beginning to see a connection between the vandalism on your car, the graffiti and the racial slur that you are now facing.

Challenge

1. How would you feel as a result of these encounters?
2. What response, if any, would you give to the student who asked the question?
3. Would you address the whole class on this subject? Why? Why not?
4. What would you say to them if you choose to address them on the topic?
5. What steps would you take to ensure that your life, property, and self-esteem are protected in this new environment?
6. What short- or long-term decision would you make concerning your decision to teach in the inner-city schools?
7. Would you involve the school administration in this matter? If yes, how and why?

Review Questions

1. What is education? In view of the insights gained from this chapter, articulate your understanding of the purpose of education within the larger society.
2. As one who sees teaching as your vocation, articulate a personal mission statement that outlines how you see your role as a teacher in the K–12 classrooms.
3. Define your role as a learner within the classroom setting, who happens to be a teacher at the same time.

Strategies for Application in the K–12 Classrooms

1. Grades K–12: Teach your students to memorize the following chant and recite it to themselves and to the class.

> I am a human being. I have a future.
> It's my honor as a Student to do my best.
> It's my honor as a Scholar to do my best.

As a follow-up activity, discuss the benefits of performing well at school and the impact it can have on their quality of life into the future. Discuss lucrative jobs and activities such as being a famous musician, actor, or athlete. Discuss the demographic representation of this population compared to the larger U.S. population and make clear that the chances of becoming one of these rich individuals may not be very high for everyone, making schooling the next best way to advance oneself.

2. Grades 4–12: Ask your students to project how much money they want to make each year to be able to live at the comfort level they desire. Secure U.S. census data on income distribution across professions, showing earning for college educated individuals and non-college-educated individuals. Lead them to use the chart you have provided to determine how many years of schooling they need in order to afford the quality of life they desire.

Chapter Eleven

Exceptionality and Learner-Centered Pedagogies for the Regular Education Classroom

Chapter Objectives:

This chapter engages the needs of exceptional students within the larger context of multicultural education. It traces the history and development of special education and similar programs aimed at meeting the needs of exceptional students within the regular school settings. Readers will be able to:

1. define the exceptional child
2. trace the history and provisions of IDEA
3. describe an individualized education program (IEP)
4. explain Section 504 and its provisions, as well as response to intervention (RTI)

DEFINING THE EXCEPTIONAL CHILD

The concept of the exceptional child in the educational setting suggests a paradigm shift in the way we see students who do not fit into the conventional mold of the average student. The exceptional child is that student who may be achieving significantly above or below grade level. They are exceptional because they are outside the bell curve. These students present unique challenges to teachers, who must get to know them as individuals before they can reasonably provide meaningful support for their academic achievement. The exceptional child may be gifted and talented, often ahead of the class, or simply gifted in one area and struggling in others. It may be the child that is deaf or hard of hearing, or the child that has dyslexia. Whatever challenge or opportunities confront the exceptional child, it simply means that we cannot adopt a cookie-cutter approach to teaching in such a classroom.

In this chapter, we will explore the various characteristics that make the exceptional child exceptional. We will explore efforts that have been made through legislation along with proven pedagogical practices that meet the needs of the exceptional child. We will propose more ways to provide support to these students in a multicultural classroom.

The Disabled or Differently Gifted Child

Without in any way discarding such words as disabled or handicapped, which have been used to describe these categories of students within the law, academic literature, and pedagogical practices, there is the need to see these students as differently gifted or differently "abled." Every human being has at least one area of strength and weakness, and it is only appropriate that we begin to see people through the lenses of their strengths rather than their weaknesses. There is a need for this paradigm shift in the way we see students with disabilities. Let's think about this as we review the conventional labels we have used over the years to describe these students, such as handicapped, disabled, and others, and attempt to modify them.

Handicap

This term has been used to refer to the challenges or hindrances a person with a disability would experience in an attempt to interact with the everyday environment. A handicapped person has been defined as anyone who has a physical or mental handicap that substantially limits one or more of major life activities, has a record of such impairment, or is regarded as having such impairment.[1] States are required under section 612 of the Education of All Handicapped Children Act to provide children in this category from preschool to high school and sometimes college with free and appropriate public education.

Part 104.43 of the Code of Federal Regulations, Title 34 states as follows,

> No qualified handicapped student shall, on the basis of handicap, be excluded
> from participation in, be denied the benefits of, or otherwise be subjected to
> discrimination under an academic, research, occupational training, housing,
> health insurance, counseling, financial aid, physical education, athletics, recre-

ation, transportation, other extracurricular, or other post secondary education aid, benefits, or services to which this subpart applies.[2]

This demonstrates how far reaching the need for educational accommodation for the handicapped from preschool to college is.

Disability

Students with disability are students who have a loss or reduced function of certain parts of their body or organs. A disability does not necessarily mean a handicap unless it interferes with the child's educational, social, vocational, and personal opportunities.

At Risk

This refers to children who have not yet been identified as disabled but are considered to have a higher-than-normal chance of developing a handicap. Due to certain biological, environmental, or economic factors surrounding the child's life, the likelihood that the child will develop a disability is high. Hunt and Marshall grouped the risk factors into three categories: biological, established risk, and environmental risk.[3]

1. Biological risks: Biological risk factors have been subdivided into three categories: prenatal (from conception to birth), perinatal (from twentieth week of pregnancy to the end of the fourth week after birth), and postnatal (after the fourth week of birth). Prenatal risk factors include incidents that affect gestation, growth and development of the fetus, maternal illnesses, maternal alcohol, drug, and substance abuse, and even HIV or AIDS. Perinatal factors include incidents that take place during labor and delivery such as oxygen deprivation, prematurity or low birth weight, or infections from the birth canal. Postnatal factors include childhood diseases.
2. Established risk factors: This occurs in infants that are born with medically diagnosed disorders such as Down syndrome, spina bifida, hearing or vision impairments, or even mental retardation.
3. Environmental risk factors: These are from environmental toxins such as lead, exposure to radiation, postnatal infections like HIV, accidents, abuse, neglect, and poverty.

HISTORY AND DEVELOPMENT OF SPECIAL EDUCATION AND THE INDIVIDUALS WITH DISABILITIES EDUCATION ACT (IDEA)

The U.S. Congress enacted a law in 1975 addressing the needs of students with disabilities. This law, which was called Education for All Handicapped Children Act (P.L. 94-142), was a fundamental shift from the way the government had addressed the needs of children with disabilities up to that point. It mandated free, appropriate public education for all children regardless of the degree of the severity of their disability. It made provisions to protect the rights of disabled children and their parents to have decision-making power over their education. It mandated an individualized education program (IEP) for every child with disability. It also required that educational services be provided to children with disabilities in the least restrictive environment. This law was changed to the Individuals with Disabilities Education Act (IDEA) in 1990 (P.L. 101-336). The new law made provisions to protect the rights of citizens with disabilities from discrimination in employment, public services, public accommodation, transportation, and telecommunication. Amendments were made to this law to include autism and traumatic brain injury on the list of disabilities that require an IEP and to include rehabilitation counseling in the definition of related services for individuals with disabilities.

A major provision of this law for identifying learning disabilities is discrepancies in one of the following areas: reading comprehension, written expression, oral language expression, basic reading skills, mathematical calculation, and mathematical reasoning.

Among the general provisions of the IDEA is the need to locate and identify children with disabilities, a role that falls within the parameters of the general education teacher. Another provision is the need to identify and place the child by means of testing and evaluations in the appropriate educational setting without prejudice or discrimination. There is also the need to protect the rights of the child with a disability and those of the family by ensuring due process and confidentiality of record and personal information.

From 1990 to date, this law has gone through many revisions and updates. The most current version of this law was passed by a congressional act in 2004. The sections that follow examine certain specific provisions of the IDEA.

Free and Appropriate Education (FAPE)

The idea of free and appropriate education is to ensure that essential services are not denied students because their parents cannot afford to pay for them. This provision removes the likelihood of asking parents to pay for any part of the educational and support services given to children under this law. There have been times when this provision has been challenged, especially in cases of autism and related illness, where parents have sought out high-cost services from private agencies or university research programs and demanded that the public schools pay for those services for their children. The dilemma has been whether to pay for one child's expensive private service and compromise the services required by many other children who are receiving their services from the public school system.

Zero Reject

The idea of zero reject is a federal mandate that no child is to be refused appropriate education by any school. This provision makes it possible for children in private schools who have identified disabilities to have access to free educational services that are obtainable from neighborhood public schools. A major significance of this law is that it is the basis on which children identified with HIV or AIDS cannot be excluded from schools. Turnbull, Huerta, and Stowe put the idea of zero reject succinctly, "The Principle of Zero Reject commands the school to enroll all and exclude none with disabilities."[4]

Least Restrictive Environment

Given the fact that a wide range of educational programs have been developed to meet the needs of children with disabilities, this law demands that care be taken to ensure that disabled children are being educated in environments that do not unduly isolate them from the rest of the population without disability. The ultimate desire for the disabled child is full inclusion in the regular education class. The range of educational settings includes the following (not an exhaustive listing):

1. Pullout programs: A Special Education student goes into another class for group instruction or into the resource room for small group or individualized

instruction. The Special Education teacher may also go into the classroom, pull out the students to a corner of the room and work with him/her individually.

2. Resource room: Students leave their regular classrooms and come into a resource room at specific times each day for individualized or small-group instruction. A credentialed special education teacher usually runs the resource room.

3. Expert consultation: The nature of this consultation varies, depending on needs and the qualifications of the general education teacher. The special education teacher serves as a consultant to the general education teacher providing guidance, special lessons and strategies, planning together with the regular education teacher, or coming into the regular education classroom for a period of time each day to provide one-to-one assistance to the child with disability.

4. Special classes: This is a setting in which children with the same type of need are grouped together and taught together. This is common with children with aphasia, deaf children, or children with speech-related disabilities. To provide the least restrictive environment, these students are often integrated with the general population for physical education, art classes, or any other subject, as well as for recesses.

5. Special schools: Special schools often mean that children with disabilities are segregated from the general education population. Under this law, the least restrictive environment requirement demands that there is proof that this is the most effective way these children can be educated, and structures must be put in place to create opportunities for them to interact with general education students.

6. Home or hospital-based instruction: Children with disabilities are often given home-based or hospital-based education when there is injury or illness. This is usually a temporary arrangement, and they go back to their regular educational setting once they improve in their health.

7. Residential schools: Residential schools are probably one of the most restrictive educational settings. There are limited opportunities for these children to interact with the general education population.

The IDEA mandate makes it imperative that school authorities ensure that they have explored all options and determined that the placement they are giving a child with a disability is the least restrictive educational placement for that child.

Individualized Education Program (IEP)

The IEP is an educational document that outlines the identified disabilities and educational challenges facing a child, the educational plans for meeting the identified challenges, responsible individuals, required resources and services, and a time line of implementation and evaluation. The idea is that a child with a disability be provided with a range of options toward meeting his or her educational needs, and the IEP is the avenue for making these options available to the child.

The IEP process must include the child's teacher or teachers (general and special education), the child's parents, and a district representative (could be the school principal or any other assigned administrator), and sometimes the child is present during the IEP meeting. If a child is receiving any transitional services from outside agencies, the agency's representative is required to be present. Some of the basic sections of the IEP are as follows:

1. identification of child's present level of academic performance/achievement
2. statement of projected measurable annual goals for the child
3. specific measurable short-term objectives that target the annual goals
4. clear and specific identification of special education and related regular and supplemental services, which the child needs
5. clear and specific explanation of inclusion programs for a child learning in non-general education settings
6. specific accommodations for standardized and local testing
7. needed transition services and plans for meeting those needs
8. list of individuals responsible for providing the individualized education programs and services
9. statement on how progress will be measured
10. dates for services, evaluations, and places where these are to be provided

The general education teacher who has this child in his or her classroom is expected to be an active participant throughout the process of planning, implementing, and evaluating the IEP.

Nondiscriminatory Evaluation

The nondiscriminatory provision of the IDEA is to ensure that bias does not play a role in the identification, evaluation, and placement of a child in special education programs. To ensure this, the tests used in making placement decisions must meet certain benchmarks, namely: test must be age appropriate, must be administered in the child's native language, must be administered and interpreted by a knowledgeable professional in the field, and requires more than one form of assessment to make a valid evaluation and placement decision. It is also important to ensure that all necessary accommodations are in place for the evaluation to be valid. According to Turnbull, Huerta, and Stowe, "all of IDEA makes sense as a sensible, seamless approach to educating students with disabilities: Enroll all, evaluate fairly, offer benefits, do it in the general education setting, be fair about what you do and how you settle disputes, and be partners with parents and students."[5]

SECTION 504 OF THE FEDERAL REHABILITATION ACT

Section 504 of the Federal Rehabilitation Act of 1973 (P.L. 93-112) protects the rights of people with disabilities in programs and activities that receive federal funding. This law, which does not provide any federal funding, depends on state and local funding to cover the general education responsibilities. This law offers protection beyond the scope of what has been defined as special education. For example, while drug use is not considered a disability, a student who has used drugs in the past and is currently undergoing rehabilitation could become eligible for accommodation under this law.

An individual is considered disabled under section 504 if that individual has had any form of mental or physical impairment that substantially limits the person's ability to care for him- or herself, walk, see, speak, learn, hear, breathe, work, or perform manual tasks. A person qualifies if that individual has had a record of such impairment in the past or if that individual is regarded as having such impairment.[6]

For successful implementation of section 504 provisions, every school is expected to have a school-based support team (SBST), whose task is to suggest steps needed to address the identified difficulties. Some schools use the student study team (SST) as a standing body that handles Section 504 matters. Referrals for Section 504 are considered appropriate and legitimate when they come from the parents or guardians, professional staff at school, student, or a community agency. The district will consequently conduct the necessary evaluations and make placement determinations as appropriate.

On the cases that are deemed appropriate under section 504, the assistant secretaries for the Office of Special Education and Rehabilitative Services, the Office of Civil Rights, and the Office of Elementary and Secondary Education, issued a joint memorandum in 1991, which reads as follows,

> Under Section 504, an LEA must provide a free appropriate public education to each qualified child with disability. A free appropriate public education, under Section 504, consists of regular or special education and related aids and services that are designed to meet the individual student's needs and based on adherence to the regulatory requirements on educational setting, evaluation, placement, and procedural safeguards. . . . A student may be handicapped within the meaning of section 504, and therefore entitled to regular or special education and related aids and services under the Section 504 regulation, even though the student may not be eligible for special education and related services under Part B.[7]

This means that certain disabilities that may not necessarily qualify for special education services can and will qualify for Section 504 aids and services. This memorandum was specific as it relates to ADD and ADHD when it stated that under IDEA children with ADD or ADHD could qualify for special education and related services under the categories of "other health impairment," "specific learning disability," or "serious emotional disturbance." The memorandum went further to state,

> Should it be determined that the child with ADD is handicapped for purposes of Section 504 and needs only adjustment in the regular classroom, rather than special education, those adjustments are required by Section 504. A range of strategies is available to meet the educational needs of children with ADD. Regular classroom teachers are important in identifying the appropriate educational adaptations and interventions for many children with ADD.[8]

Whereas many regular education teachers think that since they are not trained special education teachers, they are not required to provide these special services to children with disabilities, under Section 504, they are required by law to provide those services in the regular education classroom, where determination has been made that the students will be better served in a regular classroom instead of a special education classroom. This means that students who may be refused services under IDEA because they do not meet the established criteria, may actually request evaluation for services under Section 504. This is a right both parents and students have to ensure that they are receiving free appropriate public education (FAPE). Such evaluation is supposed to be done by qualified professionals and care is taken to ensure that the evaluation is unbiased. Once disabilities have been established, an IEP (for special education students) or Section 504 plan is put in place to track the identified needs and services provided.

RESPONSE TO INTERVENTION (RTI)

The idea of response to intervention is to clear the way for students to begin to receive some help as soon as they are identified as having academic problems. This new provision under the IDEA 2004 reauthorization aims at cutting through the delay that often accompanies the evaluation and placement process in special education, which often works against students. Under this new arrangement, students can begin to receive help as early as kindergarten, within the general education setting. This process is prereferral, and is required to utilize scientifically based research intervention strategies to help struggling students.

As part of the RTI process, the general education teacher is expected to embark on continuous monitoring of the student's learning, documenting struggles, challenges, accommodations, and accomplishments. Data from these sources will combine to inform the school psychologist, the administration, and other concerned individuals on the need to have this child assessed for special education. This process provides for early intervention, which enables students to reverse course and begin to succeed, as well as possibly reduce misplacement of children who are struggling with academics into special education programs.[9]

RTI requires a written intervention plan, which clearly describes the specific intervention, the length of time required for such intervention, minutes per day for intervention services, persons responsible for providing intervention, location of intervention services, criteria for measuring success, and a progress-monitoring schedule. This written plan may be the most significant element that has been added to the prereferral process. This guarantees that clear and specific modifications have been implemented, their outcomes evaluated, and informed decision made as a result of the outcomes.

UNDERSTANDING DISABILITIES IN GENERAL EDUCATION CLASSROOMS

Learning Disability

The definition of *learning disability* by the federal government is articulated in the Individuals with Disability Education Act (IDEA) of 1975 as "a disorder in one or more of the basic psychological processes involved in understanding or in using language, spoken or written, that may manifest itself in imperfect ability to listen, think, speak, read, write, spell, or do mathematical calculation, including conditions such as perceptual disabilities.[10] A learning disability therefore, is a disorder that affects an individual's ability to understand and interpret what he or she sees or hears. The problem here is often interference in the individual's ability to integrate information from one part of the brain to the other. This interference manifests itself in various ways, including speech, attention, coordination, and functionality. Learning disabilities are multiple and varied, and are presumed to be a result of some central nervous system dysfunction.[11]

A more common indicator of learning disabilities is significant underachievement. When students are achieving significantly below grade level, it is often an indication of a learning disability. Table 11.1 lists the various categories of learning disorders and their common characteristics.[12]

Mental Retardation

Mental retardation is defined as significant subaverage general intellectual functioning, which exists concurrently with deficits in adaptive behaviors. This is usually manifested during the developmental period, and adversely affects a child's educational achievement.[13]

More than 250 causes of mental retardation have been identified. The causes of a significant measure of mental retardation remain unknown. The known causes are overwhelmingly biological or medical; often referred to as clinical or pathological retardation.[14] The American Association for Mental Retardation (AAMR) has categorized the causes into seven groups:

1. infections and intoxications (e.g., rubella, syphilis, encephalitis, meningitis, exposure to drugs or poisons, blood group incompatibility)
2. trauma and physical agents (e.g., accidents before, during, or after birth)

Table 11.1. Learning Disorders and Their Common Characteristics

Category	Description/Characteristics
Academic readiness disorders	Deals with issues relating to knowledge of the alphabet, print directions and flow, and quantitative concepts.
Reading disorders	One of the most commonly seen reading disorders is dyslexia. Reading disorders often border on interference with visual perception. The learner sees something and his or her brain processes and interprets it differently.
Mathematical skills disorders (dyscalculia)	This deals with difficulties understanding and interpreting spatial relations, place value, decimals, logical sequence, fractions, time, etc., and problems understanding and following mathematical steps.
Verbal skills disorders	Verbal disorders are complex and varied. They include difficulties using the appropriate words, speech sounds, sentence structure, and grammar or language convention: phonology, morphology, syntax, and pragmatics.
Receptive language disorders	Receptive language disorder involves the student's inability to process, understand, and interpret information, make meaning of implied language, figures of speech, or imagery.
Expressive language disorders	Expressive language disorder focuses on what has been referred to as functional flexibility. This is the student's difficulty in being able to appropriately apply a variety of language forms interchangeably to address different issues in different settings.
Visual perception disorders	This disorder addresses learners' inability to discriminate between letters, words, and sometimes sentence structures. Sometimes students learn a word within a particular context, but when they see it outside that contest they are unable to relate to it.
Auditory perception disorders	This disorder deals with letter-sound discrimination, as well as vowel and consonants sounds. Auditory perception disorder deals with the child's inability to hear sounds correctly and recognize specific characteristics of a given sound.
Written language disorders (dysgraphia)	Students in this category struggle with putting ideas down on paper. They are deficient in the ability to plan, organize, and complete a written project. Sentence structure, ideas organization, and flow may come to them freely when they are speaking, but they struggle when asked to write them down.

Category	Description/Characteristics
Social-emotional disorders	This refers to a spectrum of disorders that may range from withdrawal, inability to connect with people emotionally, antisocial behaviors, and other behavioral issues, which negatively affect academic achievement.
Attention disorders	These students may have short attention span or be easily distracted or frequently daydreaming. They are often unable to attend to given tasks, have frequent purposeless movements, and hyperactivity. Both Attention Deficit Disorder (ADD) and Attention Deficit Hyperactivity Disorder (ADHD) fit into this category.

3. metabolic and nutritional factors
4. gross postnatal diseases
5. other prenatal influences
6. chromosomal abnormalities
7. gestational disorders (e.g., low birth weight)

These causes can be grouped into three simple categories as follows,

- Prenatal: genetic, malnutrition (including smoking, alcohol, drugs, or infections)
- Perinatal (during birth): anoxia (oxygen deprivation), breach birth, etc.
- Postnatal (after birth): childhood diseases (meningitis, encephalitis, accidents, abuse, etc.); environment (toxins)

Table 11.2 gives the levels of mental retardation and was developed on information from the American Association on Mental Retardation and Marilyn Friend.[15]

Table 11.2. Levels of Mental Retardation

Level of Retardation	Intelligence Quotient Test Score
Mild Retardation	55 to approximately 70 (+/– 5) IQ score.
Moderate Retardation	40 to 54 IQ score.
Severe Retardation	25 to 39 IQ score.
Profound Retardation	Below 25 IQ score.

Behavioral/Emotional Disorders

The definition of behavioral/emotional disorders under the IDEA uses the umbrella term of serious emotional disturbance to describe this problem. This term combines children with schizophrenia and children with one or more of the following challenges.

1. an inability to learn, which cannot be explained by intellectual, sensory, and health factors
2. an inability to build or maintain satisfactory interpersonal relationships with peers and teachers
3. inappropriate behaviors or feelings under normal circumstances
4. a general pervasive mood of unhappiness or depression
5. a tendency to develop physical symptoms or fears associated with personal or school problems[16]

Different groups have presented different systems for classifying behavioral and emotional disorders. *The Diagnostic and Statistical Manual of Mental Disorders* (DSM-III-R), which was developed by the American Psychiatric Association in 1987, has 230 separate categories that label the many disorders in this category identified in clinical practice.[17] Kerr and Nelson presented them in five categories: disruptive behaviors, socially inadequate and immature behaviors, social withdrawal, stereotypic behaviors, and aggressive behaviors.[18] For our purposes in this work, we will engage the five categories identified in the *Diagnostic and Statistical Manual of Mental Health* (DSM-IV-TR). We will add to the list childhood schizophrenia and autism (see table 11.3).

Communicative Disorders

Communicative disorders include a wide range of disorders that span the fields of speech, language, and communication. Whereas each of these aspects has its unique characteristic, there are elements that are common to them. Communication focuses on the exchange of ideas, but it uses among other vehicles, language and speech (as well as listening, reading, and writing skills). Most forms of communication occur through speech and language (written or spoken).

Table 11.3. Categories of Behavioral/Emotional Disorders

Category	Description
Anxiety disorders	Characterized by an overwhelming sense of fear or dread. Examples include obsessive-compulsive disorder (OCD), phobias, and posttraumatic stress disorder (PSTD).
Disruptive behavior disorders	Characterized by a tendency to be disruptive, bossy, defiant, or have temper tantrums and get into fights. Examples include attention deficit/hyperactivity disorder (ADHD), oppositional defiant disorder (ODD), and conduct disorder, which manifests in bullying, cruelty to animals, and similar behaviors.
Eating disorders	Eating disorders can come in two extreme forms of overeating as a way to handle anxiety and stress or near starvation as a way to build self-image.
Mood disorders	This comprises of a range of disorders including simple depression, bipolar disorders, and manic depression.
Tic disorders	These are ranges of involuntary rapid, stereotyped movement of the whole body or a particular part of body. One common form of this disorder is called Tourette's syndrome, involving facial tics and tics on other parts of the body.
Autism	Added to the list of disabilities in 1990, autism is a severe disorder that ranges from behavioral, through language, to health impairment. Autism is added to this category because it is a developmental disability that significantly affects verbal and nonverbal communication and social interaction. Signs of autism are usually evident before age three, and it adversely affects a child's educational performances. Common Characteristics of autistic children include engagement in repetitive activities, stereotyped movements, resistance to environmental change or change of daily routines, unusual responses to sensory experiences, and lack of creativity or imagination.
Childhood schizophrenia	Schizophrenia generally refers to a psychiatric problem involving split personality. Rosengberg, Wilson, Maheady, and Sindelar[19] identified three main characteristics of childhood schizophrenia: disorders in speech and language, disorders in the ability to relate to other people or the environment, and emotional disorders.[20]

Whereas speech and language disorders are found within a larger range of communicative disorders, *communicative disorders* is a broader term that includes discrepancies in communication reception, which may take place as a result of hearing impairment or reading disorders.[21] Since we have already discussed both hearing and learning disabilities, we will restrict this section to speech and language issues. Table 11.4 shows a listing of the various categories of speech disorders. Table 11.5 presents a listing of the categories of language disorders.

Blindness and Visual Impairments

The National Federation of the Blind uses the word *blind* to refer to persons who have no vision at all as well as persons with a certain degree of limited vision. The term *legally blind* is used for persons whose visual acuity, measured in both eyes while wearing corrective lenses, is 20/200, or whose visual field is no more than twenty degrees. Decreased vision, regardless of degree of decrease, is generally referred to as *visual impairment*.

Visual impairment comprises two different categories of visual disorder, namely, low vision and blindness. Individuals with low vision are able to use "compensatory strategies, technology, and environmental modifications" to aid vision and enhance their ability to perform tasks.[22] Blind people are often

Table 11.4.   Categories of Speech Disorders

Speech Disorders	Description
Articulation disorders	These are also referred to as phonological disorders. They are disorders in the use of sounds in common communication. This occurs in many forms, including omission of sounds, substitution, addition, or distortion of sounds.
Voice disorders	There are disorders in the use of pitch, intensity, resonance, or vocal quality. This often occurs as a result of abnormalities in the function of the larynx or the oral and nasal cavities. Some children can only whisper and will struggle with speaking loud. Others are unable to maintain a loud or constant voice tone.
Fluency disorders	This label generally refers to an interruption in the flow of speech. It occurs in a variety of ways, for example: (1) stuttering—excessive and uncontrolled sound, syllable, and word repetitions—and (2) cluttering—random and unnecessary bursts and or pauses during speech.
Apraxia of speech	An extraordinary difficulty producing speech that ordinary people have no difficulty producing. This individual may come across as unintelligible or extremely soft-spoken.

Table 11.5. Categories of Language Disorders

Language Disorders	Descriptions
Receptive language disorder	A child suffering from receptive language disorders has difficulties using written or spoken commands to follow direction. May be unable to follow commands that have more than one step involved.
Expressive language disorder	This is limitation in vocabulary and language forms necessary to communicate to other people, either for spoken or written expressions. This child may have a very limited vocabulary bank to draw from, or limited knowledge of sentence structures and forms to make expressive communication free and effective.
Aphasia	This is a difficulty with both expressive and receptive language. This occurs mostly as a result of traumatic brain injuries or other accidents. When this occurs in childhood it affects reading skills.
Central auditory processing disorder (CAPD)	This is an interruption in the brain's ability to process and interpret the information that comes to it from the ears.

defined as having profound visual impairment or as functionally blind. A representative sampling of the various vision impairments (not an exhaustive listing) is presented in table 11.6.

Physical and Other Health Impairments

Individuals with conditions that, to a certain degree, incapacitate the skeletal, muscular, and/or neurological systems of the body are referred to as physically impaired. *Health impairment* on the other hand, refers to conditions in which one or more of the body systems are affected by disease or debilitating conditions.[23]

The Massachusetts Department of Elementary and Secondary Education provides a more in-depth definition of *health impairment* as follows:

A chronic or acute health problem such that the physiological capacity to function is significantly limited or impaired and results in one or more of the following: limited strength, vitality or alertness including a heightened alertness to environmental stimuli resulting in limited alertness with respect to the educational environment. The term shall include health impairments due to asthma, attention deficit disorder or attention deficit with hyperactivity disorder, diabetes, epilepsy, a heart condition, hemophilia, lead poisoning, leukemia, nephritis, rheumatic fever, sickle cell anemia, and Tourette's syndrome, if such health impairment adversely affects a student's educational performance.[24]

Table 11.6.   Vision Impairments

Visual Impairments	Description
Congenital visual impairments	Visual impairments or conditions that occur at or near birth.
Adventitious visual impairments	Visual impairments or conditions occurring after birth, either at childhood or later in life.
Strabismus	An inability to focus on an object with both eyes due to the inability of the muscles of the eye to hold both eyes in proper alignment.
Ocular motility	This is impairment of the eye's ability to move.
Amblyopia	Loss of vision in one eye, usually the weaker one, due to lack of use.
Photophobia	Extreme sensitivity to light. Tinted glasses are usually used to reduce glare.
Cataract	This is a clouding of the lens making it unable to transmit light through the retina.
Glaucoma	This is damage to the optic nerve caused when the aqueous humor (a watery liquid that fills the front chamber of the eye) does not flow properly.
Refractive errors	This is an error that occurs when light rays do not focus properly on the retina. This correctible error can lead to permanent damage if not corrected quickly. The various impairments in this group include astigmatism (distorted or blurred vision), myopia (nearsightedness), and hyperopia (farsightedness).
Cortical visual impairment	Damage to a part of the brain that deals with sight, leading to errors in the brain's interpretation of visual data.
Macular degeneration	Gradual deterioration of the central area of the retina leading to a loss in the ability to see clearly in the central visual fields.

Types of Physical Impairments

The different categories of physical disorders include, but are not limited to, neurological disorders, musculoskeletal disorders, and traumatic brain injury. See table 11.7 fore neurological disorders and table 11.8 for musculoskeletal disorders.

Other forms of physical and health impairments include traumatic head injuries, chronic illnesses, convulsions or epilepsy, juvenile diabetes, asthma, cystic fibrosis, HIV/AIDS, sickle-cell disease, serious burns, and hemophilia. Children with these diseases and conditions require special accommodations in class, physical education, and other educational environments.

Table 11.7. Neurological Disorders

Neurological Disorder	Description
Spina bifida	Split or divided spine. This often leads to seizure and bladder and bowel-related problems.
Cerebral palsy	This is a paralysis of the brain, involving muscle control, posture, and movement. It is often caused by a lesion to the brain or an abnormal brain growth. This impairment is often accompanied by low academic achievement.
Spinal cord injury	Results from a break, bruise, or other kinds of damage to the spinal cord. This affects the motor and sensory organs and results in paralysis.
Quadriplegia	Impairment of all four limbs, face, and trunk.
Diplegia	Significant impairment of the legs, but not the arms.
Paraplegia	Impairment of the legs only.
Monoplegia	Impairment of only one limb.
Double hemiplegia	Significant impairment of the arms, but less severe impairment of the legs.
Triplegia	Impairment of three limbs.

Table 11.8. Musculoskeletal Disorders

Disorder	Description
Muscular dystrophy	A progressive weakness of the muscular systems. Early indications in children include difficulty walking, running, or climbing.
Juvenile rheumatoid arthritis	This occurs in children sixteen years of age or less. The joints get swollen and sore.
Osteogenesis imperfecta	This is a hereditary disease that leads to abnormal skeletal growth and brittle bones, and often puts children in wheelchairs or on braces or crutches.

UNDERSTANDING THE GIFTED AND TALENTED CHILD

The U.S. Department of Education defines giftedness as the potential for remarkably high levels of accomplishment when compared to the average for the gifted child's age, experience, and environment. Giftedness is demonstrated through intellectual capacity, creative abilities, academic accomplishments, and/or artistic accomplishments.[25] Gifted and talented students are often frustrated and underserved due to the inability of teachers in the regular classrooms to teach them at what Vygotzky has called their zone of proximal development. They are either taught at the same pace and with the same learning curriculum as the other kids in class, or, in the name of differentiation, they are given excessive amounts of work that overwhelm them.

There is a whole range of discussions about the need and justification for gifted and talented education (GATE) programs, since they are often populated by predominantly white students from the middle- and upper-middle-class families, with little or no visible representation from the minority groups. The fact remains that while white students fill the GATE programs, African American and Hispanic students fill the Special Education programs. This imbalance continues to raise questions as to whether the minority kids are being tracked into special education while the white kids are given undue preference for GATE identification. It continues to be argued that little progress has been recorded in the under-representation of Hispanic and black students in gifted programs over the past twenty years.[26] This failure has been blamed on deficit thoughts and beliefs and attitudes that cause teachers to lower expectations for these demographics (Milner, Tenore, and Laughter, 2008).[27]

The need to make accommodations for gifted and talented students was addressed in the Federal Elementary and Secondary Education Act of 1965. Subpart 6, section 5462 of this act states that "The purpose of this subpart is to initiate a coordinated program of scientifically based research, demonstration projects, innovative strategies, and similar activities designed to build and enhance the ability of elementary schools and secondary schools nationwide to meet the special educational needs of gifted and talented students."[28] Giftedness and talent do not know cultural or socioeconomic limits. Children from every demographic possess these characteristics, and K–12 teachers are mandated to make special accommodations to meet their needs within the classroom.

A major problem that has been identified in studying American classrooms in the last few years is that in our attempts to meet the needs of struggling students as well as students with learning disabilities, we have often overlooked the needs of about 3 million gifted and talented students in the American classrooms.[29] Gifted and talented students are diverse and varied in their intellectual, emotional, linguistic, and cultural backgrounds, and like the students with disabilities, they require specific instructional programs and materials that target them at their own levels.[30]

A learner-centered classroom must be structured to address the needs of gifted and talented students at the same time that we are meeting the needs of struggling students and students with disabilities. A number of areas where differentiation has to be made for gifted and talented students in a reading class have been identified by Wood as assessment, grouping, acceleration, enrichments, opportunities for discussion, challenging literature, critical reading, creative reading, and inquiry reading.[31] Whether in reading or any other subject areas, differentiation has to be made in assessment, grouping, provision of enrichment materials and resources, opportunities for creativity, originality, and critical thinking, The learner's thinking skills and creativity have to be continuously challenged, depending on their areas of giftedness and talent. These students must be allowed to think outside the box. In fact, all children need to be empowered to think outside the box.

LEARNER-CENTERED PEDAGOGY IN CLASSROOMS WITH EXCEPTIONAL CHILDREN

A fundamental principle that should underlie teaching in a classroom with exceptional students is diagnostic instruction. Just as a medical doctor is not expected to prescribe treatment for an illness until the illness has been properly diagnosed, teachers should not teach until they have properly diagnosed the academic, emotional, and intellectual levels of their students.

Diagnostic instruction can be visualized in the form of an isosceles triangle. Each of the three sides of the isosceles triangle is equal and important. The three parts are assessment, planning, and instruction. Diagnostic instruction begins with assessment, which allows the teacher to know who the students are, what they already know, and what they are ready to learn. Then the teacher plans the instruction using the collected data and appropriate curriculum. The learning is delivered using appropriate strategies and instructional resources that would communicate to the identified needs. Assessment is done again to determine what the students have learned, and the cycle begins all over again (see figure 11.1).

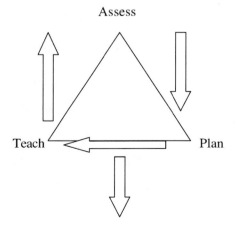

Figure 11.1.
Cycle of Diagnostic Instruction

There are six essential steps to this idea of diagnostic instruction. These six steps include (1) knowing the students, (2) knowing the curriculum, (3) planning appropriate instructional and assessment activities for the students, (4) making appropriate adaptations for the exceptional students and struggling students, (5) planning and implementing appropriate assessment and evaluations of the students and the teaching activities, and (6) constructively reflecting on one's practice as a teacher.

Know the Students

The principle behind this step is that in a learner-centered classroom, the teacher does not plan instruction for a hypothetical group of students; neither does he or she plan for the average student. The teacher plans instruction with a thorough knowledge of his or her classroom demographics. The teacher asks, "Who are my students? What issues and concerns are they dealing with that could enhance or interfere with this instructional activity?"

Knowledge of the students should include their names and faces, but also their cultural and linguistic backgrounds, ability levels in relation to the academic content, and issues that they are dealing with in relation to emotional, physical, and social concerns. What health and other personal issues are they dealing with? What extracurricular activities are they involved in? Admittedly, this level of knowledge is more easily gained in a self-contained K–6 classroom than in a departmentalized classroom setting in grades 7–12, yet some secondary level teachers have successfully done this.

For the exceptional child, the teacher should be familiar with their specific disabilities or giftedness and ensure to put those into consideration in planning instruction.

For all students, learner-centered teaching requires that we know their strengths, abilities, and giftedness.

Know the Content Area

Content area knowledge not only demonstrates the teacher's professional competency, it also demonstrates respect for the learners. Content area knowledge requires thorough knowledge of the subject matter in question. Beyond subject matter knowledge, the teacher also needs to know the academic content standards and frameworks the subject in question is supposed to address.

The era of English-language majors who teach mathematics and arts majors who teach chemistry and physics must come to an end if the educational setting is to value and respect the learners. Teachers must not be just a few chapters ahead of their students in subject matter knowledge. They need to possess a measurable degree of expertise in the subject they teach.

Instructional Planning in a Learner-Centered Classroom

Instructional planning involves a detailed outline of the learning that a teacher expects to take place in the lesson. The detailed plan must address the standards, goals and objectives, anticipatory sets, and instructional input, which includes vocabulary development. It must include guided practice and independent practice, and finally assessment.[32]

In learner-centered teaching the appropriate strategies and principles are used to connect students to the learning content and assist them to interact and retain the material. There must be a connectedness between the identified academic content standards, the instructional content, the grade level, the identified student needs, and the established academic goals or objectives for the lesson. The instructional plan should include appropriate student activities and student groupings, as well as ways of properly communicating the teacher's expectations for the lessons. Good instructional planning also involves proper time allocation for the different activities in the lessons, including guided and independent activities.

Make Adaptations

In a learner-centered classroom, the teacher is efficient in adapting lessons to meet the specific needs of the different students represented in the classroom. The scope of the adaptation would vary depending on class demographics. A classroom with English-language learners would require adaptations that address the needs and levels of these students. If the classroom has special needs students, adaptations are made to accommodate their needs as well. The same applies for students who are gifted.

The nature of the adaptations would also vary. Adaptations can be made on content material. Some students are able to handle grade-level content material, but there may be other students who need only some exposure to grade-level material while their actual instruction would be below grade level. Some students may require modifications in terms of volume of work, while others would require modification in the amount of time needed to complete the work. Some gifted students may need above-grade-level content to be challenged, while others may require analytical or investigative activities to keep them interested, engaged, and learning.

A learner-centered classroom does not operate on a one-size-fits-all model. It is the ideal context for differentiated instruction. In such an environment the teacher becomes a facilitator of learning, while students and the learning content take the central focus. Learning and instruction takes place within students' zone of proximal development.

Engage in Continuous Assessment and Evaluation

Learner-centered teaching relies heavily on an ongoing practice of assessment, which in turn informs instruction. New topics are not introduced without the teacher taking time to assess the prior knowledge students are bringing to the topic, which will necessarily inform what is taught. When the teacher is aware of the prior knowledge students are bringing to a topic, care is taken to avoid repetitions and pertinent aspects of the subject in question that need to be addressed in depth are clearer. Formative assessments are also planned and implemented to continuously monitor what students are learning so as to be sure the pacing is appropriate, and no one is left behind. When a topic is completed, summative assessment is administered to determine how well the students learned the topic, and to determine their readiness level to move on to the next topic. When assessment drives instruction in this fashion, teachers can easily measure their students' skills and ability levels, as they can use feedback from multiple sources of performance-based assessments and standardized tests to make judgments on students' abilities, rather than rely on one snapshot of data from standardized testing.

Reflect on Practice

The final step in a learner-centered instructional practice is personal reflection on one's teaching practices. A learner-centered teacher focuses attention on personal evaluation and reflection on planning, instruction, and assessment practices. The teacher does not see a unit of study as finished until he or she has taken the time to reflect on what was done in the planning, teaching, and assessments that were all parts of the unit. The teacher is continuously asking such questions as, "What did I do at the planning stage, instructional stage, and assessment stages?" "Why did I do what I did?" "How effective were strategies and activities that I implemented?" and "What do I need to do differently the next time I am teaching a similar unit?"

The teacher is supposed to be a reflective practitioner. Part of this reflective practice should focus on how the needs of the various individuals within the classroom community are being met. A learner-centered teacher knows the students using a variety of assessments, plans for the specific needs, makes adaptations to address those needs, and reflects on how effective the planning and adaptations are in meeting the identified needs.

~

QUESTIONS AND ACTIVITIES

Case Study: Working with an Exceptional Student

Background

You are a fourth-grade teacher at Walkman Elementary School. Your school is populated mostly by Hispanic and Asian students. Mike Medina is a student in your class. Mike has been recently identified to have Attention Deficit Hyperactivity Disorder (ADHD). Whereas Mike is maintaining an average level of academic achievement, you are aware that he can achieve better. You have patiently worked with Mike and his mother, who recently confessed to you that she was diagnosed with ADD as an adult, having suffered through all kinds of mistreatment and disregard in her schools days, since neither her, her parents, nor her teachers knew what was wrong with her.

Challenge

On Valentine's Day, as was the practice in many schools, your students exchanged Valentine's Day cards, and everything seemed normal. The following day, Mike's mother shows up in class with all the cards Mike received the previous day. She gives back the cards to you with tears in her eyes and asks you to read them. As you read through the cards you are shocked to notice that more than two-thirds of the cards contain negative words and insults to Mike. These students, who did not understand why Mike was always hyperactive and often played rough during recess, were basically telling him how they hated his behavior and manners. Unfortunately, these regular-education students have no idea that Mike suffers.

Follow-Up Questions

1. What will you say to Mike's mother?
2. What will you say to Mike?
3. What will you say to your students?
4. What lessons and/or activities would you develop to address the problem of tolerance, lack of empathy, and the need to understand and respect differences in your classroom?

Review Questions

1. How would you define exceptional children?
2. Use a Venn diagram to illustrate the similarities and differences that exist between students who are gifted and talented and those who are handicapped.
3. Distinguish between the IDEA and section 504.
4. Discuss the circumstances under which ADHD, which typically belongs to section 504, could qualify for IDEA.
5. Define *response to intervention* (RTI). Discuss how it differs from individualized education plan (IEP).

Strategies for Application in the K–12 Classrooms

1. Grades K–12: Identify specific students in your class with disabilities, who may not have IEPs. These could be students with ADD or ADHD or students who are simply below grade level. Develop a plan of action that identifies their challenges and struggles. Identify the subject matter where they are weakest and develop a plan of action to remediate learning for them. Make weekly lesson plans that target particular students in specific subject matter areas and provide appropriate accommodation that would make the subject matter accessible and comprehensible to them.
2. Grades K–12: Discuss with your class the role nondisabled students can play to make life at school more comfortable for disabled students. Identify things and events in class that may distract the attention of students with ADD and ADHD and discuss how to remediate them to help these students learn. Discuss physical obstacles that may interfere in the abilities of other students with disabilities to learn and discuss what the class can do to remediate these situations.

Chapter Twelve

Standards-Based Planning and Teaching in a Multicultural Classroom

Chapter Objectives:

This chapter provides a step-by-step approach to planning and teaching a multicultural lesson. It provides model multicultural lessons and other resources needed by K–12 teachers. Readers will be able to:

1. describe Banks's four levels of multicultural education
2. explain the seven-step lesson plan and vital elements needed in each section to plan a multicultural lesson
3. define *social action objective*, and be able to articulate an example for a given lesson
4. create a social action project as a culminating activity for a multicultural lesson plan

STANDARDS-BASED PLANNING AND TEACHING

This chapter attempts to present practical steps to planning and teaching multicultural lessons in the K–12 classrooms. The American educational setting has seen a major push toward standards-based instruction, pacing of instructions, and benchmark assessments. This movement, which has been fast-tracked by the "No Child Left Behind" Act of 2001, has changed the educational culture in America. There has come to be a tension between the standards movement and multicultural education. The tension between the standards movement and the multicultural education movement is only one of the oppositions facing the future of education today. According to Thompson, "One thing the standards movement will never be accused of is a lack of critical opposition."[1] Some educators and critics tend to see an irreconcilable polarity between the standards movement and the multicultural education movement. A question that must be addressed, however, is whether such polarity must exist. Thompson argues that there is a mistaken assumption that authentic standards-based reforms and test-based reforms are one and the same thing. He defines authentic standards-based reform as "fundamentally concerned with equity," and radically departs from tracking and what he calls, the "factory-style school,"[2] which is evident in test-based reforms. Standards-based instruction, distinct from test-based reform can, therefore, be defined as *instructional practices that anchor on a state-approved guide, which outlines essential learning and curriculum content for every grade level from Kindergarten to twelfth grade.* A lot of the resistance that has been rightly directed toward the standards movement arises as a reaction against the accompanying standardized tests, and reasons for such resistance are many, among which are: (1) the fact that standardized tests are inaccurate measures of learning and (2) standardized testing hijacks instruction and converts it to test preparation instead of real learning for students.[3] It is difficult to argue against the standardization of learning and curriculum alone, a necessary evil that has become part of the school system as we experience more and more governmental involvement. The possibility of pursuing standards at the expense of real individual needs of students is what makes it a little more difficult for many educators to accept.

One of the fundamental points of confusion in understanding standards-based instruction is the assumption that it suggests a one-size-fits-all approach to teaching. Several research projects cited by Wang and Odell provide a variety of ways for looking at standards-based teaching. They cited Romberg, Cobb, and Cohen as presenting standards-based instruction as student-centered instruction that focuses on progressive ideas and constructivist ideas of learning and constructing knowledge; as active sense-making by students; and as collaborative inquiry. According to them, knowledge is seen as "consisting of cultural artifacts constructed by individuals and groups."[4] If these ideas of standards-based instruction are to be taken seriously, one can logically argue that there might be a positive relationship that exists between standards-based instruction and multicultural education, contrary to the general perception.

According to Beverly Falk, standards-based instruction and assessments sometimes can stimulate teachers and their students to "get clear about their purposes, to develop coherent goals for learning, and to make use of a range of instructional strategies to support students' varying approaches to learning."[5] A more appropriate argument is that high standards, when required for all, may make it possible to invest resources into providing assistance to those who need extra help.[6]

The argument must be presented, however, that despite the possible symbiotic relationship that may be found between the standards-based instructional reform and the multicultural education movement, multicultural education seems to have suffered grave casualties in states where the standards-based reform movement has been the strongest. One of the fundamental issues that have often crippled the implementation of multicultural education in today's classrooms is time for another "subject." Many teachers and school administrators look at the idea of multicultural education as the inroad of a new subject into the school curriculum. This perception of multicultural education is based on the forms multicultural education has traditionally taken in schools.

James Banks presented four levels of multicultural education: contributions, additive, transformational, and social action approaches. According to him, the first level deals with heroes, holidays, and discrete cultural elements. Teachers conveniently infuse cultural issues like holidays and heroes into their curriculum. Banks refers to this approach as the easiest approach for teachers to integrate multicultural content into their curriculum, but one may argue against that assumption, because amid the contemporary standards-based instructions, "scripted teaching," "pacing," and "benchmarking," it is more and more difficult to integrate cultural contributions and holidays into the main curriculum unless it comes with the scripted teaching package.

At the second level, additive approach, teachers add content, concepts, themes, and perspectives that are multicultural without changing the structure of their instructional materials, infusing multicultural themes, contents and perspectives into the main curriculum. When many teachers do this, it often involves worksheets and reading materials on specific cultural activities related to the main topic being taught. The problem with this approach is that whereas it may work perfectly well in history and social studies or language classes, it may be hard to do in mathematics, science, and other technical classes. In mathematics and science classrooms you may see multicultural games used to teach mathematics or science concepts, for example, mankala (also called Okwe), an African game used in teaching addition, subtraction, and multiplication. When such games are used, their multicultural emphases are often lost, as nothing is done or said to connect the activity to the culture from which it originated.

The contemporary standards-based curriculum is crammed with lots of reading, writing, and arithmetic, as schools are struggling to meet the various state academic standards as well as score high on high-stakes tests. It is known that local schools should hold the power on how they constitute and deliver instruction.[7] With the standards movement and its accompanying evils of pacing and scripted teaching, that right and power has been significantly taken away from schools; requiring them to spend extra time teaching heroes and holidays, as well as multicultural games is to require the impossible from them. Added to the lack of time and space in the curriculum is the fact that the first two approaches have little or no value in transforming students' worldview or enhancing cultural appreciation, respect and tolerance. The first two approaches are superficial, and they place lots of demands on teaching time and curriculum space.

In this age of standards-based instruction and assessments, any attempt to implement multicultural education, which follows the first level, will require a significant curriculum adjustment, as teachers would be required to teach heroes, holidays, and cultural events outside of the state academic content standards. Some types of academic activities that take place as a part of the cultural emphasis program are done as extracurricular activity rather than as part of the academic curriculum. Other times it is done as part of the academic curriculum but with the use of worksheets that have little or no connection to the academic standards. It is indeed an additional piece of work that many teachers don't have time and resources to undertake, given the pressures they face now. The second level is an improvement over the first, but it remains significantly insufficient for today's classroom, as many schools are demanding that all learning activities be tied to the academic content standards. Thus, even if the multicultural activity would be relevant and helpful to students, if it is not clearly tied to the standards, teachers would be reluctant to have their supervisors walk in on them doing an activity that they cannot readily link to the standards.

The last two approaches—the transformation approach, and the social action approach, do not necessarily require a separate curriculum. According to Banks, in these two approaches, "ethnic content is added to the mainstream core curriculum without changing its basic assumptions, nature, and structure."[8] It is also at these two levels that we can see the possibility of integrating standards-based instruction and multicultural education. First, let's look at the two levels. The transformation approach requires teachers to change the structure of their curriculum to enable students to engage concepts, issues, events, and themes from a multicultural perspective. Here teachers use the mainstream subject areas like mathematics, the arts, language, and literature to acquaint students with the ways the common U.S. culture and society has "emerged from a complex synthesis and interaction of the diverse cultural elements that originated within the various cultural, racial, ethnic, and religious groups that make up U.S. society."[9] Here students engage and critique issues and concepts that deal with diversity and social justice. They learn to take a stand.

Banks's fourth level of multicultural education, *the social action approach*, "allows students to make decisions on important social issues and take actions to help solve them."[10] The last two approaches are best implemented by weaving culture appreciation and cultural awareness issues into the existing curriculum: mathematics, language arts, history/social studies, and science. Using this approach, the teachers are able to teach the standards, follow whatever pacing guides are stipulated by their districts, while teaching equity and social justice without having to look for extra time in their day to teach multicultural awareness.

It is in the planning of their instruction for the basic subjects that teachers are able to weave in multicultural education. A legitimate question that follows would be: "How can we do this?" In the section that follows we will explore how teachers can develop standards-based lessons across various disciplines and weave in multicultural education effectively. The fact that this can be done, and the fact that instruction can be delivered at the highest level of cultural integration, makes it a better approach, as it could prove to be the most effective and yet least time-consuming approach to teaching both standards and multicultural education. It does not require separate time for planning and teaching.

LESSON PLANNING FOR THE
MULTICULTURAL CLASSROOM

Lesson planning in a multicultural classroom needs to depart from the exclusively traditional subject matter focus to a broader view of the need of the classroom community. The basic steps for preparing a lesson often vary from one teacher to the other, one teacher education institute to another, yet the basic elements required remain the same.

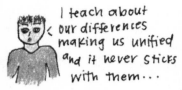 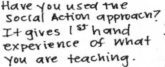

Figure 12.1.   Chat

There are seven steps that would be found in any standard lesson plan; the order may vary, but the content remains the same: (1) goals and objectives, (2) materials and resources, (3) anticipatory set or entry, (4) instructional input, (5) guided practice, (6) independent practice, and (7) assessment/evaluation. Using these steps we will explore ways to integrate multicultural education into standards-based instructional planning and teaching.

Step 1: Goals and Objectives

For a standards-based lesson plan in the state of California, for example, teachers should familiarize themselves with two basic tools. The goals should usually be derived from the state academic content standards, which address the concepts being taught, and the state framework for that subject matter. These are two separate but closely related documents. Oftentimes the two are combined in one volume, but they are nevertheless two separate entities. The framework provides guidelines and "research-based approaches" for implementing the standards. It is an organized approach to implementing the standards from kindergarten to twelfth grade. The standards, however, provide the required learning and curriculum content needed for each grade level. The two combine to make for a standards-based curriculum.

For a standards-based instruction, the standards remain the first point of call. Both national and state standards, for example, California Academic Content Standards, provide us with the broad and specific goals to be pursued in every lesson. Assume that a California art teacher wants to teach art critique and analysis to her seventh-grade class. Let's plan the lesson for her.

Goals and Standards Statement

The lesson is anchored on seventh-grade California academic content standards for visual and performing arts, standard 4.0 (aesthetic valuing), which reads: *"Students analyze, assess, and derive meaning from works of art, in-cluding their own, according to the elements of art, the principles of design, and aesthetic qualities."*

Let's narrow our focus down to substandard 4.2, which reads: "Analyze the form (how a work of art looks) and content (what a work of art com-municates) of works of art." The standards provide us with the goal of the lesson, which specifies where this lesson is going, yet the teacher is required to isolate certain measurable objectives that would convince him or her at the end of this lesson that the destination was reached. This refers to the learning objectives.

Learning Objectives

In a multicultural classroom there is a need to ensure that objectives consider cognitive as well as affective domains of learning.[11] The objective is what the teacher articulates as his or her expectations from students in relation to the stated goals, and it is here that the teacher articulates any multicultural and behavioral objective he or she wants to achieve through this lesson. In keeping with Banks's third and fourth levels of multicultural education, the objectives here must not only be measurable, they must have transforma-tional and social action focus.

The task of the teacher is to teach a standards-based lesson, cleverly in-fusing multicultural education in such a way that students' worldviews are not only transformed, but they are led to do something to positively impact the world around them. What is social action? Banks explains: "When you identify concepts and generalizations, you should select those that will help students make decisions and take personal, social, or civic actions that re-duce prejudice and discrimination in their personal lives, in the school, and, when possible, in the other social settings in which they function."[12]

Social action, therefore, is an action that is taken with the objective of enhancing the social status of another person or group of persons. Whatever thing we do to enhance the social status of another person or group is a so-cial action. A social action objective, therefore, is an objective that aims at enhancing an individual's or group's social status.

In the case of this art lesson, this teacher may want to state the following academic objective: *"Students will be able to create a collage of pictures representing the theme of homelessness, and subsequently identify the thoughts and feelings associated with each art work."* Homelessness is in itself a social as well as a multicultural issue, as it addresses a people's group within the larger society. The homeless represent marginal life and destitution. However, the objective does not contain any social action. Should the lesson end here, the academic goal would be fully met, but the multicultural impact will be very minimal. To take it to the higher level, a second objective may need to be added: "*After identifying the thoughts and feelings that those homeless scenes represent, students will list positive actions society can take to engage and mediate those feelings and thoughts, and the problem of homelessness in general.*"

The second objective brings in transformation, as students are led to critically engage the topic in question and propose solutions. However, there is no explicit social action yet. To bring in the social action part of the objective, let's add that "*Students will hold an exhibition of their art work on homelessness and the suggested strategies that can be used in addressing it. This may assist people to begin to adjust their attitudes toward the homeless.*" Thus, a simple art lesson can produce change of attitude and a changed society. This is social action.

The goal and objective parts of a lesson may be considered the most crucial part, as time needs to be spent articulating its academic and social objectives and merging them in one lesson plan. One of the areas teachers may face challenges in is articulating a valid social action for primary-grade students. In responding to this challenge, Banks argues, "Primary grade students cannot take actions that will reduce discrimination in the larger society. However, they can make a commitment to not tell or laugh at racist jokes, [and] to play with and make friends with students from other racial, ethnic, religious groups."[13] Banks seems to have a narrow view of social action in submitting that primary grades "cannot take social actions." Social action can be undertaken at any grade level. Choosing not to tell or laugh at racist jokes is an action. Primary-grade students have been known to undertake fund raising to help the poor and homeless as well, so they can do social action. According to Taylor and Whittaker, "Once the major goals for implementing a change process have been chosen and prioritized, the steps for achieving these goals must be delineated."[14] A plan of action thus may involve reference to the time and place of the action, such as the next classroom, the assembly ground, or the community or neighborhood. This specific detail is not expected to be part of the objectives statement. It is usually best presented as part of the independent practice. Moving on from goals and objectives, therefore, let's go to the next level.

Step Two: Materials Needed

The materials that will be needed for this lesson would include poster boards, magazines and newspapers (which will have pictures of the homeless from different genders and ethnicities), glue sticks, markers, pens and pencils, and paper to write with.

Step Three: Anticipatory Set or Entry

This step is often called "entry," as it excites, arouses interest in, and prepares the students for the learning experience. A good reading that can accomplish these for this lesson and provoke student curiosity about the homeless or art appreciation can be selected. Kathleen Krull's *Lives of the Artists: Masterpieces, Messes (and What the Neighbors Thought)*, could make a good anticipatory. The story is read and briefly discussed, and the teacher quickly transitions into the lesson. Another form of anticipatory may be to preview the lesson by checking to know what the students already know on the topic so as to avoid repeating what they already know.

One good way is to use the KWL chart. This chart asks students for what they already know on the subject (K), what they want to know about the subject (W), and what they have learned (L). The good thing about the KWL chart is that it serves as an anticipatory as well as a way to summarize and assess learning. In this case, students can tell what they already know about collages, the homeless, and so on. They can state what they want to learn about each of the concepts to be addressed. At the end they will summarize what they learned in terms of art analysis and critique, as well as the homeless.

Step Four: Instructional Input

This is the place where the teacher presents and explains basic concepts, definitions, and clarifications students need to comprehend the lesson. Here is where new concepts are introduced. According to Barba, decisions about your instructional strategies need to depend on the characteristics of your students, information to be learned, and your goals and objectives.[15] This is the right place to specify what scaffolds you intend to use in delivering instruction to special needs students or English learners as you plan.

For this lesson, the teacher will need to define and explain such words as *collage*, *homelessness*, and *aesthetic valuing*. Word study (along with pictures) may be additional scaffolds for students who are English learners. The teacher will need to present a variety of collages for illustration and to explain to students how pulling together different shapes and forms that were otherwise unrelated created the collages. The teacher could separate the various parts of a collage to demonstrate to students what a collage means and how they are formed.

Now the teacher needs to demonstrate the process involved in making collages by starting a collage from scratch and finishing it as students watch. This is called modeling. After the demonstration, the first part of the direct instruction has ended.

Step Five: Guided Practice

Here, the teacher hands the students a set of arts activity materials containing blank paper and cut-out parts of various magazines. Each student would have the same set of items. The teacher will then lead them to make a collage, giving them step-by-step direction. The instructions on the activity can also be typed up and given to individual students. The teacher walks around, making sure everyone is following the instructions. He or she ensures that each step is clear and comprehensible to everyone. When everyone has completed that task, the teacher leads them through a discussion of the art principles (form and content) as well as social/multicultural issues represented by the collages they have made. The teacher models for them how to analyze a piece of art and how to decipher their hidden messages. He or she models all these for the students so that the whole process is clear to them.

Given the fact that the homeless present the object of analysis and critique, a discussion of the hidden messages in the art piece would reveal the plight of the homeless and the social questions it would provoke. This way, the discussion of the multicultural objectives of this course is not pursued outside of the scope of the lesson's academic goals and objectives—form and content of art.

Step Six: Independent Practice

At this point, the students have fully experienced the process of making collages as well as deciphering the hidden messages through analysis and critique. They have also discussed the social implications of the feeling aroused by homelessness and how the art pieces portray them. Now they are going to create their own unique collages of homelessness and use them to communicate unique messages about homelessness. It will be the task of classmates to decipher the message contained in other classmates' artwork as they work in pairs or small groups to analyze their works. Part of the independent practice may be to work individually or in small groups to produce collages that would present positive ways to respond to the feelings and faces of hopelessness in the homeless.

It could also be a written piece that analyzes the feelings and thoughts. The two pieces of work can then be published to the public (which could be school community, school bulletin board, open house day, community center, etc.) for viewing. Now social action is completed. The message has been communicated outside the classroom.

Step Seven: Assessment and Evaluation

At this point, the teacher may choose to require a written piece of analysis of at least one piece of art from each student. Each assessment may be placed beside the artist's own piece of communicative intent, and the success may depend on how closely the critic comes to the artist's communicative intent. The evaluation may also be anchored on the exhibition. Written comments can be solicited from viewers, and such comments would indicate whether the artists were successful in presenting the two views of homelessness through their works of art or not.

Lesson Extension

Extending the lesson beyond visual and performing arts, a language arts lesson can be developed for the same seventh-grade classroom with the following goals and objectives:

Standard: Students will write a summary of a reading material—California seventh-grade academic content standard 2.5.

Objective: Students will identify and write the main idea of the story "Bums in the Attic" from the book *The House on Mango Street,* with supporting details.

Social action: Students will go to neighborhood grocery stores and solicit enough supplies to make 101 lunches for the homeless. The supplies will be donated to a homeless shelter.

ANOTHER EXAMPLE OF A
STANDARDS-BASED MULTICULTURAL LESSON

Racial Percentage

Grade: 5

I. Goals and Objectives:

Goal: Standard 1.3. (Data Analysis) —Use fractions and percentages to compare data sets of different sizes.

Objective:

- Students will search information online regarding American racial distribution.
- Students will research the Internet for the racial makeup of their city.
- Students will discuss the racial makeup of their city and identify ethnicities that are absent or inadequately represented in their city. They will explore ways to attract these minorities to their neighborhood to make for more diversity.
- The class will write a letter to the mayor of their city presenting their suggestions on how to attract other ethnicities to their community. The list will also be taken to the city library and posted for public reading.

II. Materials:

- Basic instructional tools (e.g., overhead projector, compass, protractor).
- Computers with online access.
- Textbook—Chapter 7.6, "Exploring Percents" of *Passport to Algebra and Geometry.*

III. Anticipatory:

Teacher will read the story, *Nino's Pizzeria.*

IV. Instructional Input:

Teacher will first teach students on how to convert between fraction, decimal, and percentage. Then teacher will do a poll and find out about classroom students' racial distribution and use percentage to present the data collected in a list and in a pie chart.

V. Guided Practice:

Teacher will guide students to take a poll of the entire student population and break them down to percentages to show the ethnic distribution.

Then they will search online about the racial distribution of a U.S. city of their choice, find out the percentage of each race in that city and draw a pie chart. (They might start to notice that America is a mixed pot and that sometimes it is not easy to clearly indicate which race one person belongs to; some useful websites are www.itc.virginia.edu/research/splus/graphlets/map.html and www.psc.isr.umich.edu/census2000/subject/choices-max.html.)

VI. Independent/Group Activities:

Groups of students will research the Internet for the demographics of their city and report to the class on the ethnic makeup of their city in fractions and percentages. The following day, using their research results, students will work in groups to compare the percentage of each racial group in their city to that of different U.S. cities. They will discuss why certain populations are missing in their city, and others only lightly represented. Issues like equal housing opportunities law, housing segregation, and economic opportunities will be discussed. Each group will devise ways to attract the underrepresented group to their city. This list will be sent to the mayor of their city and taken to the city library and posted for public reading.

VII. Evaluation/Assessment:

- The homework will be graded in the next class session to see if students get the math concepts.
- Students will share their project's findings on the racial distribution of a U.S. city in a list and in a pie chart in groups of four. Each student will be graded by teacher and also by peers on their online project's final product.
- The list of polarizing issues in our city and things that can be done to combat them will merge into one whole class project before it is published. The success of this work will inform the teacher on the success of collaborative activities as well as students' ability to engage sensitive social issues and find solutions to them.

~

QUESTIONS AND APPLICATION

Case Study

Background

Norton Elementary School in South Hollywood was committed to educating students about cultural diversity. They have always celebrated the cultural holidays in a big way. This year the plan was to celebrate *Cinco de Mayo* in a special way. They invited a *folklorico* dance group from Baja California to come to the school and perform during a special assembly for the occasion. Students and teachers had a great time dancing and interacting with the special dance group that most of them were unfamiliar with.

The Challenge

During this special assembly no attempt was made to explain to the students and the audience of interested parents what *Cinco de Mayo* celebration was all about. No attempt was made to explain the history and significance of the *folklorico* dance in the Mexican culture. No attempt was made to address the issue of Mexican immigration challenges in the United States, either at the assembly or in the classrooms. Apart from the entertainment from the performance, nothing was done to highlight the values and challenges the Mexican culture presents to the United States.

Follow-Up Questions

1. What level of multicultural education would you say the activity represented?
2. What are the different ways the *folklorico* group would have been utilized to make multicultural education more in-depth and possibly reach the transformation and social action levels at this school?
3. What other activities could have been carried out at this school that would have been even more effective than inviting the *folklorico* group?

Review Questions

1. Describe the four levels of multicultural education according to James Banks.

2. Compare and contrast the transformation level and the social action level.
3. Define a social action objective. Distinguish a social action objective from a regular academic objective.
4. Select any standard lesson from either the Internet or other source and articulate a social action objective that can fit that lesson.

Strategies for Application in the K–12 Classrooms

Here are some social action projects that can be used across disciplines and grade levels in the K–12 classrooms:

1. Grades 7–12, for lessons on discrimination, students can write papers or make collages of actions that can be taken to engage discrimination and can display them in conspicuous place at the school.
2. Grades K–12, students can develop plans for peaceful engagement of a current social problem. The entire class can implement the plan.
3. Grades 4–12, language arts, Spanish language, or history and social studies lessons can deal with biographies of Latinos, African Americans, Jews, and non-Western Europeans. Each student can make a pictorial biography of one of the characters studied, and the class work can be posted on the school bulletin board.
4. Grades 7–12, a physical education lesson on soccer can focus on the HIV/AIDS issue in Brazil or Africa, homes of the game of soccer, and engage students to become actively involved in combating this disease.
5. K–12, a language arts lesson can use the story of Jackie Robinson as its context either for reading comprehension, literary analysis, or other forms of language arts activities. This will provide the forum for discussing discrimination. Students can write papers, draw pictures, or make posters on their personal experiences of unfair treatment: being picked last in a game, or being left out altogether.
6. Grades 9–11, language arts lessons can focus on an analysis of recent court rulings involving civil rights, such as a recent U.S. Supreme Court ruling that strengthened and expanded the rights of cities and counties to enforce the "eminent domain" laws. The class can discuss these rulings and use notes from their discussions to write an open letter to their city, county, or state leaders expressing their personal opinions on those rulings.

Glossary

14th Amendment: An amendment to the U.S. Constitution, ratified in 1868, defining national citizenship and forbidding the states to restrict the basic rights of citizens to minorities and women.

19th Amendment: An amendment to the U.S. Constitution, ratified in 1920, guaranteeing women the right to vote.

abolition movement: An 1800s movement toward bringing an end to the practice of slavery.

Academic Performance Index (API): A measurement in California of academic performance and progress of individual schools in California using students' scores in standardized test.

AIDS (Acquired Immune Deficiency Syndrome): A severe immunological disorder caused by the retrovirus HIV, resulting in a defect in cell-mediated immune response that is manifested by increased susceptibility to opportunistic infections and to certain rare cancers, especially Kaposi's sarcoma. It is transmitted primarily by exposure to contaminated body fluids, especially blood and semen.

American Woman Suffrage Association (AWSA): An organization in the U.S. during the 19th century, which pursued the right of women to vote and be voted for.

Anne Hutchinson: English-born American colonist and religious leader (1591–1643) who was banished from Boston (1637) for her religious beliefs, which included an emphasis on personal intuition as a means toward salvation.

anti-Catholic sentiments: Negative sentiments and treatment of Roman Catholics.

anti-defamation leagues (ADLs): International nongovernmental organizations based in the United States and committed to civil rights.

antinomianism: The doctrine or belief that the Gospel frees Christians from required obedience to any law, whether scriptural, civil, or moral, and that salvation is attained solely through faith and the gift of divine grace. This was regarded as heretical by the mainstream Christian community.

antisemitism: Discrimination against or prejudice or hostility toward Jews.

Anti-Slavery Society: An abolitionist society founded by William Lloyd Garrison and Arthur Tappan.

assimilation: The process by which a person or persons acquire the social and psychological characteristics of a group in order to fit in and become part of the group.

atheism: The doctrine or belief that there is no God or gods.

at risk: Children who have the predisposition based on biological, environmental, social, or economic factors toward disabilities.

attention deficit hyperactivity disorder (ADHD): A condition characterized by inattention, hyperactivity, and impulsiveness.

autism: A pervasive developmental disorder characterized by severe deficits in social interaction and communication, often resulting in an extremely limited range of activities and interests, and often the presence of repetitive, stereotyped behaviors.

basic interpersonal communication skills (BICS): Strategies by which English language learners acquire English language skills through social interactions.

bias: A personal and often unreasoned judgment for or against one side in a dispute, or against an ethnic, cultural, or gender group.

biculturalism: The tendency of individuals within one social setting to possess and function effectively within the norms of two different cultures existing concurrently in the same social setting.

***Brown v. Board of Education of Topeka*:** A landmark decision of the United States Supreme Court that declared state laws establishing separate public schools for black and white students denied black children equal educational opportunities, and was consequently unlawful.

Buddhism: A religion, originated in India by Buddha (Gautama) and later spreading to China, Burma, Japan, Tibet, and parts of southeast Asia, holding that life is full of suffering caused by desire and that the way to end this suffering is through enlightenment that enables one to halt the endless sequence of births and deaths to which one is otherwise subject.

capitalism: An economic system based on a free market, open competition, profit motive and private ownership of the means of production. Capitalism encourages private investment and business, contrary to a government-controlled economy. Investors in private companies called shareholders own the firms. Individuals who invest in private or corporate businesses are known as capitalists.

childhood schizophrenia: A chronic mental illness in which reality is interpreted abnormally (psychosis). Childhood schizophrenia includes split personality, hallucinations, delusions, irrational behavior and thinking, and problems carrying out routine daily tasks, such as bathing.

Cinco de Mayo: May 5, observed by Mexican communities in Latin America and Mexican-American communities in the United States in commemoration of the 1862 defeat of French troops at the Battle of Puebla.

civil rights movement: The national effort made by African Americans and others in the United States and their supporters in the 1950s and 1960s to eliminate segregation and gain equal rights.

cognitive academic language development (CALP): Academic language learning in which learners of English language in the K–12 school setting are taught the grammatical and structural forms of the language in an academic setting, unlike language learned in a social setting.

Confucianism: The system of ethics, education, and statesmanship taught by Confucius and his disciples, stressing love for humanity, ancestor worship, reverence for parents, and harmony in thought and conduct.

Continental Congress: The two legislative congresses during and after the American Revolutionary War. The first was in session from September 5 to October 26, 1774, to petition the British government for a redress of grievances. The second existed from May 10, 1775, to 1789, which issued the Declaration of Independence from Great Britain.

cultural pluralism: The idea of more than one culture coexisting and becoming commonly acceptable by citizens of the same nation. In cultural pluralism, minority groups participate fully in the dominant society; yet maintain their cultural differences, while the dominant group accepts the validity and legitimacy of the other cultures as part of the society.

cultural proficiency: The knowledge, skills, and attitudes/beliefs that enable people to work well with, respond effectively to, and be supportive of people in cross-cultural settings. The ability to function effectively and healthily in a multicultural setting.

cultural values: Values shared and held in esteem by members of a cultural group.

cultural values adjustment: The ability to subject one's personal cultural values to scrutiny and to critique using insights from other cultures and worldviews.

culture: The sum of attitudes, customs, and beliefs that distinguish one group of people from another. Culture is transmitted through language, material objects, rituals, institutions, and art, from one generation to the next.

democracy: A system of government in which power is vested in the people, who rule either directly through village or community meetings or through freely elected representatives.

disability: A disadvantage or deficiency, especially a physical or mental impairment that prevents or restricts normal achievement.

discrimination: Treatment or consideration of individuals based on gender, ethnic, class or other social categories, rather than individual merit.

diversity: The state or fact of being diverse; having differences; or being unlike the other(s).

Down syndrome: A genetic disorder, associated with the presence of an extra chromosome 21, characterized by mild to severe mental retardation, weak muscle tone, a low nasal bridge, and epicanthic folds at the eyelids.

Ebonics: A term used in describing the varieties of non-conventional English language spoken by African Americans in various U.S. communities.

elitism: The belief that certain persons or members of certain classes or groups deserve favored treatment by virtue of their perceived superiority, as in intellect, social status, or financial resources.

equity pedagogy: Using different teaching styles to meet the diverse needs of a diverse population of students in the K-12 educational settings, without allowing the differences in their ethnicity and social backgrounds to become an impediment to their learning opportunities.

ethnicity: Identification with or membership in a particular ethnic or cultural group. This includes observance of that group's customs, beliefs, and possibly the ability to speak the language of that group.

ethnocentric: The tendency to evaluate other groups according to the values and standards of one's own ethnic group, especially with the conviction that one's own ethnic group is superior to the other groups.

evangelicalism: Adherence to evangelical principles or doctrines or to an evangelical church or religious association.

gifted and talented education (GATE): Education opportunities geared towards serving the needs of children who are gifted and talented. These children may not necessarily possess superior intellectual abilities than others, but have natural giftedness that predispose them to achieve above them nor in all or select fields of learning.

glass ceiling: A discriminatory barrier that prevents women and minorities from rising to positions of power or responsibility, as within a corporation. The idea of a glass ceiling suggests that the excluded individuals are able to see the height to which they have the skills to ascend, but their ethnicity or gender becomes the only barrier preventing them from ascending to those heights.

Great Awakening: The series of religious revivals among Protestants in the American colonies with such leading names as Jonathan Edwards and George Whitefield.

hegemony: Control or dominating influence exercised by one group over others in a nation, state, or a confederation.

Hinduism: The common religion of India, based upon the religion of the original Aryan settlers as expounded and evolved in the Vedas, the Upanishads, the Bhagavad-Gita. Hinduism has an extremely diversified character comprising many schools of philosophy and theology, many popular cults, and a large pantheon symbolizing the many attributes of deity or deities.

individualized education program (IEP): An educational plan used in assessment, planning and delivering guided instruction, as well as evaluating the instructional delivery to students with disabilities with the goal of bridging the gap in learning created by their disabilities.

Individual with Disabilities Education Act (IDEA): A U.S. federal law ensuring educational services to children with disabilities throughout the nation.

Islam: The religious faith of Muslims, based on the words and religious system founded by the prophet Muhammad and taught by the Koran, the basic principle of which is absolute submission to a unique and personal god, Allah.

Jim Crow laws: A variety of state and local laws that existed mostly in the Southern states of the United States up to the 1950s with the goal of discriminating against black people and other non-white people.

Judaism: The monotheistic religion of the Jews, having its ethical, ceremonial, and legal foundation in the precepts of the Old Testament and in the teachings and commentaries of the rabbis as found chiefly in the Talmud.

lesbian: A homosexual woman.

macroculture: A cultural system that influences the majority of the people that live in a nation, region, or geographical location.

melting pot ideology: A social ideology that required European immigrants to the United States to assimilate into the Anglo-Saxon Protestant culture that had been established by the early English settlers.

microculture: The distinctive culture of a small group of people shared by a small population within a nation, a limited geographical area, or within an organization such as a school or business.

monogamy: The practice or condition of being married to only one person at a time.

multicultural education: A field of study and an emerging discipline whose major aim is to create equal access to educational opportunities for students from diverse racial, ethnic, social class, and cultural groups.

Nancy Pelosi: The first female Speaker of the United States House of Representatives. Nancy Pelosi represents a San Francisco electoral constituency.

National Association for the Advancement of Colored People (NAACP): An interracial U.S. organization working for political and civil equality of blacks and other non-white people. It was organized in 1910.

new age movements: A collection of Eastern-influenced metaphysical and religious ideologies. It comprises a variation of theologies and philosophies that are bound together by "universal tolerance," secular humanistic principles, and moral relativism.

No Child Left Behind (NCLB): Federal legislation that enacts the theories of standards-based education reform, which is based on the belief that setting high standards and establishing measurable goals can improve individual outcomes in education. The Act requires states to develop assessments in basic skills to be given to all students in certain grades as conditions to receive federal funding for schools.

pedagogy: The study of successful methods for teaching children in the K–12 settings. It includes a clear understanding and articulation of educational objectives and clear and specific strategies for targeting those goals and assessing them.

pluralism: A social system that allows the coexistence and affirmation of various religious, ethnic, racial, and political groups within a single society.

prejudice: A predisposition towards hostile opinion, attitude, and/or treatment of certain persons or class of persons within a social arrangement. Prejudice is socially learned, and often based on misconceptions, misunderstanding, and inflexible generalizations about certain groups of people.

Protestantism: Movement that began in northern Europe in the early sixteenth century as a reaction to medieval Roman Catholic doctrines and practices.

racism: A belief or doctrine that certain inherent differences exist among the various human populations often regarded as races of people. Race is often used to make erroneous generalizations towards group or individual achievement.

Response to Intervention (RTI): A federal government mandate established in 2004 as part of the IDEA reauthorization that requires early intervention for students in the K–12 educational settings who have not been identified as learning disabled, but performing below their grade level expectations.

Rosa Parks: An American civil rights leader. Her refusal to give up her seat on a bus to a white man in Montgomery, Alabama, resulted in a citywide boycott of the bus company and became the fuel that stirred the civil rights movement across the nation.

scaffolds: A temporary platform, either supported from below or suspended from above, on which workers sit or stand when performing tasks at heights above the ground. Instructional scaffolds are temporary supports used in providing instruction and learning opportunities to students who are English language learners. These temporary measures are taken away as the students become more and more competent in English language acquisition.

Section 504: A civil rights law that prohibits discrimination against individuals with disabilities. It mandates states to provide support for students who may not qualify for the IEP but still need support in the educational opportunities.

secular humanism: A set of beliefs that promotes human values without specific allusion to religious doctrines. Secular humanism may, however, be traced to the Greek philosopher Protagoras, who said that "man is the measure of all things, things that are that they are and things that are not that they are not."

social action: Individual or group behavior or activity that involves taking action to address social inequality in society and providing for equity and social justice.

social equity: A social state of affairs in which all people within a specific society have equal access to the resources of the land and the opportunities therein.

Sojourner Truth: American abolitionist and feminist. Born into slavery, she escaped in 1827 and became a leading preacher against slavery and for the rights of women.

specially designed academic instruction in English (SDAIE): A teaching approach intended for teaching various academic contents (such as sciences, social studies, academic language or literature) to learners of English language using pragmatic strategies and practices that bridge the language gap.

state academic content standards: Academic standards established by the state education boards as benchmarks for teaching and learning various subject matter and contents across the grade levels in a given U.S. state.

student study team (SST): A school-based, problem-solving group whose purpose is to assist teachers in identifying and servicing students with learning disabilities and others who may be performing below grade level. They provide assistance to teachers in the areas of instruction, curriculum, and classroom management.

Thurgood Marshall: American jurist who served as an associate justice of the U.S. Supreme Court from 1967 to 1991. As a lawyer for the NAACP Marshall argued thirty-two cases before the Supreme Court, winning twenty-nine of them, including *Brown v. Board of Education of Topeka, Kansas* (1954), which brought about the end of legal segregation in public schools.

values: The ideals, customs, institutions, and practices of a society toward which the people of the group have an affective regard.

women's suffrage: A movement organized to demand the rights of women to vote and to be voted for.

worldviews: The underlying assumptions beneath a cultural system, the overall perspective from which individuals within a cultural arrangement see and interpret their world.

Appendix A

Annotated Bibliography of Multicultural Literature for Grades K–12

Ada, A. F. *My Name Is María Isabel*. New York: Simon & Schuster, 1993.

This is a story about a new girl in school who comes from Puerto Rico. She has a difficult time adjusting to school simply because the teacher changes her name to Mary. It is a story that also captures the authentic flavor of Latino culture, while highlighting the significance of the indigenous names.

Bambara, T. C. "Raymond's Run." In *Best Short Stories—Middle Level*. Ed. Raymond Harris. Providence, RI: Jamestown Publishers, 1983.

This is a short story about a feisty, young girl who is the fastest runner in her neighborhood until a new girl moves in and it is rumored the new girl is faster. The story is about her preparations for the race and how she cares for her older brother who is mentally retarded.

Berry, J. *A Thief in the Village and Other Stories*. New York: Orchard Books, 1987.

James Berry wrote a collection of nine short stories set in Jamaica. The stories involve various youth on different adventures, ranging from a girl who longs to own a bicycle, like the boys in the neighborhood, to another girl's adventures at a coconut farm and a boy's desire to buy shoes for a cricket team.

Bruhac, J. *Many Nations*. New York: Bridge Water Books, 1997.

This is an alphabet book displaying different aspects of the Native American culture.

Bunting, E. *A Day's Work*. New York: Clarion Books, 1994.

This is a story of Mexican immigrants coming to America and trying to find work. It talks about some of the difficulties and fears they face daily, such as not being able to speak English or having to settle for day-to-day jobs and not being able to rely on steady work or income. The book opens the reader's eyes to experiences immigrants face that ordinary Americans may never experience in life.

Bunting, E. *Smoky Night*. San Diego: Harcourt Brace, 1994.

This is a story about an African American family and how they react to a Los Angeles riot. For safety reasons they are taken out of their small apartment to a shelter. While at the shelter, they face racist reactions. The way they handle the situation leads to their making friends at the shelter in the end. This book presents real-life situations and how to work around them.

Bunting, E. *The Wall*. New York: Clarion Books, 1990.

The Vietnam War deeply affected many soldiers and their families. This story illustrates the degree to which the war affected people at a personal level. It's about a young boy and his father who visit the Vietnam War Memorial in Washington, D.C. They search the wall for his grandfather's name. Once they find his name, the boy begins to reflect on all the things he could have done with his grandfather, but couldn't because he is dead. This book presents a different view of the Vietnam War from how U.S. history books present it.

Coles, R. *The Story of Ruby Bridges*. New York: Scholastic, 1995.

This is a true story of the first African American girl who attended an all-white elementary school in New Orleans. It is a story of courage and of breaking culture barriers. She defied the odds of racial prejudices and survived the hatred.

Cosby, B. *Super-Fine Valentine*. New York: Scholastic, 1998.

Little Bill has his first crush and is teased by his family and friends.

Dooley, N. *Everybody Cooks Rice*. New York: Carolrhoda Books, 1991.

Carrie is out in the neighborhood searching for her brother Anthony, who is late for dinner. In her search for her brother, many of her neighbors from different ethnic backgrounds invite her to eat with them and she discovers that they all eat rice.

Fox, M. *Whoever You Are*. New York: Harcourt Brace, 1997.

This story is about celebrating the bonds that unites us through our cultures and through many generations. Despite the differences between people around the world, there are similarities that unite us together such as pain, joy, and love.

Freschet, G. *Beto and the Bone Dance*. New York: Farrar Straus Giroux, 2001.
Beto searches for something special to put on his grandmother's grave for Day of the Dead.

Keats, Ezra J. *Goggles*. New York: Aladdin Books, 1969.
A couple of boys who find an old pair of motorcycle goggles and have to protect their find from some bigger boys who want to take their treasure.

Kricorian, N. *Zabelle: A Novel*. New York: Atlantic Monthly Press, 1998.
This novel, an excellent read for more advanced middle school and high school students, provides a look into the life of Armenian American women who survived the 1915 Armenian Genocide. The story begins with Zabelle, an elderly woman living in Boston, traveling back in time to examine her life in Turkey and the many struggles and triumphs she had experienced.

Herron, C. *Nappy Hair*. New York: Alfred A. Knopf, 1997.
Various people at a backyard picnic offer their comments on a young girl's "nappy" hair, but she discovers its meaning and strength in the African culture, and begins to value it regardless of the racial responses to her.

Lee, J. M. *Ba Nam*. New York: Henry Holt and Company, 1987.
A young Vietnamese girl visits the graves of her ancestors to find the old graves keeper frightening. Later a severe storm reveals the old woman's kindness.

Lowry, L. *Number the Stars*. New York: Bantam, 1989.
This is a story of a ten-year-old girl living in Copenhagen in 1943. It is a story that describes Annemarie's bravery in saving her best friend's life. It is a story of the Danish people who effectively resisted the Nazis and ended up saving the lives of many Jews.

McKissack, P. *Goin' Someplace Special*. New York: Scholastic, 2001.
This story is about a girl who is traveling to a special place. On her way she encounters discrimination, and she is turned away from entering through

the front door of the Grand Music Palace. Tricia Ann is reminded that she is somebody, a human being—no better, no worse than anybody else in this world. She continues her journey to that someplace special where all are welcome.

Meyer, C. *Jubilee Journey*. Orlando. FL: Harcourt Brace, 1997.

This is a tale of an African American woman in the south named Rose Lee. Her great-grandchildren come to visit her and to explore their family roots and history. They learn of the racism their great-grandmother faced throughout her life in the South, and learn that some of the racism still lingers. With vivid imagery, the reader can enter the picturesque, humid landscapes of the South and see the bond develop across the generations of this family as they spend time with one another.

Morris, A. *Bread Bread Bread*. New York: Lothrop, Lee & Shepard, 1989.

All around the world, wherever there is a human being, someone is eating bread. This picture book reveals how different people around the world eat, and some food items that are common across cultures.

Say, A. *Grandfather's Journey*. New York: Houghton Mifflin, 1993.

A Japanese American man recounts his grandfather's journey to America. He later takes a journey of his own to America, and like his grandfather, he feels torn apart by love for two different countries. Both men miss their childhood memories and long for their friends.

Schick, E. *Navajo Wedding Day*. New York: Marshall Cavendish, 1999.

This story is about a young girl who attends the wedding of her best friend's cousin. She learns about the customs and traditions of Navajo Indians living in the American Southwest. The bride's wedding clothes consist of a velvet shirt and satin skirt, silver and turquoise jewelry, and deerskin moccasins. Throughout the story, the young girl learns the significance in each of the rituals and customs of the Navajo wedding ceremony.

Soto, G. *A Summer Life*. Hanover, NH: University Press of New England, 1990.

Gary Soto uses short tales in this book to describe his life growing up as a Chicano in California. The stories take place in his home city of Fresno. He described with detail the things that fill his memory of the city streets that he knew as a child. He paints the pictures of his family, his home, and the images from his life in an elaborate and poetic way. This book celebrates the life and traditions of a Mexican American and is especially relevant for Californian students.

Wangerin, W. Jr. *Probity Jones and the Fear Not Angel*. Minneapolis: Augsburg Fortress, 1996.

Probity Jones was set to be the "Fear Not" angel in the Christmas pageant, until her coat got stolen. On the way home with no coat, she catches a cold and has to miss the pageant. But in the middle of the night, she is visited by the real "Fear Not" Angel and gets to see where Jesus was really born.

Wiesel, E. *Night*. New York: Bantam Books, 1960.

The setting for this book is World War II, as thousands of Jews are being evacuated from their homes, leaving behind their possessions, their jobs and their livelihoods. They work for hours surrounded by Nazi soldiers with no breaks, no food, and no personal considerations. The author describes scenes of the internment camps as well as the horrible conditions they are subjected to while under the watchful eyes of German Nazis. The story is told from a young boy's perspective as he lives through this unspeakable horror. In one part of the book, he describes seeing his own mother and sisters taken away to be killed in the gas chambers. He discusses hardships, struggles, pains and sorrows that scar his young life forever.

Guidance on Constitutionally Protected Prayer in Public Elementary and Secondary Schools, February 7, 2003

INTRODUCTION

Section 9524 of the Elementary and Secondary Education Act ("ESEA") of 1965, as amended by the No Child Left Behind Act of 2001, requires the Secretary to issue guidance on constitutionally protected prayer in public elementary and secondary schools. In addition, Section 9524 requires that, as a condition of receiving ESEA funds, a local educational agency ("LEA") must certify in writing to its State educational agency ("SEA") that it has no policy that prevents, or otherwise denies participation in, constitutionally protected prayer in public schools as set forth in this guidance.

The purpose of this guidance is to provide SEAs, LEAs, and the public with information on the current state of the law concerning constitutionally protected prayer in the public schools, and thus to clarify the extent to which prayer in public schools is legally protected. This guidance also sets forth the responsibilities of SEAs and LEAs with respect to Section 9524 of the ESEA. As required by the Act, this guidance has been jointly approved by the Office of the General Counsel in the Department of Education and the Office of Legal Counsel in the Department of Justice as reflecting the current state of the law. It will be made available on the Internet through the Department of Education's website (www.ed.gov/). The guidance will be updated on a biennial basis, beginning in September 2004, and provided to SEAs, LEAs, and the public.

THE SECTION 9524 CERTIFICATION PROCESS

In order to receive funds under the ESEA, an LEA must certify in writing to its SEA that no policy of the LEA prevents, or otherwise denies participation in, constitutionally protected prayer in public elementary and secondary schools as set forth in this guidance. An LEA must provide this certification to the SEA by October 1, 2002, and by October 1 of each subsequent year during which the LEA participates in an ESEA program. However, as a transitional matter, given the timing of this guidance, the initial certification must be provided by an LEA to the SEA by March 15, 2003.

The SEA should establish a process by which LEAs may provide the necessary certification. There is no specific Federal form that an LEA must use in providing this certification to its SEA. The certification may be provided as part of the application process for ESEA programs, or separately, and in whatever form the SEA finds most appropriate, as long as the certification is in writing and clearly states that the LEA has no policy that prevents, or otherwise denies participation in, constitutionally protected prayer in public elementary and secondary schools as set forth in this guidance.

By November 1 of each year, starting in 2002, the SEA must send to the Secretary a list of those LEAs that have not filed the required certification or against which complaints have been made to the SEA that the LEA is not in compliance with this guidance. However, as a transitional matter, given the timing of this guidance, the list otherwise due November 1, 2002, must be sent to the Secretary by April 15, 2003. This list should be sent to:

Office of Elementary and Secondary Education
Attention: Jeanette Lim
U.S. Department of Education
400 Maryland Avenue, S.W.
Washington, D.C. 20202

The SEA's submission should describe what investigation or enforcement action the SEA has initiated with respect to each listed LEA and the status of the investigation or action. The SEA should not send the LEA certifications to the Secretary, but should maintain these records in accordance with its usual records retention policy.

ENFORCEMENT OF SECTION 9524

LEAs are required to file the certification as a condition of receiving funds under the ESEA. If an LEA fails to file the required certification, or files it in bad faith, the SEA should ensure compliance in accordance with its regular enforcement procedures. The Secretary considers an LEA to have filed a certification in bad faith if the LEA files the certification even though it has a policy that prevents, or otherwise denies participation in, constitutionally protected prayer in public elementary and secondary schools as set forth in this guidance.

The General Education Provisions Act ("GEPA") authorizes the Secretary to bring enforcement actions against recipients of Federal education funds that are not in compliance with the law. Such measures may include withholding funds until the recipient comes into compliance. Section 9524 provides the Secretary with specific authority to issue and enforce orders with respect to an LEA that fails to provide the required certification to its SEA or files the certification in bad faith.

OVERVIEW OF GOVERNING CONSTITUTIONAL PRINCIPLES

The relationship between religion and government in the United States is governed by the First Amendment to the Constitution, which both prevents the government from establishing religion and protects privately initiated religious expression and activities from government interference and discrimination.[1] The First Amendment thus establishes certain limits on the conduct of public school officials as it relates to religious activity, including prayer.

The legal rules that govern the issue of constitutionally protected prayer in the public schools are similar to those that govern religious expression generally. Thus, in discussing the operation of Section 9524 of the ESEA, this guidance sometimes speaks in terms of "religious expression." There are a variety of issues relating to religion in the public schools, however, that this guidance is not intended to address.

The Supreme Court has repeatedly held that the First Amendment requires public school officials to be neutral in their treatment of religion, showing neither favoritism toward nor hostility against religious expression such as prayer.[2] Accordingly, the First Amendment forbids religious activity that is sponsored by the government but protects religious activity that is initiated by private individuals, and the line between government-sponsored and privately initiated religious expression is vital to a proper understanding of the First Amendment's scope. As the Court has explained in several cases, "there is a crucial difference between government speech endorsing religion, which the Establishment Clause forbids, and private speech endorsing religion, which the Free Speech and Free Exercise Clauses protect."[3]

The Supreme Court's decisions over the past forty years set forth principles that distinguish impermissible governmental religious speech from the constitutionally protected private religious speech of students. For example, teachers and other public school officials may not lead their classes in prayer, devotional readings from the Bible, or other religious activities.[4] Nor may school officials attempt to persuade or compel students to participate in prayer or other religious activities.[5] Such conduct is "attributable to the State" and thus violates the Establishment Clause.[6]

Similarly, public school officials may not themselves decide that prayer should be included in school-sponsored events. In *Lee v. Weisman*,[7] for example, the Supreme Court held that public school officials violated the Constitution in inviting a member of the clergy to deliver a prayer at a graduation ceremony. Nor may school officials grant religious speakers preferential access to public audiences, or otherwise select public speakers on a basis that favors religious speech. In *Santa Fe Independent School District v. Doe*,[8] for example, the Court invalidated a school's football game speaker policy on the ground that it was designed by school officials to result in pregame prayer, thus favoring religious expression over secular expression.

Although the Constitution forbids public school officials from directing or favoring prayer, students do not "shed their constitutional rights to freedom of speech or expression at the schoolhouse gate,"[9] and the Supreme Court has made clear that "private religious speech, far from being a First Amendment orphan, is as fully protected under the Free Speech Clause as secular private expression."[10] Moreover, not all religious speech that takes place in the public schools or at school-sponsored events is governmental speech.[11] For example, "nothing in the Constitution . . . prohibits any public school student from voluntarily praying at any time before, during, or after the school day,"[12] and students may pray with fellow students during the school day on the same terms and conditions that they may engage in other conversation or speech. Likewise, local school authorities possess substantial discretion to impose rules of order and pedagogical restrictions on student activities,[13] but they may not structure or administer such rules to discriminate against student prayer or religious speech. For instance, where schools permit student expression on the basis of genuinely neutral criteria and students retain primary control over the content of their expression, the speech of students who choose to express themselves through religious means such as prayer is not attributable to the state and therefore may not be restricted because of its religious content.[14] Student remarks are not attributable to the state simply because they are delivered in a public setting or to a public audience.[15] As the Supreme Court has explained, "The proposition that schools do not endorse everything they fail to censor is not complicated,"[16] and the Constitution mandates neutrality rather than hostility toward privately initiated religious expression.[17]

APPLYING THE GOVERNING PRINCIPLES IN PARTICULAR CONTEXTS

Prayer during Noninstructional Time

Students may pray when not engaged in school activities or instruction, subject to the same rules designed to prevent material disruption of the educational program that are applied to other privately initiated expressive activities. Among other things, students may read their Bibles or other scriptures, say grace before meals, and pray or study religious materials with fellow students during recess, the lunch hour, or other noninstructional time to the same extent that they may engage in nonreligious activities. While school authorities may impose rules of order and pedagogical restrictions on student activities, they may not discriminate against student prayer or religious speech in applying such rules and restrictions.

Organized Prayer Groups and Activities

Students may organize prayer groups, religious clubs, and "see you at the pole" gatherings before school to the same extent that students are permitted to organize other non-curricular student activities groups. Such groups must be given the same access to school facilities for assembling as is given to other non-curricular groups, without discrimination because of the religious content of their expression. School authorities possess substantial discretion concerning whether to permit the use of school media for student advertising or announcements regarding non-curricular activities. However, where student groups that meet for nonreligious activities are permitted to advertise or announce their meetings—for example, by advertising in a student newspaper, making announcements on a student activities bulletin board or public address system, or handing out leaflets—school authorities may not discriminate against groups who meet to pray. School authorities may disclaim sponsorship of non-curricular groups and events, provided they administer such disclaimers in a manner that neither favors nor disfavors groups that meet to engage in prayer or religious speech.

Teachers, Administrators, and Other School Employees

When acting in their official capacities as representatives of the state, teachers, school administrators, and other school employees are prohibited by the Establishment Clause from encouraging or discouraging prayer, and from actively participating in such activity with students. Teachers may, however, take part in religious activities where the overall context makes clear that they are not participating in their official capacities. Before school or during lunch, for example, teachers may meet with other teachers for prayer or Bible study to the same extent that they may engage in other conversation or nonreligious activities. Similarly, teachers may participate in their personal capacities in privately sponsored baccalaureate ceremonies.

Moments of Silence

If a school has a "minute of silence" or other quiet periods during the school day, students are free to pray silently, or not to pray, during these periods of time. Teachers and other school employees may neither encourage nor discourage students from praying during such time periods.

Accommodation of Prayer during Instructional Time

It has long been established that schools have the discretion to dismiss students to off-premises religious instruction, provided that schools do not encourage or discourage participation in such instruction or penalize students for attending or not attending. Similarly, schools may excuse students from class to remove a significant burden on their religious exercise, where doing so would not impose material burdens on other students. For example, it would be lawful for schools to excuse Muslim students briefly from class to enable them to fulfill their religious obligations to pray during Ramadan.

Where school officials have a practice of excusing students from class on the basis of parents' requests for accommodation of nonreligious needs, religiously motivated requests for excusal may not be accorded less favorable treatment. In addition, in some circumstances, based on federal or state constitutional law or pursuant to state statutes, schools may be required to make accommodations that relieve substantial burdens on students' religious exercise. Schools officials are therefore encouraged to consult with their attorneys regarding such obligations.

Religious Expression and Prayer in Class Assignments

Students may express their beliefs about religion in homework, artwork, and other written and oral assignments free from discrimination based on the religious content of their submissions. Such home and classroom work should be judged by ordinary academic standards of substance and relevance and against other legitimate pedagogical concerns identified by the school. Thus, if a teacher's assignment involves writing a poem, the work of a student who submits a poem in the form of a prayer (for example, a psalm) should be judged on the basis of academic standards (such as literary quality) and neither penalized nor rewarded on account of its religious content.

Student Assemblies and Extracurricular Events

Student speakers at student assemblies and extracurricular activities such as sporting events may not be selected on a basis that either favors or disfavors religious speech. Where student speakers are selected on the basis of genuinely neutral, evenhanded criteria and retain primary control over the content of their expression, that expression is not attributable to the school and therefore may not be restricted because of its religious (or anti-religious) content. By contrast, where school officials determine or substantially control the content of what is expressed, such speech is attributable to the school and may not include prayer or other specifically religious (or anti-religious) content. To avoid any mistaken perception that a school endorses student speech that is not in fact attributable to the school, school officials may make appropriate, neutral disclaimers to clarify that such speech (whether religious or nonreligious) is the speaker's and not the school's.

Prayer at Graduation

School officials may not mandate or organize prayer at graduation or select speakers for such events in a manner that favors religious speech such as prayer. Where students or other private graduation speakers are selected on the basis of genuinely neutral, evenhanded criteria and retain primary control over the content of their expression, however, that expression is not attributable to the school and therefore may not be restricted because of its religious (or anti-religious) content. To avoid any mistaken perception that a school endorses student or other private speech that is not in fact attributable to the school, school officials may make appropriate, neutral disclaimers to clarify that such speech (whether religious or nonreligious) is the speaker's and not the school's.

Baccalaureate Ceremonies

School officials may not mandate or organize religious ceremonies. However, if a school makes its facilities and related services available to other private groups, it must make its facilities and services available on the same terms to organizers of privately sponsored religious baccalaureate ceremonies. In addition, a school may disclaim official endorsement of events sponsored by private groups, provided it does so in a manner that neither favors nor disfavors groups that meet to engage in prayer or religious speech.

Appendix C

Archived Information: United States Department of Education

The Secretary

Schools do more than train children's minds. They also help to nurture their souls by reinforcing the values they learn at home and in their communities. I believe that one of the best ways we can help out schools to do this is by supporting students' rights to voluntarily practice their religious beliefs, including prayer in schools. . . . For more than 200 years, the First Amendment has protected our religious freedom and allowed many faiths to flourish in our homes, in our work place and in our schools. Clearly understood and sensibly applied, it works.

—President Clinton, May 30, 1998

Dear American Educator,

Almost three years ago, President Clinton directed me, as U.S. Secretary of Education, in consultation with the Attorney General, to provide every public school district in America with a statement of principles addressing the extent to which religious expression and activity are permitted in our public schools. In accordance with the President's directive, I sent every school superintendent in the country guidelines on *Religious Expression in Public Schools* in August of 1995.

The purpose of promulgating these presidential guidelines was to end much of the confusion regarding religious expression in our nation's public schools that had developed over more than thirty years since the U.S. Supreme Court decision in 1962 regarding state sponsored school prayer. I believe that these guidelines have helped school officials, teachers, students and parents find a new common ground on the important issue of religious freedom consistent with constitutional requirements.

In July of 1996, for example, the Saint Louis School Board adopted a district wide policy using these guidelines. While the school district had previously allowed certain religious activities, it had never spelled them out before, resulting in a lawsuit over the right of a student to pray before lunch in the cafeteria. The creation of a clearly defined policy using the guidelines allowed the school board and the family of the student to arrive at a mutually satisfactory settlement.

In a case decided last year in a United States District Court in Alabama, (*Chandler v. James*) involving student initiated prayer at school related events, the court instructed the DeKalb County School District to maintain for circulation in the library of each school a copy of the presidential guidelines.

The great advantage of the presidential guidelines, however, is that they allow school districts to avoid contentious disputes by developing a common understanding among students, teachers, parents and the broader community that the First Amendment does in fact provide ample room for religious expression by students while at the same time maintaining freedom from government sponsored religion.

The development and use of these presidential guidelines were not and are not isolated activities. Rather, these guidelines are part of an ongoing and growing effort by educators and America's religious community to find a new common ground. In April of 1995, for example, thirty-five religious groups issued "Religion in the Public Schools: A Joint Statement of Current Law" that the Department drew from in developing its own guidelines. Following the release of the presidential guidelines, the National PTA and the Freedom Forum jointly published in 1996 "A Parent's Guide to Religion in the Public Schools" which put the guidelines into an easily understandable question and answer format.

In the last two years, I have held three religious-education summits to inform faith communities and educators about the guidelines and to encourage continued dialogue and cooperation within constitutional limits. Many religious communities have contacted local schools and school systems to offer their assistance because of the clarity provided by the guidelines. The United Methodist Church has provided reading tutors to many schools, and Hadassah and the Women's League for Conservative Judaism have both been extremely active in providing local schools with support for summer reading programs.

The guidelines we are releasing today are the same as originally issued in 1995, except that changes have been made in the sections on religious excusals and student garb to reflect the Supreme Court decision in *Boerne v.*

Flores declaring the Religious Freedom Restoration Act unconstitutional as applied to actions of state and local governments.

These guidelines continue to reflect two basic and equally important obligations imposed on public school officials by the First Amendment. First, schools may not forbid students acting on their own from expressing their personal religious views or beliefs solely because they are of a religious nature. Schools may not discriminate against private religious expression by students, but must instead give students the same right to engage in religious activity and discussion as they have to engage in other comparable activity. Generally, this means that students may pray in a nondisruptive manner during the school day when they are not engaged in school activities and instruction, subject to the same rules of order that apply to other student speech.

At the same time, schools may not endorse religious activity or doctrine, nor may they coerce participation in religious activity. Among other things, of course, school administrators and teachers may not organize or encourage prayer exercises in the classroom. Teachers, coaches and other school officials who act as advisors to student groups must remain mindful that they cannot engage in or lead the religious activities of students.

And the right of religious expression in school does not include the right to have a "captive audience" listen, or to compel other students to participate. School officials should not permit student religious speech to turn into religious harassment aimed at a student or a small group of students. Students do not have the right to make repeated invitations to other students to participate in religious activity in the face of a request to stop.

The statement of principles set forth below derives from the First Amendment. Implementation of these principles, of course, will depend on specific factual contexts and will require careful consideration in particular cases.

In issuing these revised guidelines I encourage every school district to make sure that principals, teachers, students and parents are familiar with their content. To that end I offer three suggestions:

First, school districts should use these guidelines to revise or develop their own district wide policy regarding religious expression. In developing such a policy, school officials can engage parents, teachers, the various faith communities and the broader community in a positive dialogue to define a common ground that gives all parties the assurance that when questions do arise regarding religious expression the community is well prepared to apply these guidelines to specific cases. The Davis County School District in

Farmington, Utah, is an example of a school district that has taken the affirmative step of developing such a policy.

At a time of increasing religious diversity in our country such a proactive step can help school districts create a framework of civility that reaffirms and strengthens the community consensus regarding religious liberty. School districts that do not make the effort to develop their own policy may find themselves unprepared for the intensity of the debate that can engage a community when positions harden around a live controversy involving religious expression in public schools.

Second, I encourage principals and administrators to take the additional step of making sure that teachers, so often on the front line of any dispute regarding religious expression, are fully informed about the guidelines. The Gwinnett County School system in Georgia, for example, begins every school year with workshops for teachers that include the distribution of these presidential guidelines. Our nation's schools of education can also do their part by ensuring that prospective teachers are knowledgeable about religious expression in the classroom.

Third, I encourage schools to actively take steps to inform parents and students about religious expression in school using these guidelines. The Carter County School District in Elizabethton, Tennessee, included the subject of religious expression in a character education program that it developed in the fall of 1997. This effort included sending home to every parent a copy of the "Parent's Guide to Religion in the Public Schools."

Help is available for those school districts that seek to develop policies on religious expression. I have enclosed a list of associations and groups that can provide information to school districts and parents who seek to learn more about religious expression in our nation's public schools.

In addition, citizens can turn to the U.S. Department of Education web site (http://www.ed.gov/index.html) for information about the guidelines and other activities of the Department that support the growing effort of educators and religious communities to support the education of our nation's children.

Finally, I encourage teachers and principals to see the First Amendment as something more than a piece of dry, old parchment locked away in the national attic gathering dust. It is a vital living principle, a call to action, and a demand that each generation reaffirm its connection to the basic idea that is America—that we are a free people who protect our freedoms by respecting the freedom of others who differ from us.

Our history as a nation reflects the history of the Puritan, the Quaker, the Baptist, the Catholic, the Jew and many others fleeing persecution to find religious freedom in America. The United States remains the most successful experiment in religious freedom that the world has ever known because the First Amendment uniquely balances freedom of private religious belief and expression with freedom from state-imposed religious expression.

Public schools can neither foster religion nor preclude it. Our public schools must treat religion with fairness and respect and vigorously protect religious expression as well as the freedom of conscience of all other students. In so doing our public schools reaffirm the First Amendment and enrich the lives of their students.

I encourage you to share this information widely and in the most appropriate manner with your school community. Please accept my sincere thanks for your continuing work on behalf of all of America's children.

Sincerely,
Richard W. Riley
U.S. Secretary of Education

RELIGIOUS EXPRESSION IN PUBLIC SCHOOLS

Student prayer and religious discussion: The Establishment Clause of the First Amendment does not prohibit purely private religious speech by students. Students therefore have the same right to engage in individual or group prayer and religious discussion during the school day as they do to engage in other comparable activity. For example, students may read their Bibles or other scriptures, say grace before meals, and pray before tests to the same extent they may engage in comparable nondisruptive activities. Local school authorities possess substantial discretion to impose rules of order and other pedagogical restrictions on student activities, but they may not structure or administer such rules to discriminate against religious activity or speech.

Generally, students may pray in a nondisruptive manner when not engaged in school activities or instruction, and subject to the rules that normally pertain in the applicable setting. Specifically, students in informal settings, such as cafeterias and hallways, may pray and discuss their religious views with each other, subject to the same rules of order as apply to other student activities and speech. Students may also speak to, and attempt to persuade, their peers about religious topics just as they do with regard to political topics. School officials, however, should intercede to stop student speech that constitutes harassment aimed at a student or a group of students.

Students may also participate in before or after school events with religious content, such as "see you at the flag pole" gatherings, on the same terms as they may participate in other no curriculum activities on school premises. School officials may neither discourage nor encourage participation in such an event.

The right to engage in voluntary prayer or religious discussion free from discrimination does not include the right to have a captive audience listen, or to compel other students to participate. Teachers and school administrators should ensure that no student is in any way coerced to participate in religious activity.

Graduation prayer and baccalaureates: Under current Supreme Court decisions, school officials may not mandate or organize prayer at graduation, nor organize religious baccalaureate ceremonies. If a school generally opens its facilities to private groups, it must make its facilities available on the same terms to organizers of privately sponsored religious baccalaureate services. A school may not extend preferential treatment to baccalaureate ceremonies and may in some instances be obliged to disclaim official endorsement of such ceremonies.

Official neutrality regarding religious activity: Teachers and school administrators, when acting in those capacities, are representatives of the state and are prohibited by the establishment clause from soliciting or encouraging religious activity, and from participating in such activity with students. Teachers and administrators also are prohibited from discouraging activity because of its religious content, and from soliciting or encouraging antireligious activity.

Teaching about religion: Public schools may not provide religious instruction, but they may teach *about* religion, including the Bible or other scripture: the history of religion, comparative religion, the Bible (or other scripture)-as-literature, and the role of religion in the history of the United States and other countries all are permissible public school subjects. Similarly, it is permissible to consider religious influences on art, music, literature, and social studies. Although public schools may teach about religious holidays, including their religious aspects, and may celebrate the secular aspects of holidays, schools may not observe holidays as religious events or promote such observance by students.

Student assignments: Students may express their beliefs about religion in the form of homework, artwork, and other written and oral assignments free of discrimination based on the religious content of their submissions. Such home and classroom work should be judged by ordinary academic standards of substance and relevance, and against other legitimate pedagogical concerns identified by the school.

Religious literature: Students have a right to distribute religious literature to their schoolmates on the same terms as they are permitted to distribute other literature that is unrelated to school curriculum or activities. Schools may impose the same reasonable time, place, and manner or other constitutional restrictions on distribution of religious literature as they do on non-school literature generally, but they may not single out religious literature for special regulation.

Religious excusals: Subject to applicable State laws, schools enjoy substantial discretion to excuse individual students from lessons that are objectionable to the student or the students' parents on religious or other conscientious grounds. However, students generally do not have a Federal right to be excused from lessons that may be inconsistent with their religious beliefs or practices. School officials may neither encourage nor discourage students from availing themselves of an excusal option.

Released time: Subject to applicable State laws, schools have the discretion to dismiss students to off-premises religious instruction, provided that schools do not encourage or discourage participation or penalize those who do not attend. Schools may not allow religious instruction by outsiders on school premises during the school day.

Teaching values: Though schools must be neutral with respect to religion, they may play an active role with respect to teaching civic values and virtue, and the moral code that holds us together as a community. The fact that some of these values are held also by religions does not make it unlawful to teach them in school.

Student garb: Schools enjoy substantial discretion in adopting policies relating to student dress and school uniforms. Students generally have no Federal right to be exempted from religiously-neutral and generally applicable school dress rules based on their religious beliefs or practices; however, schools may not single out religious attire in general, or attire of a particular religion, for prohibition or regulation. Students may display religious messages on items of clothing to the same extent that they are permitted to display other comparable messages. Religious messages may not be singled out for suppression, but rather are subject to the same rules as generally apply to comparable messages.

THE EQUAL ACCESS ACT

The Equal Access Act is designed to ensure that, consistent with the First Amendment, student religious activities are accorded the same access to public school facilities as are student secular activities. Based on decisions of the Federal courts, as well as its interpretations of the Act, the Department of Justice has advised that the Act should be interpreted as providing, among other things, that:

General provisions: Student religious groups at public secondary schools have the same right of access to school facilities as is enjoyed by other comparable student groups. Under the Equal Access Act, a school receiving Federal funds that allows one or more student noncurriculum-related clubs to meet on its premises during noninstructional time may not refuse access to student religious groups.

Prayer services and worship exercises covered: A meeting, as defined and protected by the Equal Access Act, may include a prayer service, Bible reading, or other worship exercise.

Equal access to means of publicizing meetings: A school receiving Federal funds must allow student groups meeting under the Act to use the school media—including the public address system, the school newspaper, and the school bulletin board—to announce their meetings on the same terms as other noncurriculum-related student groups are allowed to use the school media. Any policy concerning the use of school media must be applied to all noncurriculum-related student groups in a nondiscriminatory matter. Schools, however, may inform students that certain groups are not school sponsored.

Lunch-time and recess covered: A school creates a limited open forum under the Equal Access Act, triggering equal access rights for religious groups, when it allows students to meet during their lunch periods or other noninstructional time during the school day, as well as when it allows students to meet before and after the school day.

Revised May 1998

Notes

CHAPTER 1

1. N. M. Ford, *When Did I Begin? Conception of the Human Individual in History, Philosophy and Science* (New York: Cambridge University Press, 1988).

2. H. Titus, *Living Issues in Philosophy* (New York: Van Nostrand Reinhold, 1970), p. 130.

3. Titus, *Living Issues*, p. 130.

4. See J. L. Jarrett, *The Educational Theories of the Sophists* (New York: Teachers College Press, 1969).

5. Titus, *Living Issues*, pp. 132–33.

6. Titus, *Living Issues*, p. 134.

7. Titus, *Living Issues*, p. 156.

8. The idea of family in America today has been expanded to include many different expressions of domestic partnership: Two males with children, two females with children, grandparent(s) with grandchildren, even foster homes and more, in addition to the traditional mother and father with children.

9. L. T. Diaz-Rico and K. Z. Weed, *The Crosscultural Language and Academic Development Handbook: A Complete K–12 Reference Guide* (Boston: Allyn and Bacon, 1995).

10. J. J. Romo, P. Bradfield, and R. Serrano, *Reclaiming Democracy: Multicultural Educators' Journeys toward Transformative Teaching* (Upper Saddle River, NJ: Pearson Education, 2004).

CHAPTER 2

1. Sandra Nieto, *Affirming Diversity: The Sociopolitical Context of Multicultural Education* (Boston: Pearson Education, 2004).

2. A. L. Kroeber and Clyde Kluckhohn, *Culture: A Critical Review of Concepts and Definitions* (Cambridge, MA: The Museum, 1952). p. 357

3. This image may be acting against American interests in certain circles as other nationalities have often come to interpret this behavior as arrogance and lack of consideration of others. A fellow professor from Toronto University commented that American tourists in Canada had impressed upon her this negative image, and it would be difficult to convince her otherwise.

4. The U.S. Declaration of Independence declares that "All men are created equal and endowed with such inalienable rights as life, liberty, and the pursuit of happiness." The pursuit of happiness, like the other two, have become a fundamental aspect of the American lifestyle.

5. D. M. Gollnick and P. C. Chinn, *Multicultural Education in a Pluralistic Society* (Upper Saddle River, NJ: Pearson Education, Inc., 2009).

6. Charles Kraft, *Christianity in Culture* (Maryknoll, NY: Orbis Books, 1979).

7. H. L. Tischler, P. Whitten, and D. E. K. Hunter, *Introduction to Sociology* (New York: CBS College Publishing, 1983).

8. Tischler, Whitten, and Hunter, *Introduction to Sociology*, p. 145.

9. Émile Durkheim, *The Elementary Forms of Religious Life: A Study of Religious Sociology* (New York: Macmillan, 1915).

10. Tischler, Whitten, and Hunter, *Introduction to Sociology*, p. 460.

11. The Declaration of Independence, 1776.

12. Abraham Lincoln, Address made at Gettysburg, Pennsylvania, November 19, 1863.

13. W. O. Kellog, *American History the Easy Way.* (New York: Barron's Educational Series, Inc., 1995).

14. P. Gorski, Multicultural Pavilion (2004), available at www.edchange.org/multicultural (accessed October 8, 2007).

15. Alvin Toffler, *Powershift: Knowledge, Wealth, and Violence at the Edge of the 21st Century* (New York: Bantam Books, 1990), p. 20; cf. Russell Chandler, 1992, p. 45.

16. Gorski, Multicultural Pavilion.

17. J. O. Hertzler, *Social Institutions* (Lincoln: University of Nebraska Press, 1946).

18 T. E. Lasswell, J. H. Burma, and S. H Aronson (eds.), *Life in Society: Readings in Sociology* (Glenview, IL: Scott, Foresman and Company, 1970).

19. Cf. U.S. Census Bureau; U.S. Department of Justice; the U.S. office of Management and Budget; www.edchange.org/multicultural.

20. Gorski, Multicultural Pavilion.

21. Russell Chandler, *Racing Toward 2001: The Forces Shaping America's Religious Future* (Grand Rapids: Zondervan Publishing House, 1992).

22. Kraft, *Christianity in Culture*, p. 53.

23. Amitai Etzioni, *The Active Society: A Theory of Societal and Political Processes* (New York: The Free Press 1968), pp. 13–14.

24. Max Weber, *The Protestant Ethic and the Spirit of Capitalism*, translated by Talcott Parsons (New York: Charles Scribner's Sons, 1958).

25. In Weber's analysis of Benjamin Franklin's view of money, he indicated that Franklin considered a lack of care in handling money as tantamount to murdering capital embryos and as an ethical defect on the side of the culprit (cf. Weber, *The Protestant Ethic*, p. 196).

26. R. P. Cuzzort and E. W. King, *Humanity and Modern Social Thought* (Hindsale, IL: The Dryden Press 1976), p. 48.

27. P. Schaff, *History of the Christian Church* (Peabody, MA: Hendrickson Publishing, Inc., 1888) p. 221.

28. Cuzzort and King, *Humanity and Modern Social Thought*, p. 49.

29. Robert A. Nisbet, *Emile Durkheim* (Westport, CT: Greenwood Press, 1965).

CHAPTER 3

1. Kent Koppelman and R. Lee Goodhart, *Understanding Human Differences: Multicultural Education for Diverse America* (Boston: Pearson Education, 2005).

2. Cf. D. Lindsey (ed.), *A. Lincoln/Jefferson Davis: The House Divided.* (Cleveland, OH: Howard Allen, Inc., 1960).

3. Jonathan Kozol, *The Shame of the Nation: The Restoration of Apartheid Schooling in America* (New York: Crown Publishers, 2005).

4. Jack Levin and William Levin, *The Functions of Discrimination and Prejudice*, 2nd ed. (New York: Harper and Row, 1982).

5. Stephen Covey, *The Seven Habits of Highly Effective People* (Gahanna, OH: Covey Leadership Center, 1986).

6. Janet Kalven, "Personal Value Clarification," in *Readings in Value Development*, ed. B. Hall, J. Kalven, L. Rosen, and B. Taylor (Ramsey, NJ: Paulist Press, 1982).

7. L. Raths, M. Harmin, and S. Simon, *Values and Teaching: Working with Values in the Classroom* (Columbus, OH: Charles E. Merrill, 1966).

8. Rosa Hernandez-Sheets, "What Is Diversity Pedagogy?" *Multicultural Education* (Spring 2009).

9. Randall B. Lindsey, Kikanza Nuri Robins, and Raymond D. Terrell, *Cultural Proficiency: A Manual for School Leaders* (Thousand Oaks, CA: Corwin Press, 1999); Randall B. Lindsay, Laraine M. Roberts, and Franklin CampbellJones, *The Culturally Proficient School: An Implementation Guide for School Leaders* (Thousand Oaks, CA: Corwin Press, 2005).

10. A 1993–1994 U.S. Department of Education, National Center for Educational Statistics, School Staffing Survey reported the percentage of public school teachers who are white, non-Hispanic between 84 and 87 percent (cf. http://nces.ed.gov/pubs97/97460.pdf).

11. This certification has recently changed its name to California Teachers of English Learners (CTEL).

12. L. Derman-Parks, *Anti-Bias Curriculum: Tools for Empowering Young Children* (Washington DC: National Association for the Education of You, 1993).

13. G. Allport, *The Nature of Prejudice* (Reading, MA: Addison-Wesley Publishing Company, 1954).

14. E. Weymeyer, M. Wartz, and M. Wartz, "Disproportionate Representation of Males in Special Education Services: Biology, Behavior, or Bias?" *Education and Treatment of Children* (February, 2001).

15. M. Cooper, "The Detrimental Impact of Teacher Bias: Lessons Learned from Standpoint of African American Mothers," *Teachers Education Quarterly* 30(2): 101–14; cf. L. I. Bartolomew, "Beyond the Methods Fetish: Towards a Humanizing Pedagogy." *Harvard Educational Review*, 64(2): 173–94); M. Cochran-Smith, "Knowledge, Skills, and Experiences for Teaching Culturally Diverse Learners: A Perspective for Practicing Teachers," in J. Irvine (ed.) *Critical Knowledge for Diverse Teachers and Learners*, pp. 27–88 (Washington, DC: AACTE); V. Fueyo and S. Betchtol, "Those Who Can Teach: Reflecting on Teaching Diverse Populations," *Teacher Education Quarterly* 26(3); J. Oakes and M. Litpon, *Teaching to Change the World* (Boston: McGraw-Hill College, 1999).

16. Gloria Ladson-Billings, "But That's Just Good Teaching! The Case for Culturally Relevant Pedagogy," *Theory into Practice* 34(3): 159–65.

17. Personal communication.

18. L. T. Diaz-Rico and K. Z. Weed, *The Crosscultural, Language, and Academic Development Handbook: A Study in Religious Sociology* (New York: Macmillan, 1995).

19. Ellwood Patterson Cubberly, *Changing Conceptions of Education* (Boston: Houghton Mifflin, 1909).

20. American cultural pluralism covers ethnic and religious diversities.

21. Indeed, the ideal picture of America may not be Congress in session, but rather the U.S. military, with white, African American, Hispanic, Asian, and other ethnicities bearing arms to fight a common enemy.

22. J. M. Jones, *Prejudice and Racism* (New York: McGraw-Hill, 1997).

23. Kevin Cokley, "Testing Cross's Revised Racial Identity Model: An Examination of the Relationship between Racial Identity and Internalized Racialism," *Journal of Counseling Psychology* 49(4): 476–83.

24. Cf. *Race: The Power of an Illusion* (motion picture), California Newsreel, 2003.

25. A. H. Soukhanov, ed., *Microsoft Encarta College Dictionary* (New York: St. Martin's Press, 2001).

26. J. Kozol, *Savage Inequalities: Children in America's Schools* (New York: Harper Perennial, 1991).

CHAPTER 4

1. James A. Banks and Cherry A. McGee Banks, *Handbook of Research on Multicultural Education*, 2nd ed. (San Francisco: Wiley, 2004), p. 3.

2. The U.S. Declaration of Independence states that all men are created equal and endowed with certain inalienable human rights. The right to equal treatment in educational opportunity has been viewed as a civil right by many.

3. It was June 7, 1892, when a shoemaker by the name of Homer Plessy, defined as "one-eighth black and seven-eighths white" was jailed for sitting in the "white" car of the East Louisiana Railroad. He went to court to argue that the separate car violated his Thirteenth and Fourteenth Amendment rights. The judge in the case, John Howard Ferguson, ruled that the State of Louisiana had the right to regulate different cars for different peoples for railroads operating in the state. In so ruling he found Plessey guilty of refusing to leave the white car. A U.S. Supreme Court upheld this decision in 1896.

4. M. J. Klarman, *From Jim Crow to Civil Rights: The Supreme Court and the Struggle for Racial Equality* (New York: Oxford University Press, 2004); P. Irons, *Jim Crow's Children: The Broken Promise of the Brown Decision* (New York: The Penguin Group, 2002).

5. This federal law, which was proposed by Senator Charles Sumner, a Republican congressman, guaranteed every American, regardless of race, color, or previous conditions of servitude, the same treatment in public accommodations (including transportation and access to public places).

6. This law declared all rail companies in Louisiana must provide separate but equal accommodations for white and nonwhite passengers. The penalty for sitting in the wrong car was twenty-five dollars or a twenty-day jail sentence.

7. *Plessy v. Ferguson*, 163 U.S. 537 (1896).

8. *Plessy v. Ferguson*.

9. *Plessy v. Ferguson*.

10. Michael W. LaMorte, *School Law: Cases and Concepts* (Boston, MA: Allyn and Bacon, 1999), p. 272.

11. R. J Cottrol, R. T. Diamone, and L. B. Ware, *Brown v. Board of Education: Caste, Culture, and the Constitution* (Lawrence: University Press of Kansas, 2003), pp. 128–29; M. J. Klarman, *Brown v. Board of Education and the Civil Rights Movement* (New York: Oxford University Press, 2007), pp. 55–58.

12. *Brown v. Board of Education*, 347 U.S. 483 (1954).

13. *Brown v. Board of Education*.

14. *Brown v. Board of Education*.

15. LaMorte, *School Law*, p. 356.

16. *Lau v. Nichols*, 414 U.S. 563 (1974) retrieved from http://supct.law.cornell.edu March 30, 2005.

17. U.S. Const. Fourteenth Amendment, sec. 1.

18. *Brown v. Board of Education*.

19. This book documents the most deplorable conditions America's poor and mostly minority students are subjected to in the name of schooling.

20. Jonathan Kozol, *Savage Inequalities: Children in America's Schools* (New York: Crown, 1991).

21. The No Child Left Behind Act (NCLB) was enacted in 2001 as a means toward better accountability of schools and improved student achievement.

22. G. Gay, "Educational Equality for Students of Color." In *Multicultural Education: Issues and Perspectives,* ed. James A. Banks and Cherry A. McGee Banks (New York: Wiley, 2004), p. 228.

23. Banks and Banks, *Multicultural Education*, p. 19.

CHAPTER 5

1. H. Nagai, "Multicultural Education in the United States and Japan," paper presented at the 46th Annual Conference of Comparative International Education Society (CIES) Orlando, Florida, March 6–8, 2002.

2. James A. Banks, "Multicultural Education: Characteristics and Goals," in *Multicultural Education: Issues and Perspectives*, 4th ed., ed. James A. Banks and Cherry A. McGee Banks (New York: Wiley, 2003).

3. D. Sadkler and M. Sadkler, *Teachers, Schools and Society* (Princeton, NJ: McGraw-Hill, 1994).

4. Horace Mann is regarded as one of the individuals who shaped the American educational landscape. He is often referred to as the "Father of American Education." Mann was a self-educated man who acquired learning by reading prolifically from the Franklin Town library in Franklin, Massachusetts, the town in which he was born in 1796. He studied law, served as a state legislator, became the U.S. secretary of education, and used that opportunity to sell his vision of education as part of the birth right of every American child. He referred to education as the "great equalizer."

5. J. E. Hernandez-Tutop, "Oppressor: The Educational System," opinion paper published by the U.S. Department of Education, 1998, p. 3.

6. R. Ueda, "The Construction of Ethnic Diversity and National Identity in the Public Schools," in *Historical Perspectives on the Current Education Reforms*, ed.

Diane Ravitch, and Maris Vinovskis, essays commissioned by the Office of Research (OR) in the Office of the Educational Research and Improvement (OERI) (Washington, DC: U.S. Department of Education, 1993).

7. Cf. N. V. Montalto, *A History of the Intercultural Educational Movement, 1924–1841* (New York: Garland Publishing, Inc., 1982).

8. Jim Crow laws were a series of laws that established a racial caste system primarily, but not exclusively, in the Southern and border states between 1876 and the 1960s. These laws legitimized segregation against blacks and other minorities and became the basis on which antiblack sentiments spread across the United States, so that individuals that once lived alongside their black slaves in harmony became so hostile to these now freed people that they would not share a restaurant, drinking fountain, rail car, or other public facilities with them. The laws also launched the series of lynchings that marked one of the darkest periods of the black experience in the United States.

9. See www.ferris.edu/htmls/news/jimcrow/menu.htm.

10. James A. Banks, "Multicultural Education: Historical Developments, Dimensions and Practice," in *Handbook of Research on Multicultural Education*, 2nd ed., ed. James A. Banks and Cherry A. McGee Banks (San Francisco: Wiley, 2004).

11. Williams is said to have been born in Bedford Springs, Pennsylvania, on October 16, 1849, and died in Blackpool, England, on August 1891. He is credited to have written the first objective and scientifically researched history of the African Americans. Among his works were, *History of the Negro Race in America from 1619 to 1880* (1882) and *A History of Negro Troops in the War of Rebellion.*

12. Gary Nash, "Multiculturalism and History: Historical Perspectives and Present Prospects," in *Historical Perspectives on the Current Education Reforms*, ed. Diane Ravitch, and Maris Vinovskis, essays commissioned by the Office of Research (OR) in the Office of the Educational Research and Improvement (OERI) (Washington, DC: U.S. Department of Education, 1993).

13. Banks, "Multicultural Education."

14. Cf. J. Oakes, *Keeping Track: How Schools Structure Inequality.* New Haven, CT: Yale University Press, 1985); A. Valenzuela, *Subtractive Schooling: U.S.-Mexican Youth and the Politics of Caring* (Albany: State University of New York Press, 1999); H. Mehan, I. Villanueva, L. Hubbard, and A. Lintz, *Constructing School Success: The Consequences of Untracking Low Achieving Students* (New York: Cambridge University Press, 1996); S. Yonezawa, A. S. Wells, and I Serna, "Choosing Tracks: 'Freedom of Choice' in Detracking Schools," *American Educational Research Journal*, 39(1): 37–67.

15. D. Kirp, "The Educational Equities in Historical Perspective," in *Historical Perspectives on the Current Education Reforms*, ed. Diane Ravitch, and Maris Vinovskis, essays commissioned by the Office of Research (OR) in the Office of the Educational Research and Improvement (OERI) (Washington, DC: U.S. Department of Education, 1993).

16. J. Weiler, "Recent Changes in School Desegregation," ERIC/CUE Digest Number 133 (1998); cf. H. D. Willis, "The Shifting Focus in School Desegregation," paper presented to the SWRL Board of Directors and the 1995 Equity Conference, November 1, 1994.

17. *Plessy v. Ferguson*, 163.U.S.537 [1896].

18. *Brown v. Board Education*, 347 U.S. 483 [1954] [USSC+]).

19. Rosa Parks has been labeled the "mother of the modern civil rights movement" in America. Her refusal to move was done at a risk of legal sanctions as well as physical harm. That deliberate act of defiance sparked the fire that led to the modern civil rights movement.

20. B. Brunner and E. Haney, "Civil Rights Timeline: Milestones in the Modern Civil Rights Movement," available at: www.infoplease.com/spot/civilrightstime line1.html (accessed October 9, 2006).

21. Brunner and Haney, "Civil Rights Timeline."

22. R. Moses and C. E. Cobb Jr., *Radical Equations: Math Literacy and Civil Rights* (Boston: Beacon Press, 2001).

23. See L. Barr, "The Next Step: Showing a Common History of Treatment for Minorities, Women and Gays in Media Content, Newsrooms and Journalism Schools: A Proposal for Future Research and Suggestions for a Curriculum," a paper presented at the 76th annual meeting of the Association for Education in Journalism and Mass Communication, Kansas City, MO, August 11–14, 1993.

24. Banks, "Multicultural Education."

25. C. G. Woodson and C. H. Wesley, *The Negro in Our History* (Washington, D.C: Associated Publishers, 1922).

26. W. E. B. Du Bois, *Black Reconstruction* (New York: Harcourt, 1935); *The Education of Black People: Ten Critiques, 1906–1960* (New York: Monthly Review Press).

27. Nash, "Multiculturalism and History."

28. Cf. J. D. Pulliam and J. J. Van Patten, *History of Education in America* (Upper Saddle River, NJ: Pearson Education, 2003).

29. M. F. Suleiman, "Preparing Teachers for the Culturally Diverse Classrooms," paper presented at the 7th Annual Effective Schools Conference, Topeka, Kansas, May 3–5, 1996.

30. *Brown v. Board of Education*, 347 U.S. 483 [1954] [USSC+].

31. Title VII of the Civil Rights Act of 1964.

32. Equal Educational Act of 1974.

33. Banks, "Multicultural Education."

34. James A. Banks and Cherry A. McGee Banks (eds.), *Multicultural Education: Issues and Perspectives*, 5th ed. (New York: Wiley, 2004).

35. K. Maclay, "Anthropology Professor John Ogbu Dies at Age 64," available at http://berkeley.edu/news/media/release/2003/08/26_ogbu.html (accessed October 7, 2006).

36. The most significant impact of Elliot's campaign is her insistence that one person can make a difference.

CHAPTER 6

1. Title I, sec. 1001 of the Elementary and Secondary Education Act of 1965 (20 U.S.C. 6301 et seq.), see www.ed.gov/policy/elsec/leg/esea02.

2. S. Books, "High Stakes in New York: From a 'Last Chance, First Chance' Classroom," *Educational Foundations* 15(4): 57–70.

3. Books, "High Stakes in New York."

4. Title I, sec. 1001.

5. See www.cde.ca.gov/sp/sw/t1.

6. "Geoffrey Borman, "How Can Title I Improve Achievement?" *Educational Leadership* 60(4): 49–53.

7. Two of the researched studies were D. Grissmer, A. Flanagan, and S. Williamson, "Why Did the Black-White Score Gap Narrow in the 1970s and 1980s?" in *The Black-White Test Score Gap*, ed. C. Jencks and M. Phillips, pp. 181–226 (Washington, DC: Brookings Institute, 1998); M. S. Smith and J. A. O'Day, "Educational Equality: 1966 and Now," in *Spheres of Justice in Education: The 1990 American Education Finance Association Yearbook*, ed. D. Verstgen and J. Ward, pp. 53–100 (New York: Harper Business, 1991).

8. Borman, "How Can Title I Improve Achievement?"

9. No Child Left Behind Act, available at www.ed.gov/nclb/overview/intro/presidentplan.

10. No Child Left Behind Act.

11. The New American Foundation, "No Child Left Behind Act—Title 1 Distribution Formulas," 2009, available at http://febp.newamerica.net/background-analysis/no-child-left-behind-funding (accessed August 24, 2009).

12. A. J. Townley, J. H. Schmeider-Ramirez, and L. B. Wehmeyer, *School Finance: A California Perspective* (Dubuque, IA: Kendall/Hunt Publishing Company, 1999), p. 95.

13. K. K. MacKenzie, "Using Literacy Booster Groups to Maintain and Extend Reading Recovery Success in the Primary Grades," *The Reading Teacher* 55(3): 222–34.

14. J. Fagan, "There's No Place Like School," *Principal* 80(5): 36–37.

15. Jennifer Cohen, "Examining the Data: Understanding Title I Funding Distributions," The Ed Money Watch Blog, New America Foundation, available at www.newamerica.net/blog/ed-money-watch/2009/examining-data-understanding-title-i-funding-distributions-15316 (accessed August 24, 2009).

16. R. Miller, "Interactive Map: Title 1 Education Grants, Funding Formulas Create Unfair Allocations," Center for American Progress, available at www.americanprogress.org/issues/2009/08/title1_map/htm (accessed August 24, 2009).

CHAPTER 7

1. T. G. Wiley, "Myths about Language Diversity and Literacy in the United States," *ERIC Digest*, www.ericdigests.org/1998-1/myths.htm.

2. H. W. Button and E. F. Provenzo, Jr., *History of Education and Culture in America.* (Englewood Cliffs, NJ: Prentice Hall, 1989); D. Sadkler and M. Sadkler, "Gender Bias: From Colonial America to Today's Classrooms," in *Multicultural Education: Issues and Perspectives*, ed. James A. Banks and Cherry A. McGee Banks, 4th ed. (New York: Wiley, 2004).

3. D. Calhoun, *The Educating of Americans: A Documentary History* (Boston: Houghton Mifflin Company, 1969).

4. Calhoun, *The Educating of Americans.*

5. Marion Brown, "Is There a Nationality Problem in our Schools?" in *Shaping the American Educational State 1900 to the Present*, ed. Clarence J. Karier, pp. 269–74 (New York: The Free Press, 1900).

6. Brown, "Is There a Nationality Problem," pp. 585–90.

7. Brown, "Is There a Nationality Problem," pp. 585–90.

8. J. Lessow-Hurley, *The Foundations of Dual Language Instruction* (New York: Longman, 1990).

9. L. T. Diaz-Rico and K. Z. Weed, *The Crosscultural, Language, and Academic Development Handbook: A Complete K–12 Reference Guide* (Boston: Allyn and Bacon, 1995).

10. Wiley, "Myths about Language Diversity."

11. P. Tiedt and I. Tiedt, *Multicultural Teaching: A Handbook of Activities, Information, and Resources* (Boston: Allyn and Bacon, 2002).

12. Ellwood Patterson Cubberly, *Changing Conceptions of Education* (Boston: Houghton Mifflin, 1909).

13. James A. Banks, *Cultural Diversity and Education: Foundations, Curriculum, and Teaching* (Boston: Allyn and Bacon, 2001).

14. Lessow-Hurley, *The Foundations of Dual Language Instruction.*

15. C. J. Faltis and S. J. Hudelson, *Bilingual Education in Elementary and Secondary School Communities: Towards Understanding and Caring* (Boston: Allyn and Bacon, 1998).

16. Equal Educational Opportunity Act (20 USC sec. 1703).

17. H. A. Daniels, *Not Only English: Affirming America's Multilingual Heritage* (Urbana, IL: National Council of Teachers of English, 1990).

18. A. Scheid, *Pasadena—Crown of the Valley: An Illustrated History* (Northridge, CA: Windsor Publications, 1986).

19. The information and resources used in establishing these time lines are derived from a variety of sources which include, but are not limited to the following works (see the bibliography for publication details):

Crawford, 1992; 1995; 1996; 2002; Kloss, 1998; Leibowitz, 1969; Pitt, 1966; Mailman,1995;

http://ourworld.compuserve.com/homepages/JWCRAWFORD/lau.htm;

http://ourworld.compuserve.com/homepages/JCRAWFORD/Adams.htm;

www.ed.gov/updates/Working/title-7.html; www.loc.gov/rr/hispanic/ghtreaty/;

www.usnews.com/usnews/opinion/baroneweb/mb_020208.htm; http://coe.sdsu .edu/people/jmora/pages/HistoryBE.htm;

www.ssbb.com/article1.html.

20. J. Crawford, "Language Politics in the U.S.A.: The Paradox of Bilingual Education," *Social Justice* 25(3); J. Crawford, "Language Politics in the United States: The Paradox of Bilingual Education," in *The Politics of Multiculturalism and Bilingual Education: Students and Teachers Caught in the Cross-Fire*, ed. Carlos J. Ovando and Peter McLaren (Boston: McGraw-Hill, 2000).

21. Ralph Yarborough was a Texas Democratic member of the U.S. Senate from 1957 to 1971. He was the leader of the progressive wing of the party, and championed lots of civil rights issues as well as advocated for Medicare and Medicaid.

22. Crawford, "Language Politics in the U.S.A."

23. Diaz-Rico and Weed, *The Crosscultural, Language, and Academic Development Handbook*.

CHAPTER 8

1. The First Amendment to the U.S. Constitution.

2. *Reynolds v. United States*, 98 U.S. 145 (1878).

3. *Reynolds v. United States*.

4. *Abington School District v. Schemp*, 374 U.S. 203 (1963).

5. *Abington School District v. Schemp*.

6. U.S. Department of Education, "Guidance on Constitutionally Protected Prayer in Public Elementary and Secondary Schools," February 7, 2003, available at www.ed.gov/policy/gen/guid/religionandschools/prayer_guidance.html (see appendix B).

7. Richard W. Riley, "Religious Expression in Public Schools," U.S. Department of Education, available at www.ed.gov/Speeches/08-1995/religion.html (see appendix C).

8. U.S. Department of Education, "Guidance on Constitutionally Protected Prayer in Public Elementary and Secondary Schools."

9. Riley, "Religious Expression in Public Schools."

CHAPTER 9

1. W. Blackstone, *Commentaries of England* (Oxford: Clarendon Press, 1765–1769).

2. D. H. Fischer, *Liberty and Freedom: A Visual History of America's Founding Ideas* (New York: Oxford University Press, 2005), p. 263.

3. Fischer, *Liberty and Freedom*, p. 263.

4. H. W. Button and E. F. Provenzo, Jr., *History of Education and Culture in America* (Englewood Cliffs, NJ: Prentice Hall, 1989).

5. Button and Provenzo, *History of Education*.

6. M. P. Winship, *The Times and Trials of Anne Hutchinson* (Lawrence: University Press of Kansas, 2005), p. 11.

7. F. C. Huber, "Hutchinson, Ann," American National Biography Online, February 2000, available at http://0-www.anb.org.patris.apu.edu/articles/01/01-00437-print.html (accessed September 12, 2008).

8. Fischer, *Liberty and Freedom*, p. 263.

9. J. F. Cooper, Jr., *Tenacious of Their Liberties: The Congregationalists in Colonial Massachusetts* (New York: Oxford University Press, 1999), pp. 46–53.

10. M. Kelley, "A More Glorious Revolution: Women's Antebellum Reading Circles and the Pursuit of Public Influence," *New England Quarterly* 76(2): 1963.

11. Button and Provenzo, *History of Education*.

12. See G. S. Jones, "An End to Poverty: The French Revolution and the Promise of a World Beyond Want," paper presented at the Anglo-American Conference of Historians at the University of London, July 7–9, 2004, p. 193.

13. C. W. Akers, *Abigail Adams: An American Woman* (New York: Longman, 2000), p. 37.

14. C. F. Adams, *Letters of Mrs. Adams, the Wife of John Adams*, vols. 1 and 2 (Boston: Freeman and Bolles, 1840).

15. Adams, *Letters of Mrs. Adams*.

16. Adams, *Letters of Mrs. Adams.*

17. A. S. Myers, "Emma Hart Willard (1787–1870)," in *Collier's Encyclopedia* (New York: MacMillan Educational Company, 1992), p. 489.

18. Fischer, *Liberty and Freedom*, p. 265.

19. B. A. Zink-Sawyer, "From Preachers to Suffragists: Enlisting the Pulpit in the Early Movement for Woman's Rights," *American Transcendental Quarterly* 14(3): 193–209.

20. "Report of the Woman's Rights Convention Seneca Falls, New York," available at www.hbci.com/~tgort/convent.htm (accessed September 12, 2008).

21. M. Washington, "From Motives of Delicacy: Sexuality and Morality in the Narratives of Sojourner Truth and Harriet Jacobs," *Journal of African American History* 92(1): 59.

22. N. I. Painter, "Truth, Sojourner," American National Biography Online, February 2002, available at http://0-www.anb.org.patris.apu.edu/ articles/15/15 -00706.html (accessed September 12, 2008); Zink-Sawyer, "From Preachers to Suffragists."

23. Painter, "Truth, Sojourner."

24. Cf. L. Chessum, "Race and Gender in the United States of America," *Gender & History* 12(1): 228–31.

25. J. L. Lebedun, "Harriet Beecher Stowe's Interest in Sojourner Truth, Black Feminist," in *American Literature* 46 (1974): 359–63, at 360.

26. Zink-Sawyer, "From Preachers to Suffragists"; W. H. Venet, "The Emergence of a Suffragist: Mary Livermore, Civil War Activism, and the Moral Power of Women," *Civil War History* 48(2): 143–64; A. Leuchtag, "Elizabeth Cady Stanton, Freethinker and Radical Revisionist," *Humanist* 56 (1996): 29–32.

27. James A. Banks and Cherry A. McGee Banks, *Multicultural Education: Issues and Perspectives* (Hoboken, NJ: Wiley, 2007).

28. It is documented that the chief justice in this case stated that women should be able to sit upon grand juries, which would give them the best opportunity to uplift the country's morals.

29. J. D. Pulliam and J. J. Van Patten, *History of Education in America* (Upper Saddle River, NJ: Pearson Education, 2003).

30. Pulliam and Van Patten, *History of Education in America*, p. 148; P. W. Kaufman, *Women Teachers on the Frontier* (New Haven, CT: Yale University Press, 1984).

31. E. H. Clark, *Sex in Education; Or, a Fair Chance for Girls* (Boston: Houghton Mifflin, 1873); D. Sadkler and K. Zittleman, "Gender Bias: From Colonial America to Today's Classrooms," in *Multicultural Education: Issues and Perspectives*, ed. James A. Banks and Cherry A. McGee Banks (Hoboken, NJ: Wiley, 2007).

32. Sadkler and Zittleman, "Gender Bias."

33. Fischer, *Liberty and Freedom*, pp. 598–602.

34. N. Beisel and T. Kay, "Abortion, Race, and Gender in Nineteenth-Century America," *American Sociological Review* 69 (2004): 498–518.

35. Cf. *United States v. Virginia*, 518 U.S. 515; Banks and Banks, *Multicultural Education*.

CHAPTER 10

1. *Webster's New Twentieth Century Dictionary of English Language*, 1968, p. 576.

2. B. F. Skinner, *The Technology of Teaching* (New York: Meredith Corporation, 1968), p. 3.

3. Skinner, *The Technology of Teaching*, p. 3.

4. Skinner, *The Technology of Teaching*, p. 3.

5. Skinner, *The Technology of Teaching*, pp. 2–3.

6. Abraham Maslow, *Towards a Psychology of Being* (New York: Van Nostrand Reinhold, 1968).

7. Within the educational contexts, you construct knowledge, personalities, and social arrangements. Education shapes and molds the lives that shape and mold society.

CHAPTER 11

1. "Nondiscrimination on the Basis of Handicap in Programs or Activities Receiving Federal Financial Assistance," Title 34, Code of Federal Regulations, Part 104 (Washington DC: Office for Civil Rights, Dept. of Education, 2000), p. 6.

2. "Nondiscrimination," p. 22.

3. N. Hunt and K. Marshall, *Exceptional Children and Youth: An Introduction to Special Education* (Boston: Houghton Mifflin Company, 1994), p. 247.

4. R. Turnbull, N. Huerta, and M. Stowe, *The Individuals with Disabilities Education Act as Amended in 2004* (Upper Saddle River, N.J: Pearson Education, 2006), p. 17.

5. Turnbull, Huerta, and Stowe, *Individuals with Disabilities Education Act*, p. 17.

6. *Students with Attention Deficit Disorders ADD/ADHD: Eligibility Issues and Service Options under the Individuals with Disabilities Education Act (IDEA) and Section 504* (Logan: Utah State University, 1998), p. 21.

7. *Students with Attention Deficit Disorders*, p. 30.

8. *Students with Attention Deficit Disorders*, p. 30.

9. Candace Cortiella, *IDEA Parent Guide* (New York: National Center for Learning Disability, 2006), p. 13.

10. *Individuals with Disability Education Act* of 1975 (P.L. 94-142).

11. National Joint Committee on Learning Disabilities (1990).

12. Sources used for table 11.1: Marilyn Friend, *Special Education: Contemporary Perspectives for School Professionals* (Boston: Pearson Education, 2008); Hunt and Marshall, *Exceptional Children and Youth*; W. L. Heward and M. D. Orlansky, *Exceptional Children: An Introductory Survey of Special Education* (New York: Macmillan Publishing Company, 1992).

13. S. J. Salend, *Creating Inclusive Classrooms: Effective and Reflective Practices* (Columbus, OH: Pearson Education, 2008), p. 76.

14. Heward and Orlansky, *Exceptional Children*, pp. 105–6.

15. Friend, *Special Education*, p. 245; American Association on Mental Retardation, Washington, D.C.

16. Cf. Hunt and Marshall, *Exceptional Children and Youth*, p. 247.

17. Heward and Orlansky, *Exceptional Children*, p. 202.

18. M. M. Kerr and C. M. Nelson, *Strategies for Managing Behavior Problems in the Classrooms* (New York: Merrill/Macmillan, 1989).

19. M. S. Rosenberg, R. Wilson, L. Maheady, and P. T. Sindelar, *Educating Students with Behavior Disorders* (Boston: Allyn & Bacon, 1992).

20. Hunt and Marshall, *Exceptional Children and Youth*.

21. Cf. Friend, *Special Education*, p. 273.

22. Friend, *Special Education*, p. 345.

23. Hunt and Marshall, *Exceptional Children and Youth*, p. 429.

24. Massachusetts Department of Elementary and Secondary Education, "Health Impairment," available at www.doe.mass.edu/sped/links/healthimpair.html (accessed September 24, 2008).

25. U.S. Department of Education (USDE), *National Excellence: A Case for Developing America's Talent* (Washington, DC: USDE, 1993).

26. Part of the problem behind the gap is the continuous use of assessment instruments that are often culturally biased.

27. H. R. Milner, F. B. Tenore, and J. Laughter, "What Can Teacher Education Programs Do to Prepare Teachers to Teach High-Achieving Culturally Diverse Male Students," *Gifted Child Today* 31 (Winter 2008).

28. *Elementary and Secondary Education Act of 1965*, Title V, Part D, Subpart 6; sec. 5462.

29. S. Philips, "Are We Holding Back Our Students That Possess the Potential to Excel?" *Education* 129(1): 50.

30. P. F. Wood, "Reading Instruction with Gifted and Talented Readers: A Series of Unfortunate Events or a Sequence of Auspicious Results?" *Gifted Child Today* 31(3).

31. Wood, "Reading Instruction," p. 20.

32. See Madeline Hunter, *Mastery Teaching* (El Segundo, CA: TIP Publications, 1982).

CHAPTER 12

1. S. Thompson, "The Authentic Standards Movement and Its Evil Twin," *Phi Delta Kappan* 82(5): 358.

2. Thompson, "The Authentic Standards," p. 358.

3. E. G. Cohen, "Talking and Working Together: Status, Interactions, and Learning," in *The Social Context of Instruction: Group Organization and Group Process*, ed. P. L. Peterson, L. C. Wilkerson, and M. Hallinan, pp. 171–87 (New York: Academic Press, 1984).

4. J. Wang and S. J. Odell, "Mentored Learning to Teach according to Standards-Based Reform: A Critical Review," *Review of Educational Research* 72 (3): 481–546; T. A. Romberg, "Problematic Features of the School Mathematics Curriculum," in *Handbook of Research on Curriculum*, ed. P. N. Sackson, pp. 749–88 (New York: Macmillan, 1992); P. Cobb, "Where Is the Mind? Constructivist and Sociocultural Perspectives on Mathematical Development," *Educational Researcher*, 23(7): 13–20; E. G. Cohen, "Talking and Working Together: Status, Interactions, and Learning," in *The Social Context of Instruction: Group Organization and Group Processes*, ed. P. L. Peterson, L. C. Wilkerson, and M. Hallinan, 171–87 (New York: Academic Press, 1984).

5. B. Falk, "Standards-Based Reforms: Problems and Possibilities," *Phi Delta Kappan,* 83(8): 612–620.

6. EdSource, "Standards in Focus," *Leadership* 33(1): 28–31.

7. M. Chatterji, "Models and Methods for Examining Standards-Based Reforms and Accountability Initiatives: Have the Tools of Inquiry Answered Pressing Questions and Improving Schools?" *Review of Educational Research* 72(3): 345–86.

8. Banks, 2003, p. 250.

9. Banks, 2003, p. 235.

10. Banks, 2003, p. 229.

11. Pamela Tiedt and Iris Tiedt, *Multicultural Teaching: A Handbook of Activities, Information, and Resources* (Boston: Allyn and Bacon, 2002), p. 41.

12. Banks, 2003, p. 109.

13. Banks, 2003, p. 108.

14. L. S. Taylor and C. R. Whittaker, *Bridging Multiple Worlds: Case Studies of Diverse Educational Communities* (Boston: Pearson Education Group, 2003), p. 76.

15. R. H. Barba, *Science in the Multicultural Classroom* (Boston: Allyn and Bacon, 1998).

APPENDIX B

1. The relevant portions of the First Amendment provide: "Congress shall make no law respecting an establishment of religion, or prohibiting the free exercise thereof; or abridging the freedom of speech . . . ." U.S. Const. amend. I. The Supreme Court has held that the Fourteenth Amendment makes these provisions applicable to all levels of government—federal, state, and local—and to all types of governmental policies and activities. *See Everson v. Board of Educ.*, 330 U.S. 1 (1947); *Cantwell v. Connecticut*, 310 U.S. 296 (1940).

2. See, e.g., *Everson*, 330 U.S. at 18 (the First Amendment "requires the state to be a neutral in its relations with groups of religious believers and non-believers; it does not require the state to be their adversary. State power is no more to be used so as to handicap religions than it is to favor them"); *Good News Club v. Milford Cent. Sch.*, 533 U.S. 98 (2001).

3. *Santa Fe Indep. Sch. Dist. v. Doe*, 530 U.S. 290, 302 (2000) (quoting *Board of Educ. v. Mergens*, 496 U.S. 226, 250 (1990) (plurality opinion)); *accord Rosenberger v. Rector of Univ. of Virginia*, 515 U.S. 819, 841 (1995).

4. *Engel v. Vitale*, 370 U.S. 421 (1962) (invalidating state laws directing the use of prayer in public schools); *School Dist. of Abington Twp. v. Schempp*, 374 U.S. 203 (1963) (invalidating state laws and policies requiring public schools to begin the school day with Bible readings and prayer); *Mergens*, 496 U.S. at 252 (plurality opinion) (explaining that "a school may not itself lead or direct a religious club"). The Supreme Court has also held, however, that the study of the Bible or of religion, when presented objectively as part of a secular program of education (e.g., in history or literature classes), is consistent with the First Amendment. *See Schempp*, 374 U.S. at 225.

5. *See Lee v. Weisman*, 505 U.S. 577, 599 (1992); *see also Wallace v. Jaffree*, 472 U.S. 38 (1985).

6. *See Weisman*, 505 U.S. at 587.

7. 505 U.S. 577 (1992).

8. 530 U.S. 290 (2000).

9. *Tinker v. Des Moines Indep. Community Sch. Dist.*, 393 U.S. 503, 506 (1969).

10. *Capitol Square Review & Advisory Bd. v. Pinette*, 515 U.S. 753, 760 (1995).

11. *Santa Fe*, 530 U.S. at 302 (explaining that "not every message" that is "authorized by a government policy and take[s] place on government property at government-sponsored school-related events" is "the government's own").

12. *Santa Fe*, 530 U.S. at 313.

13. For example, the First Amendment permits public school officials to review student speeches for vulgarity, lewdness, or sexually explicit language. *Bethel Sch.*

Dist. v. Fraser, 478 U.S. 675, 683–86 (1986). Without more, however, such review does not make student speech attributable to the state.

14. *Rosenberger v. Rector of Univ. of Virginia*, 515 U.S. 819 (1995); *Board of Educ. v. Mergens*, 496 U.S. 226 (1990); *Good News Club v. Milford Cent. Sch.*, 533 U.S. 98 (2001); *Lamb's Chapel v. Center Moriches Union Free Sch. Dist.*, 508 U.S. 384 (1993); *Widmar v. Vincent*, 454 U.S. 263 (1981); *Santa Fe*, 530 U.S. at 304 n.15. In addition, in circumstances where students are entitled to pray, public schools may not restrict or censor their prayers on the ground that they might be deemed "too religious" to others. The Establishment Clause prohibits state officials from making judgments about what constitutes an appropriate prayer, and from favoring or disfavoring certain types of prayers—be they "nonsectarian" and "nonproselytizing" or the opposite—over others. *See Engel v. Vitale*, 370 U.S. 421, 429–30 (1962) (explaining that "one of the greatest dangers to the freedom of the individual to worship in his own way lay in the Government's placing its official stamp of approval upon one particular kind of prayer or one particular form of religious services," that "neither the power nor the prestige" of state officials may "be used to control, support or influence the kinds of prayer the American people can say," and that the state is "without power to prescribe by law any particular form of prayer"); *Weisman*, 505 U.S. at 594.

15. *Santa Fe*, 530 U.S. at 302; *Mergens*, 496 U.S. at 248–50.

16. *Mergens*, 496 U.S. at 250 (plurality opinion); *id.* at 260–61 (Kennedy, J., concurring in part and in judgment).

17. *Rosenberger*, 515 U.S. at 845-46; *Mergens*, 496 U.S. at 248 (plurality opinion); *id.* at 260–61 (Kennedy, J., concurring in part and in judgment).

Bibliography

Abington School District v. Schemp, 374 U.S. 203 (1963).

Adams, C. F. *Letters of Mrs. Adams, the Wife of John Adams.* Vols. 1 and 2. Boston: Freeman and Bolles, 1840.

Aguilar v. Felton 473 U.S. 402 (1985). Available online at http://religiousfreedom .lib.viginia.edu/court/agui_v_felt.html.

Akers, C. W. *Abigail Adams: An American Woman.* New York: Longman, 2000.

Allen, A., and Stegmeir, C. *Civics.* New York: American Book Company, 1956.

Baer, J. W. "The Pledge of Allegiance: A Short History." Available online at http:// oldtimeislands.org/pledge/pledge.htm.

Banks, James A. "A Content Analysis of the African American in Textbooks. *Social Education* 33 (1969): 954–57, 963.

———. *Teaching the African American Experience: Methods and Materials.* Belmont, CA: Fearon, 1970.

———. *Teaching Ethnic Studies: Concepts and Strategies* (43rd yearbook). James A. Banks (ed). Washington, D.C: National Council for Social Studies, 1973.

———. African American Youths in Predominantly White Suburbs: An Exploratory Study of Their Attitudes and Self-Concepts. *Journal of Negro Education* 53 (1984): 3–17.

———. Ethnicity, Class, Cognitive, and Motivational Styles: Research and Teaching Implications. *Journal of Negro Education* 57 (1988): 452–66.

———. The Dimensions of Multicultural Education. *Multicultural Leader* 4 (1991): 5–6.

———. Multicultural Education: Its Effects on Students' Ethnic and Gender Role Attitudes. In J. P. Shaver (ed.), *Handbook of Research on Social Studies Teaching and Learning* (pp. 459–69). New York: Macmillan, 1991.

———. Multicultural Education: Approaches, Developments, and Dimensions. In J. Lynch, C. Modgil, and S. Modgil (eds.), *Cultural Diversity and the Schools, Vol. 1, Education for Cultural Diversity: Convergence and Divergence* (pp. 83–94). London: The Falmer Press, 1992.

——. The Canon Debate, Knowledge Construction, and Multicultural Education. *Educational Researcher* 22(5): 4–14.

——. Multicultural Education for Young Children: Racial and Ethnic Attitudes and Their Modification. In B. Spodek (ed.), *Handbook of Research on the Education of Young Children* (pp. 236–50). New York: Macmillan, 1993.

——. *Multicultural Education, Transformative Knowledge, and Action: Historical and Contemporary Perspectives.* New York: Teachers College Press, 1996.

——. The Lives and Values of Researchers: Implications for Educating Citizens in a Multicultural Society. *Educational Researcher* 27(7): 4–17.

——. *Cultural Diversity and Education: Foundations, Curriculum and Teaching* (4th ed.). Boston: Allyn & Bacon, 2001.

——. Approaches to Multicultural Curricular Reform. In James A. Banks and Cherry A. McGee Banks (eds.), *Multicultural Education: Issues and Perspectives* (4th ed., rev., pp. 225–46). New York: Wiley, 2003.

——. Approaches to Multicultural Curriculum Reform. In James A. Banks and Cherry A. McGee Banks (eds.) *Multicultural Education: Issues and Perspectives* (pp. 242–61). Hoboken, NJ: Wiley, 2003.

——. Multicultural Education: Characteristics and Goals. In James A. Banks and Cherry A. McGee Banks (eds.), *Multicultural Education: Issues and Perspectives* (4th ed., rev., pp. 3–30). New York: Wiley, 2003.

——. *Teaching Strategies for Ethnic Studies* (7th ed.) Boston: Allyn & Bacon, 2003.

——. *Teaching Strategies for Ethnic Studies.* Boston: Pearson Education Group, 2003.

Banks, James A., and Cherry A. McGee Banks (eds.). *Multicultural Education: Issues and Perspectives* (4th ed., rev.). New York: Wiley, 2003.

——. *Handbook of Research on Multicultural Education* (2nd ed.). San Francisco: Wiley, 2004.

——. *Multicultural Education: Issues and Perspectives* (5th ed., update). New York: Wiley, 2004.

Barba, R. H. *Science in the Multicultural Classroom.* Boston: Allyn and Bacon, 1998.

Barone, Michael. Debating Bilingual Education: The California State Board of Education Is on the Verge of Undoing Proposition 227. Available online at www.usnews.com/usnews/opinion/baroneweb/mb_020208.htm.

Barr, L. The Next Step: Showing a Common History of Treatment for Minorities, Women and Gays in Media Content, Newsrooms and Journalism Schools: A proposal for Future Research and Suggestions for a Curriculum. A paper presented at the 76th annual meeting of the Association for Education in Journalism and Mass Communication, Kansas City, MO, August 11–14, 1993.

Bartolomew, L. I. Beyond the Methods Fetish: Towards a Humanizing Pedagogy. *Harvard Educational Review* 64(2): 173–94.

Bearman, C. J. An Examination of Suffragette Violence. *The English Historical Review* 120 (2005): 365–97.

Beisel, N., and T. Kay. Abortion, Race, and Gender in Nineteenth-Century America. *American Sociological Review* 69 (2004): 498–518.

Board of Education v. Allen. 392 U.S. 236 (1968). Available online at http://reli giousfreedom.lib.virginia.edu/court/boar_v_allen.html.

Books, Sue. High Stakes in New York: From a "Last Chance, First Chance" Classroom. *Educational Foundations* 15(4): 57–70.

Borman, G. D. How Can Title I Improve Achievement? *Educational Leadership* 60(4): 49–53.

Borman, G. D., and J. V. D'Agostino. Title I and Student Achievement: A Meta-Analysis of Federal Evaluation Results. *Educational Evaluation and Policy Analysis* 4 (1996): 309–26.

———. Title I and Student Achievement: A Quantitative Synthesis. In G. D. Borman, S. Springfield, and R. E. Slavin (eds.), *Title I: Compensatory Education at the Crossroads* (pp. 25–57). Mahwah, NJ: Lawrence Erlbaum Associates, 2001.

Brown, M. Is There a Nationality Problem in Our Schools? In Clarence J. Karier (ed.), *Shaping the American Educational State 1900 to the Present* (pp. 269–74). New York: The Free Press, 1900.

Brown v. Board of Education, 347 U.S. 483 (1954).

Brown v. Board of Education. Available online at Resource. www.coreoline .org/History/brown_vs_hoard.htm.

Brunner, B., and E. Haney. Civil Rights Timeline: Milestones in the Modern Civil Rights Movement. Available online at www.infoplease.com/spot/civilrightstime line1.html.

Button, H. W., and E. F. Provenzo, Jr. *History of Education and Culture in America.* Englewood Cliffs, NJ: Prentice Hall, 1989.

Calhoun, D. *The Educating of Americans: A Documentary History.* Boston: Houghton Mifflin Company, 1969.

California Coalition for Immigration Reform. History of Proposition 187. Available online at http://ccir.nt/REFERENCE/187-History.html.

California Newsreel. *Race: The Power of an Illusion* [motion picture].

Chandler, R. *Racing Toward 2001: The Forces Shaping America's Religious Future.* Grand Rapids, MI: Zondervan, 1992.

Chatterji, M. Models and Methods for Examining Standards-Based Reforms and Accountability Initiatives: Have the Tools of Inquiry Answered Pressing Questions on Improving Schools? *Review of Educational Research*, 72(3): 345–86.

Chessum, L. Race and Gender in the United States of America. *Gender & History* 12(1): 228–31.

Clark, E. H. *Sex in Education; Or, a Fair Chance for Girls.* Boston: Houghton Mifflin, 1873.

Cline, A. Prayers at Graduation. Available online at http://atheism.anbout.com/od/churchstatedecisions/a/leeWeisman.htm.

CNN. Most of California's Prop. 187 Ruled Unconstitutional. Available online at www.cnn.com/ALLPOLITICS/1998/03/19/propo.187.

Cobb, P. Where Is the Mind? Constructivist and Sociocultural Perspectives on Mathematical Development. *Educational Researcher* 23(7): 13–20.

Cochran-Smith, M. Knowledge, Skills, and Experiences for Teaching Culturally Diverse Learners: A Perspective for Practicing Teachers. In J. Irvine (ed.), *Critical Knowledge for Diverse Teachers and Learners* (pp. 27–88). Washington, DC: AACTE, 1997.

Cohen, E. G. Talking and Working Together: Status, Interactions, and Learning. In P. L. Peterson, L. C. Wilkerson, and M. Hallinan (eds.), *The Social Context of Instruction: Group Organization and Group Processes* (pp. 171–87). New York: Academic Press, 1984.

Cohen, J. Examining Fund Distribution for Title 1. The Ed Money Watch Blog. New America Foundation. Available online at www.newamerica.net/blog/ed-money-watch/2009/examin.

Cokley, Kevin O. Testing Cross's Revised Racial Identity Model: An Examination of the Relationship Between Racial Identity and Internalized Racialism. *Journal of Counseling Psychology* 49(4): 476–83.

Cooper, C. M. The Detrimental Impact of Teacher Bias: Lessons Learned from Standpoint of African American Mothers. *Teacher Education Quarterly* 30(2):101–14.

Cooper, J. F., Jr. *Tenacious of Their Liberties: The Congregationalists in Colonial Massachusetts.* New York: Oxford University Press, 1999.

Cottrol, R. J., R. T. Diamone, and L. B. Ware. *Brown v. Board of Education: Caste, Culture, and the Constitution.* Lawrence: University Press of Kansas, 2003.

Covey, S. The Seven Habits of Highly Effective People. Gahanna, OH: Covey Leadership Center, 1986.

———. *Language Loyalties: A Source Book on the Official English Controversy.* Chicago: University of Chicago Press, 1992.

———. *Bilingual Education: History, Politics, Theory and Practice* (3rd ed. revised and expanded). Los Angeles: Bilingual Educational Services, 1995.

Crawford, J. Anatomy of the English-Only Movement. Paper presented at University of Illinois at Urbana-Champaign, March 21, 1996.

———. Obituary, The Bilingual Education Act 1968–2002. Available online at http://ourworld.compuserve.com/homepages/JWCRAWFORD/T7obit.htm.

———. Language Politics in the U.S.A.: The Paradox of Bilingual Education. *Social Justice* 25(3).

———. Language Politics in the United States: The Paradox of Bilingual Education. In Carlos J. Ovando and Peter McLaren (eds.), *The Politics of Multiculturalism and Bilingual Education: Students and Teachers Caught in the Cross-Fire*. Boston: McGraw-Hill, 2000.

Cubberley, E. P. *Changing Conceptions of Education*. Boston: Houghton Mifflin, 1909).

Cuzzort, R. P., and E. W. King. *Humanity and Modern Social Thought*. Hindsale, IL: The Dryden Press, 1976.

Daniels, Harvey A. *Not Only English: Affirming America's Multilingual Heritage*. Urbana: National Council of Teachers of English, 1990.

Declaration of Independence. Available online at http://members.tripod.com~candst/thompson.htm.

Derman-Sparks, L. *Anti-Bias Curriculum, Tools for Empowering Young Children*. Washington DC: National Association for the Education of Young Children, 1989.

Dever, M., M. Whitaker, and D. Byrnes. The 4th R: Teaching about Religion in the Public Schools. *Social Studies* 92: 220–29.

Diaz-Rico, Lynne T., and Kathryn Z. Weed. *The Crosscultural, Language, and Academic Development Handbook: A Complete K–12 Reference Guide*. Boston: Allyn and Bacon, 1995.

———. *The Crosscultural, Language, and Academic Development Handbook: A Complete K–12 Reference Guide*. Boston: Pearson Education, 2006.

Doer, E. Religion and Public Education. *Phi Delta Kappan* 80 (1998): 223–25.

Dubois, W. E. B. *Black Reconstruction*. New York: Harcourt Brace, 1935.

———. *The Education of Black People: Ten Critiques, 1906–1960*. New York: Monthly Review Press, 1973.

Durkheim, E. *The Elementary Forms of the Religious Life: A Study in Religious Sociology*. New York: Macmillan, 1915.

EdSource. Standards in Focus. *Leadership* 33(1): 28–31.

Edwards, Governor of Louisiana, et al. v. Aguillard et al. 482 U.S. 578 (1986). Available online at www.talkorigins.org/faqs/edwards v-aguilard.html.

Eliezer Williams v. State of California. Superior Court of the State of California County of San Francisco, No. 312236.

Elliot, J. (Producer). *A Class Divided* [motion picture], 1984. Available online at https://janeelliott.com/contactjane.htm.

———. *Essential Blue Eyed* [motion picture], 1986. Available online at https://janeelliott.com/contactjane.htm.

———. *Blue Eyed* [motion picture], 1996. Available online at https://janeelliott.com/contactjane.htm.

———. *The 30 Minute Blue Eyed* [motion picture], 1996. Available online at https://janeelliott.com/contactjane.htm.

———. *The Angry Eye* [motion picture], 2001. Available online at https://janeelliott.com/contactjane.htm.

Etzioni, A. *The Active Society: A Theory of Societal and Political Processes.* New York: The Free Press, 1968.

Fagan, J. There's No Place Like School. *Principal* 80(5): 36–37.

Falk, B. Standards-Based Reforms: Problems and Possibilities. *Phi Delta Kappan* 83(8): 612–20.

Faltis, C. J., and S. Hudelson. *Bilingual Education in Elementary and Secondary School Communities: Towards Understanding and Caring.* Boston: Allyn And Bacon, 1998.

Fischer, D. H. *Liberty and Freedom: A Visual History of America's Founding Ideas.* Oxford University Press, 2004.

Ford, N. M. *When Did I Begin? Conception of the Human Individual in History, Philosophy and Science.* New York: Cambridge University Press, 1988.

Freedman, M. K. Non-Standard Accommodations (Hereinafter called Modifications): Just the Legal Basics. Paper presented at the Annual Conference on Large-Scale Assessment of the Council of Chief State School Officers. Houston, TX, June 24–27, 2001.

Freire, P. *Pedagogy of the Oppressed.* New York: Herder & Herder, 1970.

———. *Education for Critical Consciousness.* New York: Seabury Press, 1973.

Friend, M. *Special Education: Contemporary Perspectives for School Professionals.* Boston: Pearson Education, 2008.

Fryer, R. G., Jr., and S. D. Levitt. *The Causes and Consequences of Distinctively African American Names.* Center for Advanced Study in the Behavioral Sciences in Stanford, 2003. Available online at www.cramton.umd.edu/workshop/papers/fryer-levitt-distinctively-African-American-names.pdf.

Fueyo, V., and S. Bechtol. Those Who Can Teach: Reflecting on Teaching Diverse Populations. *Teacher Education Quarterly*, 26(3).

Futrell, M., and P. Geisert, P. Religious Neutrality (2001). Available online at www.teachingaboutreligion.org/CriticalConcepts/religious_neutrality.htm.

Gay, G. Educational Equality for Students of Color. In James A. Banks and Cherry A. McGee Banks (eds.), *Multicultural Education: Issues and Perspectives* New York: Wiley, 2004).

Gollnick, D. M., and P. C. Chinn. *Multicultural Education in a Pluralistic Society.* Upper Saddle River, NJ: Pearson Education, 2009.

Gorski, P. Multicultural Pavilion (2004). Available online at www.edchange.org/multicultural.

Grissmer, D., A. Flanagan, and S. Williamson. Why Did the African American–Caucasian Score Gap Narrow in the 1970s and 1980s? In C. Jencks and M. Phillips (eds.), *The African American-Caucasian Test Score Gap* (pp. 181–226). Washington DC: Brookings Institution, 1998.

Haynes, C. C. *A Teacher's Guide to Religion in the Public Schools.* Nashville, TN: First Amendment Center, 1999.

Hernandez-Tutop, J. E. Oppressor: The Educational System. Opinion paper. Washington, DC: U.S. Department of Education, 1998.

Hertzler, J. O. *Social Institutions.* Lincoln: University of Nebraska Press, 1946.

Heward, W. L., and M. D. Orlansky. *Exceptional Children: An Introductory Survey of Special Education.* New York: Macmillan, 1992.

Huber, E. C. Hutchinson, Anne. American National Biography Online. Available online at http://0www.anb.org.patris.apu.edu/articles/01/01-00437-print.html.

Hunt, N., and K. Marshall. *Exceptional Children and Youth: An Introduction to Special Education.* Boston: Houghton Mifflin Company, 1994.

Hunt v. McNair, 413 U.S. 734 (1973). Available online at http://caselaw.lp.findlaw.com/scripts/getcase.pl?court=us&vol=413&invol=734.

IDEA Parent Guide. New York: National Center for Learning Disability, 2006.

Ides, A. Court Grants Class Certification in Williams Case. Available online at www.aclu-sc.org/News/Releases/2001/100026/.

Improving Academic Achievement. Title I (CA Department of Education). Available online at www.cde.ca.gov/sp/sw/t1.

Improving the Academic Achievement of the Disadvantaged. Title I of the Elementary and Secondary Education Act of 1965 (20 U.S.C. 6301 et seq.) Available online at www.ed.gov/print/policy/elsec/leg/esea02/pg1.html.

Irons, P. *Jim Crow's Children: The Broken Promise of the Brown Decision.* New York: Penguin, 2002.

Jarrett, J. L. *The Educational Theories of the Sophists.* New York: Teachers College Press, 1969.

Jim Crow Laws. Available online at www.ferris.edu/jimcrow/what.htm.

Jones, G. S. An End to Poverty: The French Revolution and the Promise of a World beyond Want. Paper presented at the Anglo-American Conference of Historians at the University of London, July 7–9, 2004.

Jones, J. M. *Prejudice and Racism.* New York: McGraw-Hill, 1997.

Kalven, J. Personal Value Clarification. In B. Hall, J. Kalven, L. Rosen, and B. Taylor, (eds.), *Readings in Value Development.* Ramsey, NJ: Paulist Press, 1982.

Kaufman, P. W. *Women Teachers on the Frontier.* New Haven, CT: Yale University Press, 1984.

Kellog, W. O. *American History: The Easy Way.* New York: Barron's, 1995.

Kirp, D. The Educational Equities in Historical Perspective. In Diane Ravitch and Maris Vinovskis (eds.), *Historical Perspectives on the Current Education Reforms.* Essays commissioned by the Office of Research (OR) in the Office of Educational Research and Improvement (OERI), U.S. Department of Education, 1993.

Klarman, M. J. *From Jim Crow to Civil Rights: The Supreme Court and the Struggle for Racial Equality.* New York: Oxford University Press, 2004.

———. *Brown v. Board of Education and the Civil Rights Movement.* New York: Oxford University Press, 2007.

Kloss, H. *The American Bilingual Tradition* (2nd ed.). Washington DC: ERIC Clearing House on Languages and Linguistics, 1998.

Kohn, A. Fighting the Tests. *Phi Delta Kappan* 28(5): 348–60.

Koppelman, K. L., and R. L. Goodhart. *Understanding Human Differences: Multicultural Education for a Diverse America.* New York: Pearson Education, 2008.

Kozol, J. *Savage Inequalities: Children in America's Schools.* New York: Harper Perennial, 1991.

———. *The Shame of the Nation: The Restoration of Apartheid Schooling in America.* New York: Crown Publishers, 2005.

Kraft, C. *Christianity in Culture.* Maryknoll, NY: Orbis Books, 1979.

Kroeber, A. L., and C. Kluckhohn. *Culture: A Critical Review of Concepts and Definitions.* Cambridge, MA: The Museum, 1952.

Ladson-Billings, G. But That's Just Good Teaching! The Case for Culturally Relevant Pedagogy. *Theory Into Practice* 34(3): 159–65.

LaMorte, M. W. *School Law: Cases and Concepts.* Boston: Allyn and Bacon, 1999.

Larson v. Valente 456 U.S. 228 (1982). Available online at http://religiousfreedom .lib.virginia.edu/courts/lars_v_vale.html.

Larson v. Valente. Supreme Court Decisions on Religious Liberty. Available online at http://atheism.about.com/library/decisions/religion/bllLarsonValente .htm/terms=Larson.

Lasswell, T. E., J. H. Burma, and S. H. Aronson (eds.). *Life in Society: Readings in Sociology.* Glenview, IL: Scott, Foresman and Company, 1970.

Lau v. Nichols No. 72-6520 (1973). Available online at http://supct.law.cornell .edu/supct/html/historics/USSC.

Lebedun, J. L. *American Literature.* Ipswich, MA: EBSCO Publishing, 2003.

Leibowitz, A. H. English Literacy: Legal Sanction for Discrimination. *Notre Dame Lawyer* 45(7): 7–67.

Lessow-Hurley, J. *The Foundations of Dual Language Instruction.* New York: Longman, 1990.

Leuchtag, A. Elizabeth Cady Stanton: Freethinker and Radical Revisionist. *The Humanist* 56 (1996): 29–32.

Levin, J., and W. Levin. *The Functions of Discrimination and Prejudice* (2nd ed.). New York: Harper & Row, 1982.

Levitt v. Committee for Public Education, 413 U.S. 472 (1973). Available online at http://caselaw.lp.findlaw.com/scripts/getcase.pl?court=us&vol=413&invol=472.

Lincoln, A. Gettysburg Address, November 19, 1863.

Lindsey, D. (ed.). *A. Lincoln/Jefferson Davis: A House Divided.* Cleveland, OH: Howard Allen, Inc., 1960.

Lindsey, R. B., K. N. Robins, and R. D. Terrell. *Cultural Proficiency: A Manual for School Leaders.* Thousand Oaks, CA: Corwin Press, 1999.

MacKenzie, K. K. Using Literacy Booster Groups to Maintain and Extend Reading Recovery Success in the Primary Grades. *The Reading Teacher* 55(3): 222–34.

Maclay, K. Anthropology Professor John Ogbu Dies at Age 64. Available online at http://berkeley.edu/news/media/release/2003/08/26_ogbu.html.

Mailman, S. California's Proposition 187 and Its Lessons. *New York Law Journal*, January 3, 1995.

Mehan, H., I. Villanueva, L. Hubbard, and A. Lintz. *Constructing School Success: The Consequences of Untracking Low-Achieving Students*. New York: Cambridge University Press, 1996.

Michael A. Newdow v. U.S. Congress et al. (2002). Available online at http://fl1 .findlaw.com/news.findlaw.com/hdocs/docs/conlaw/newdowus62602opn.pdf.

Miller, R. Interactive Map: Title 1 Education Grants, Funding Formulas Create Unfair Allocations (2009). Center for American Progress. Available online at www .americanprogress.org/issues/2009/08/title1_map.html.

Milner, H. R., F. B. Tenore, and J. Laughter. What Can Teacher Education Programs Do to Prepare Teachers to Teach High-Achieving Culturally Diverse Male Students. *Gifted Child Today* 31 (Winter 2008).

Missouri Department of Elementary and Secondary Education. Grading, Awarding Credit, and Graduation for Students with Disabilities: Issues in Education. *Technical Assistance Bulletin*. Jefferson City: Missouri Department of Elementary and Secondary Education, Division of Special Education, 1999.

Montalto, N. V. *A History of the Intercultural Educational Movement, 1924–1841*. New York: Garland, 1982.

Moses, R., and C. E. Cobb, Jr. *Radical Equations: Math Literacy and Civil Rights*. Boston: Beacon Press, 2001.

Murdock, G. P. *How Culture Changes in Life and Society: Readings in Sociology*. Glenview, IL: Scott, Foresman and Company, 1970.

Murray vs. Curlett, 374 U.S. 203. (1963). Available online at www.atheists.org/ courthouse/prayer.html.

Myers, A. S. Emma Hart Willard (1787–1870). *Collier's Encyclopedia*. New York: MacMillan Educational Company, 1992.

Nagai, H. Multicultural Education in the United States and Japan. Paper presented at the 46th Annual Conference of Comparative International Education Society (CIES), Orlando, FL, March 6–8, 2002.

Nash, G. Multiculturalism and History: Historical Perspectives and Present Prospects. In Diane Ravitch and Maris Vinovskis (eds.). *Historical Perspectives on the Current Education Reforms*. Essays commissioned by the Office of Research (OR) in the Office of Educational Research and Improvement (OERI), U.S. Department of Education, 1993.

New American Foundation. No Child Left Behind Act—Title 1 Distribution Formulas. Available online at http://febp.newamerica.net/background-analysis/no-child-left-behind-act-title-i-distribution-formulas.

Nieto, S. *Affirming Diversity: The Sociopolitical Context of Multicultural Education*. Boston: Pearson Education, 2004.

Nisbet, R. A. *Emile Durkheim*. Westport, CT: Greenwood Press, 1965.

No Child Left Behind Act. Available online at www.ed.gov/nclb/overview/intro/presidentplan.

Oakes, J. *Keeping Track: How Schools Structure Inequality*. New Haven, CT: Yale University Press, 1985.

Oakes, J., and M. Lipton. *Teaching to Change the World*. Boston: McGraw-Hill College, 1999.

Ogbu, J. Culture and Intelligence. In R. Stenberg (ed.), *Encyclopedia of Intelligence* (pp. 328–38). New York: MacMillan, 1994.

———. African American–American Students and the Academic Achievement Gap: What Else You Need to Know. *Journal of Thought* 37(4): 9–33.

———. Beyond Language: Ebonics, Proper English, and Identity in an African American–America Speech Community. *American Educational Research Journal* 36(2).

———. Voluntary and Involuntary Minorities: A Cultural-Ecological Theory of School Performance with Some Implications for Education (with H. D. Simons). *Anthropology and Education Quarterly* 29(2):155–88.

———. Educational Anthropology. In *Encyclopedia of Cultural Anthropology*. Vol. 2 (pp. 371–77). New York: Henry Holt and Company, 1996.

———. Speech Community, Language Identity and Language Boundaries. In A. Sjogren (ed.) *Language and Environment: A Cultural Approach to Education for Minority and Migrant Students* (pp. 17–42). Stockholm, Sweden: Botkyrka, 1997.

———. Racial Stratification in the United States: Why Inequality Persists. In A. H. Halsey, H. Lauder, P. Brown and A. S. Wells (eds.), *Education: Culture, Economy, and Society*, Oxford: Oxford University Press, 1997.

———. Understanding the School Performance of Urban African Americans: Some Essential Background Knowledge. In H. J. Walberg, O. Reyes, and R. P. Weissberg (eds.) *Children and Youth: Interdisciplinary Perspectives*, Newbury Park, CA: Sage, 1997.

———. Foreword to *Reconstructing "Dropout": A Critical Ethnography of the Dynamics of African American Students' Disengagement from School*, by G. J. S. Dei, J. Mazzuca, E. McIsaac, and J. Zine. Toronto: University of Toronto Press, 1997.

———. Cultural Context of Children's Development. In H. E. Fitzgerald, B. M. Lister, and B. S. Zuckerman (eds.), *Children of Color: Research, Health, and Policy Issues* (pp. 73–92). New York: Garland, 1999.

———. Collective Identity and Schooling. In H. Fujita (ed.), *Education, Knowledge and Power* (in Japanese). Tokyo, Japan: Shinyosha Ltd., 2000.

———. *African American Students in an Affluent Suburb: A Study of Academic Disengagement*. Mahwah, NJ: Lawrence Erlbaum, 2003.

———. Differences in Cultural Frame of Reference. *International Journal of Behavioral Development* 16(3): 483–506.

———. Anthropology at Berkeley. Overview of Title VI of the Civil Rights Act of 1964. Available online at www.usdoj.gov/crt/cor/coord/titlevi.htm.

Ogbu, J., and P. Stern. Cultural Amplifiers of Intelligence. In J. Fish (ed.), *Understanding Race and Intelligence*. Mahwah, NJ: Lawrence Erlbaum Associates, 2001.

———. Caste Status and Intellectual Development. In R. J. Sternberg and E. Grigorenko (eds.), *Environmental Effects on Cognitive Abilities* (pp. 1–37). Mahwah, NJ: Lawrence Erlbaum Associates, 2001.

Painter, N. I. Truth, Sojourner. American National Biography Online. Available online at http://0www.anb.org.patris.apu.edu/articles/15/15-00706.html.

Philips, S. Are We Holding Back Our Students That Possess the Potential to Excel? *Education* 129(1).

Pitt, L. *The Decline of the Californios: A Social History of the Spanish-Speaking Californians, 1846–1890*. Berkeley: University of California Press, 1966.

Plessy v. Ferguson, 163 U.S. 537 (1896).

Proposition 13 Peoples Advocate. Available online at www.peoplesadvocate.org/english.html.

Pulliam, J. D., and J. J. Van Patten. *History of Education in America*. Upper Saddle River, New Jersey: Pearson Education, 2003.

Raths, L., M. Harmin, and S. Simon. *Values and Teaching: Working with Values in the Classroom*. Columbus, OH: Charles E. Merrill, 1966.

Report of the Woman's Rights Convention, Seneca Falls, NY. Available online at www.hbci.com.

Reynolds v. United States. 98 U.S. 145 (1878). Available online at www.law.umkc.edu/faculty/projects/ftrials/conlaw/reynoldsvus.html.

Riley, Richard W. Religious Expression in Public Schools. U.S. Department of Education. Available online at www.ed.gov/policy/gen/guid/religionandschools/prayer_guidance.html.

Romberg, T. A. Problematic Features of the School Mathematics Curriculum. In P. N. Sackson (ed.), *Handbook of Research on Curriculum* (pp. 749–88). New York: Macmillan, 1992.

Romo, J. J., P. Bradfield, and R. Serrano. *Reclaiming Democracy: Multicultural Educators' Journeys Towards Transformative Teaching*. Upper Saddle River, NJ: Pearson Education, 2004.

Rycenga, J. A Greater Awakening: Women's Intellect as a Factor in Early Abolitionist Movements, 1824–1834. *Journal of Feminist Studies in Religion* 21(2):
31–59.

Sadkler, D., and M. Sadkler. *Teachers, Schools and Society.* Princeton, NJ: Mc-
Graw-Hill, 1994.

———. Gender Bias: From Colonial America to Today's Classrooms. In James A.
Banks and Cherry A. McGee (eds.), *Multicultural Education: Issues and Perspectives* (pp. 125–51). New York: Wiley, 2001.

Schaff, P. *History of the Christian Church.* Peabody, MA: Hendrickson Publishing,
Inc., 1888.

Scheid, A. *Pasadena—Crown of the Valley: An Illustrated History.* Northridge, CA:
Windsor Publications, 1986.

Scherer, M. Is School the Place for Spirituality? A Conversation with Rabbi Harold
Kushner. *Educational Leadership* 56(4): 18–22.

School District of Abington Township, Pennsylvania, et al. v. Schempp et al. 374
U.S. 203 (1963). Available online at www.nationalcenter.org/scot63.htm.

Seat, K. K. The Legacy of Elizabeth Russell. *International Bulletin of Missionary
Research* 32 (2): 93–99.

Skinner, B. F. *The Technology of Teaching.* New York: Meredith Corporation,
1968.

Smith, M. S., and J. A. O'Day. Educational Equality: 1966 and Now. In D. Verstgen
and J. Ward (eds.), *Spheres of Justice in Education: The 1990 American Education Finance Association Yearbook* (pp. 53–100). New York: Harper Business,
1991.

Soukhanov, A. H. (ed.). *Microsoft Encarta College Dictionary.* New York: St. Martin's Press, 2001.

Stone v. Graham, 449 U.S. 39 (1980). Available online at http://caselaw.lp.findlaw
.com/scripts/getcase.pl?court=us&vol=449&invol=39.

Students with Attention Deficit Disorders ADD/ADHD: Eligibility Issues and Service Options under the Individuals with Disabilities Education Act (IDEA) and
Section 504. Report. Logan: Utah State University, 1998.

Study Guide to the History of United States Symbols and Mottos. Available online
at http://members.tripod.com/~candst/studygd5.htm/pledge.

Suleiman, M. F. Preparing Teachers for the Culturally Diverse Classrooms. Paper
presented at the 7th Annual Effective Schools Conference, Topeka, KS, May 3–5,
1996.

Supreme Court of the United States Syllabus: *Lee et al. v. Weisman.* Personally and
as Next Friend of Weisman: Certiorari to the United States Court of Appeals for
the First Circuit. (1992). Available online at http://supct.law.cornell.edu/supc/
html/90-1014.ZS.html.

Taylor, L. S., and C. R. Whittaker. *Bridging Multiple Worlds: Case Studies of Diverse Educational Communities.* Boston: Pearson Education, 2003.

Thompson, S. The Authentic Standards Movement and Its Evil Twin. *Phi Delta Kappan* 82(5): 358–62

Tiedt, Pamela, and Iris Tiedt. *Multicultural Teaching: A Handbook of Activities, Information, and Resources.* Boston: Allyn and Bacon, 2002.

Tilton v. Richardson 403 U.S. 672. (1971). Available online at http://religiousfree dom.lib.virginia.edu/court/tilt_v_rich.html.

Tischler, H. L., P. Whitten, and D. E. K. Hunter. *Introduction to Sociology.* New York: CBS College Publishing, 1986.

Title VI of the 1964 Civil Rights Act. Available online at www.usdoj.gov/crt/cor/ coord/titlevistat.htm.

Titus, H. *Living Issues in Philosophy.* New York: Van Nostrand Reinhold Company, 1970.

Toffler, A. *Powershift: Knowledge, Wealth, and Violence at the Edge of the 21st Century.* New York: Bantam Books, 1990.

Townley, A. J., J. H. Schmeider-Ramirez, and L. B. Wehmeyer. *School Finance: A California Perspective.* Dubuque, IA: Kendall/Hunt, 1999.

Treaty of Guadalupe Hidalgo. Available online at www.loc.gov/rr/hispanic/ghtreaty/.

Ueda, R. The Construction of Ethnic Diversity and National Identity in the Public Schools. In Diane Ravitch and Maris Vinovskis (eds.), *Historical Perspectives on the Current Education Reforms.* Essays commissioned by the Office of Research (OR) in the Office of Educational Research and Improvement (OERI), U.S. Department of Education, 1993.

U.S. Court of Appeals for the Sixth Circuit: John Doe, Individually; Mary Doe, Individually and as Natural mother of A. Roe, B. Roe, and C. Roe, . . . v. Sue Porter, Individually and as Superintendent of the Rhea County School System, . . . (2004). Retrieved December 14, from U.S. Supreme Court Electronic citation database.

U.S. Department of Education (USDE). *National Excellence: A Case for Developing America's Talent.* Washington DC: USDE, 1993.

Valenzuela, A. *Subtractive Schooling: U.S.-Mexican Youth and the Politics of Caring.* Albany: State University of New York Press, 1999.

Venet, W. H. The Emergence of a Suffragist: Mary Livermore, Civil War Activism, and the Moral Power of Women. *Civil War History* 48(2): 143–64.

Walz v. Tax Commission of City of New York. Religious Tax Exemptions: Property Taxes. Available online at http://atheism.about.com/library/decisions/tax/bldec _WalzTaxComm.htm?terms=tax+co.

Wang, J., and S. J. Odell. Mentored Learning to Teach According to Standards-Based Reform: A Critical Review. *Review of Educational Research* 72(3): 481–546.

Washington, M. From Motives of Delicacy: Sexuality and Morality in the Narratives of Sojourner Truth and Harriet Jacobs. *Journal of African American History* 2007 92(1): 57–73.

Weber, M. *The Protestant Ethic and the Spirit of Capitalism.* Translated by Talcott Parsons. New York: Charles Scribner's Sons, 1958.

Weiler, J. Recent Changes in School Desegregation. *ERIC/CUE Digest* Number 133 (1998).

Weymeyer, M., and M. Schwartz. Disproportionate Representation of Males in Special Education Services: Biology, Behavior, or Bias? *Education and Treatment of Children* 24 (February 2001).

Wiley, T. G. Myths about Language Diversity and Literacy in the United States. Washington, DC: ERIC Clearinghouse on ESL Literacy Education, 1997.

Williams, G. W. *History of the Nero Race in America from 1619 to 1880: Negroes as Slaves, as Soldiers, and as Citizens* (2 vols.). New York: Putnam, 1882–1883.

Willis, H. D. The Shifting Focus in School Desegregation. Paper presented to the SWRL Board of Directors and the 1995 Equity Conference, November 1, 1994.

Wilson, J. Q. *American Government: Brief Version.* Sixth Edition. Boston: Houghton Mifflin, 2003.

Winship, M. P. *The Times and Trials of Anne Hutchinson.* Lawrence: University Press of Kansas, 2005.

Wood, P. F. Reading Instruction with Gifted and Talented Readers: A Series of Unfortunate Events or a Sequence of Auspicious Results? *Gifted Child Today* 31(3).

Woodson, C. G., and C. H. Wesley. *The Negro in Our History.* Washington, DC: Associated Publishers, 1922.

Yonezawa, S., A. S. Wells, and I. Serna. Choosing Tracks: "Freedom of Choice" in Detracking Schools. *American Educational Research Journal* 39(1): 37–67.

Zink-Sawyer, B. A. From Preachers to Suffragists: Enlisting the Pulpit in the Early Movement for Woman's Rights. *American Transcendental Quarterly* 14(3): 193–209.

Index

About the Author

Chinaka Samuel DomNwachukwu is professor of multicultural education and chair of the Department of Teacher Education at Azusa Pacific University, Azusa, California.